Rand McNally
Atlas of
AMERICAN
FRONTIERS

Rand McNally
Atlas of
AMERICAN
FRONTIERS

Martin Ridge

Professor of History, California Institute of Technology
Senior Research Associate, Henry E. Huntington Library

Rand McNally
Chicago • New York • San Francisco

Rand McNally Atlas of American Frontiers

General manager: Russell L. Voisin
Managing editor: Jon M. Leverenz
Editor: Elizabeth Fagan Adelman
Cartographic editor: V. Patrick Healy
Art director: John Nelson
Designer: Vito M. DePinto
Production editor: Laura C. Schmidt
Manufacturing planner: Marianne Abraham

Photograph credits
10–11: Colorado: David Muench. 12–13: Cahokia: Cahokia Mounds State Historic Site. 14–15: New Mexico: John Running. Blackfeet: National Anthropological Archives, Smithsonian Institution. Shoshone: National Anthropological Archives, Smithsonian Institution. 16–17: Navajo: Arizona Office of Tourism. Tlingit: National Anthropological Archives, Smithsonian Institution. 18–19: St. John: David Muench. 20–21: Henry Hudson: Milwaukee Public Museum. Ponce de Leon: The Bettmann Archive. Florida: David Muench. 22–24: Marquette and Joliet: Milwaukee Public Museum. Minnesota: David Muench. Sir Walter Raleigh: The Bettmann Archive. Fort: National Park Service. 26–27: 1612 map: Princeton University. Massachusetts: David Muench. 28–29: Jamestown: National Park Service. 30–31: Portaging: Milwaukee Public Museum. Great Smoky Mountains: David Muench. 32–33: Fort James: The Bettmann Archive. Fort Ticonderoga: The Bettmann Archive. 34–35: Settlement: The Bettmann Archive. Pennsylvania: David Muench. 36–37: 1783 map: The British Library. Maine: David Muench. 38–39: Daniel Boone: The Bettmann Archive. Newfound Gap: David Muench. 40–41: Traders: Milwaukee Public Museum. Ohio: David Muench. 42–43: Tecumseh: Smithsonian Institution. Fort Mackinaw: Milwaukee Public Museum. 44–45: Creek: National Museum of the American Indian, Smithsonian Institution. Cherokee: National Anthropological Archives, Smithsonian Institution. Seminole: National Museum of the American Indian, Smithsonian Institution. 46–47: Wagons: U.S. Department of Agriculture. 48–49: Erie Canal: The Bettmann Archive. Transcontinental railroad: Milwaukee Public Museum. New York: David Muench. 50–52: St. Louis: The Bettmann Archive. New York: The Bettmann Archive. New Orleans: The Bettmann Archive. Chicago: The Bettmann Archive. 54–55: 1856 map: Reproduction from Mitchell's *Universal Atlas.* Arizona: David Muench. 56–57: Trading post: Milwaukee Public Museum. Cheyenne: National Anthropological Archives, Smithsonian Institution. North Dakota: David Muench. 58–59: Lewis and Clark: National Park Service. Wyoming: David Muench. 60–61: Grand Canyon: National Park Service. Havasu Falls: David Muench. 62–63: Men: U.S. Department of Agriculture. South Dakota: David Muench. 64–65: Hopi: Milwaukee Public Museum. Bison: Milwaukee Public Museum. Hogan: David Muench. 66–67: Wagons: Milwaukee Public Museum. Nebraska: David Muench. 68–69: Mormons: Milwaukee Public Museum. Two of Utah: David Muench. 70–71: Alamo: The Bettmann Archive. Texas: David Muench. 72–73: Miners: Milwaukee Public Museum. Montana: David Muench. 74–75: African-American soldiers: Carlisle Barracks. Colorado soldiers: Colorado Historical Society. 76–77: Arapaho: National Anthropological Archives, Smithsonian Institution. Reservation Indians: Milwaukee Public Museum. Wyoming: David Muench. 78–79: "Bronc to Breakfast": Montana Historical Society, Mackay Collection. Lone cowboy: Milwaukee Public Museum. River crossing: Milwaukee Public Museum. 80–81: Branding: Milwaukee Public Museum. "A Hard Trail": Denver Public Library. Montana: David Muench. 82–83: Butch Cassidy: Denver Public Library. James Brothers: Denver Public Library. Pony Express: Denver Public Library. Arizona: David Muench. 84–85: Saloon: Milwaukee Public Museum. Camp: Milwaukee Public Museum. Chinese miners: The Bettmann Archive. 86–87: Land rush: U.S. Department of Agriculture. Land rush: U.S. Department of Agriculture. "Rush for the Oklahoma Land": U.S. Department of the Interior, Washington, DC. 88–89: Sod house: U.S. Department of Agriculture. Women and children: U.S. Department of Agriculture. Plowing: Milwaukee Public Museum. 90–91: Homestead: Milwaukee Public Museum. Refugees: The Bettmann Archive. 92–93: Farmers: Milwaukee Public Museum. Loggers: Milwaukee Public Museum. Factory: Chicago Historical Society. California: David Muench. 94–96: Store: U.S. Department of Agriculture. Auto: Milwaukee Public Museum. Census: The Bettmann Archive. Hawaii: David Muench. 98–99: Alaska: David Muench. 100–101: Nat Love: The Bettmann Archive. Little Bighorn: Little Bighorn Battlefield National Monument. 102–103: Gold dredge: The Bettmann Archive. Nevada: David Muench. 104–105: Wright brothers: Wright Brothers National Memorial. Utah: David Muench. Mississippi: David Muench. 106–107: Wyatt Earp: Ben Traywick. Maine: David Muench. 108–109: California: David Muench. 110–111: Suffragettes: The Bettmann Archive. George Washington Carver: The Bettmann Archive. Doctor: The Bettmann Archive. 112–113: Space shuttle: NASA. Nebraska: David Muench. 114–116: Washington: David Muench. Earth: NASA. 118–119: 1776 map: William L. Clements Library. 120–121: 1816 map: National Archives and Records Administration. 122–123: 1856 map: Reproduction from Mitchell's *Universal Atlas.* All other maps copyright © Rand McNally & Company.

Rand McNally Atlas of American Frontiers
copyright © 1993 by Rand McNally & Company

Library of Congress Cataloging-in-Publication Data

Ridge, Martin.
    Atlas of American frontiers / text by Martin Ridge.
       p.   cm.
    Includes indexes.
    ISBN 0-528-83493-2
    1. Frontier and pioneer life—United States.   2. Frontier and pioneer life—United States—Pictorial works.   3. Frontier and pioneer life—United States—Maps.   4. United States—Historical geography.   5. United States—Historical geography—Maps.   6. United States—Historical geography—Pictorial works.   I. Title.
E179.5.R53   1992
973—dc20   92-4647
                                     CIP

Contents

Foreword

When an eighteenth-century English bishop uttered his now-famous line, "Westward the course of Empire takes its way," he did not have in mind what the world knows today as the American West—the wide open spaces, big skies, and infinitely varied landscape said to have given rise to a new democracy and to symbolize the essence of freedom. But the good bishop nonetheless sensed that "out there" was the frontier of European civilization. Winston Churchill surely entertained a similar notion whenever he quoted a favorite line of poetry: "Westward, look, the land is bright." And when Andrew Carnegie, the iron and steel baron, and Samuel Gompers, the labor leader, dreamed in the British Isles about a future in America and joyfully sang a ditty that began, "To the west, to the west, to the land of the free...," they were feeling the same magnetic pull. Even in our own tumultuous time, the story of the United States is still most dramatically revealed in how a vast multitude from every place on earth carried "the American idea" from ocean to ocean and made it work.

The region called "the West" has been changing constantly since the country began, but it was always a synonym for "the frontier." In the seventeenth century, it was the wilderness area beyond the Fall Line of Virginia; in the eighteenth century, it was what is now Kentucky and Tennessee; in the nineteenth century, it moved ever more rapidly from Ohio to the trans-Mississippi region, and then across the Great Plains and the Rockies to the Pacific coast. At present, "the frontier" may chiefly be in the realm of the spirit, wherever people envision a better life and aim to rely on their own courage and determination to make it a reality.

This atlas, based on the latest scholarship and cartographic craftsmanship, is both a reference and a reading book, for it not only maps afresh the development of the West from its beginnings but also is enriched by the learned text provided by Dr. Martin Ridge. The book is designed to instruct as well as to inspire and narrates a tale that is beyond compare in the history of nation-states.

Henry F. Graff

Henry F. Graff
Professor Emeritus of History
Columbia University

Blackfeet woman and children

Mississippi River

Erie Canal, New York

Navajo hogan, Monument Valley, AZ-UT

P A R T O N E

The Frontier's Dawning

The Frontier's Dawning

At the close of the fifteenth century, Europeans encountered what they called a New World. The two continents of the Western Hemisphere were a new world only to them, however, as the Americas had been peopled and developed for centuries. Native Americans had already come from Asia, and during their years of migration across the Bering Land Bridge and settlement in the Americas, they had domesticated both plants and animals.

American Indian societies were quite diverse. Many were based on strongly held spiritual views. Native Americans created their own forms of government and family structure. And if they had not been successful in utilizing many of the mineral resources of the land, especially iron, they had devised patterns of food production that sustained substantial populations, especially in Central and South America. And they did so for centuries without significantly depleting resources.

The European encounter with the Western Hemisphere brought together two societies with different levels of material culture. Native Americans relied primarily on stone tools and weapons; the Europeans lived in an age of metals. The world of most American Indians was defined by limited surplus production, trade, and barter. Most Europeans, regardless of how isolated their villages or farms, lived in a world of commercial exchange of surplus production and the use of money. In fact, the "discovery" of America was an effort by the rulers and merchants of newly emerging European nation-states to control and increase commerce with the wealthy peoples of India and Asia. Little wonder that the extended conflict between American Indians and Europeans resulted from efforts to integrate American economies and cultures into those of Europe.

However, contact between the two groups often resulted in cultural exchange as well as conflict. Native Americans not only intermarried with Europeans, especially in South and Central America, but also contributed to the dissemination of both mineral wealth and food products to other parts of the world. From their gold and silver to the potato and some diseases, the Americas were part of a massive cultural interchange that ushered in a new world order after A.D. 1500.

There was never a one-way passage from Europe to America. People, products, and ideas moved both ways across the oceans of the world. Not only would Europeans never be the same after Columbus's voyage to America, but their descendants who lived in America became different from those who stayed behind. The initial experience and the continuing encounter, especially in the United States, of European men and women with both the new land and the native peoples contributed to the formation of the American nation, especially during the nineteenth century.

Marquette and Joliet

The first to depict only the Western Hemisphere, this map was the creation of Sebastian Münster in 1546. The map, called "The New Islands," helped perpetuate the misconception that Japan (Zipangri) and China (Cathay) lay just beyond North America; it thus encouraged European explorers and fortune seekers.

Within Mesa Verde National Park, Colorado (below), ruins and artifacts document over one thousand years of Native American habitation. Two thousand years ago, American Indians who lived here cultivated such crops as beans, corn, and squash and kept domesticated dogs and turkeys.

Sir Walter Raleigh

The First Discovery of America

Although no one knows the precise date when the ancestors of American Indians began crossing from Siberia to Alaska, the migration probably occurred between thirty and forty thousand years ago. The last wave may have been as recent as eight thousand years ago. During this prehistoric period, the Bering Sea fell perhaps as much as three hundred feet, which allowed a series of migrating peoples, following herds of animals in quest of food, to pass over the Bering Land Bridge to North America. As the later arrivals pushed into Alaska, the earlier migrants drifted southward and eastward through river valleys created as the great glaciers of the Ice Age melted. In time, Native Americans settled over the whole of the Western Hemisphere.

The migrating peoples gradually adjusted to the variety of climatic conditions they encountered, fought for dominance over territories large enough to sustain themselves, and developed their own styles of farming, trading, and hunting that suited their environment. Their strategies for survival included acquiring such new skills as weaving and such tools as the bow and arrow, the fishing net, and the basket.

Although the earliest bands probably lived in isolation from one another, over the centuries the gradual increase in communication, borrowing, and trade, as well as continued migrations and intermixing, led to the creation of regional tribal cultures, such as the Iroquois League. Some American Indian groups differed from their neighbors as completely as did the nations of Europe. Even small bands often had widely different styles of decorative art and levels of cultural achievement. But almost all of them shared some activities. Even those who were most sedentary, who planted corn, peas, and squash, usually had to hunt, fish, and trade for products that they lacked such as salt. This was true at least as far north as the 45th degree. There were, of course, exceptions, such as the Pueblo Indians and some tribes along the Northwest Coast who were relatively more self-sufficient.

Native Americans were more often divided by language than by cultural practices. Over two thousand Indian languages were spoken in the Americas, with more than two hundred in use in what is now the United States and Canada. American Indians who lived in close proximity sometimes could not understand one another's language.

On the eve of the European intrusion into America, none of the North American tribes could match the high material achievements of the peoples to the south, such as those in the Valley of Mexico, the Yucatan, or the Andean Coast. Nonetheless, Native American technology remained within the Neolithic level of development; that is, they practiced farming and had advanced in the development of stone tools. Although copper was used for ornaments, there is scant evidence to indicate that it was employed in toolmaking and weaponry. In the north, weaving was restricted to a few areas. The only domesticated animal was the dog, which Native Americans used as a beast of burden but also ate at ceremonial functions. Most political organizations north of the Valley of Mexico were very small and loosely structured. Even such large confederations as the Iroquois League, which created the greatest degree of intertribal unity north of Mexico, exercised very little direct control over individual behavior.

Cahokia Mounds, in what is now Illinois, date from A.D. 700 to 1500. Among the most impressive representations of Mississippian Native American culture, the mounds contain the remains of the domestic arts and crafts of the pre-Columbian period, including copper ornaments, pottery, and stone statuary. The mounds stand today as silent witnesses to the many changes in the land surrounding them over the last thousand years.

Homelands of the Native Americans

Ancestors of American Indians crossed the land bridge from Asia to North America, and the people that Christopher Columbus named "Indians" became widely dispersed throughout the Americas. Shown here are the Indian culture areas of what is now the United States and some important Native American groups.

United States Vegetation Regions

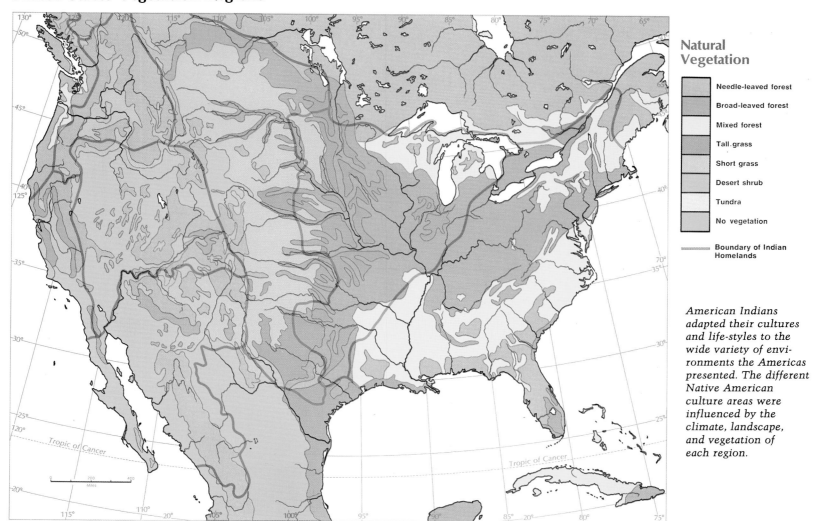

Natural Vegetation

- Needle-leaved forest
- Broad-leaved forest
- Mixed forest
- Tall.grass
- Short grass
- Desert shrub
- Tundra
- No vegetation
- Boundary of Indian Homelands

American Indians adapted their cultures and life-styles to the wide variety of environments the Americas presented. The different Native American culture areas were influenced by the climate, landscape, and vegetation of each region.

The Original Americans

From about 300 B.C. to A.D. 1300, three early desert cultures shaped life in the Southwest—the Mogollon, the Hohokam, and the Anasazi. The Mogollon (southwestern New Mexico) and Hohokam (southeastern Arizona) Indians farmed mountain valleys to grow tobacco, cotton, corn, beans, and squash. The Anasazi developed a new form of architecture after about A.D. 750, constructing stone apartment dwellings, or pueblos, on the tops of mesas. After A.D. 1000, they began building these villages on the ledges of cliffs, which provided better protection against invaders. The ancient cliffside homes of the Rio Grande Anasazi now stand in ruin at Bandelier National Monument, New Mexico. A group of Anasazi inhabited these dwellings from about A.D. 1400 to the late 1500s.

The Paleo-Indians

Between 10,000 and 5,000 B.C., the North American climate warmed, and the vast glaciers and ice sheets retreated northward. The big game upon which Paleo-Indians depended became extinct. Native Americans began to hunt and trap, and fish and wild plants played a more important role in their diet. They developed new tools and used a wider variety of materials, including wood, antler, and bone. They began to store and preserve food, weave plant fibers into clothing and baskets, and build boats.

When American Indians no longer tracked the movements of great herds, they wandered less and less. They began cultivating plants instead of simply collecting them. American farming began in Mexico, but some knowledge had filtered north into what is now the southwestern United States by about 3500 B.C. With the development of a stable food supply, Native American cultures became more organized.

Shown here is a pipe carved from stone by an eastern Indian well over twelve hundred years ago.

Stretching from the Rocky Mountains to the Mississippi River, from southern Canada to the Gulf of Mexico, the rolling grasslands of the Great Plains held some sixty million bison, incorrectly known as buffalo, that roamed freely in enormous herds. Dozens of American Indian groups depended on this incredible resource: the Arapaho, Blackfeet, Cheyenne, Crow, Iowa, Pawnee, Sioux, Plains Cree, and many more. Plains Indians may be the most familiar to us today, but the culture we know did not emerge until long after the arrival of Europeans, specifically the Spanish who explored far into the Americas in the 1500s. The horses they brought and then left behind reshaped the bison-hunting life-style that characterized the Native Americans of this region. Plains Indians had used the travois, a drag frame made of poles, with dogs, but the device became more useful with horses. This Blackfeet woman was still using a travois as late as 1900.

Native American dwellings displayed as much variety as any other part of Indian culture. Eastern Indians inhabited longhouses and wigwams; some Inuit, or Eskimo, built igloos in winter; Native Americans of the Southwest lived in pueblos, hogans, and wickiups. Tepees were favored by Plains Indians, in part because they were portable and thus suited to a seminomadic Plains lifestyle. Shown here is a Northern Shoshone community in Wyoming in 1870.

Native American Life

Why had American Indians in the north failed to develop more complex social, political, and technical organizations? The answer may be due in part to their relatively low population. There may have been as few as ten million Native Americans thinly scattered over what is now the entire United States. It may also in part have been due to their great skill in adapting to their environment and capitalizing on the richness of the land. In achieving a successful way of life based on combinations of farming, fishing, hunting, and gathering, American Indians relied on repetitive patterns for sustenance that required little variation over time.

It would be a mistake, however, to assume that Indian life was static. Although changes took place slowly, Native Americans proved capable of amazing flexibility, as demonstrated by their remarkable response to European culture. Within three centuries, from 1500 to 1800, many American Indian groups made a successful transition from the Stone Age to the Iron Age.

The remarkable capacity of some Native Americans to adapt to new opportunities is clearly evidenced by how quickly the horses brought by the Spanish to America revolutionized the lives of the people of the Great Plains. Mastery of the horse gave them greater mobility, a new way to wage war, and greater skill in hunting bison. Some of the Indians who had the greatest contact with Europeans gradually accepted iron tools and new skills such as using iron traps for hunting beaver. These changes brought them out of their relative isolation and subsistence living and toward integration with the commercial world of modern Europe.

Indian religious and social organizations proved more resistant to European institutions. For example, many Native Americans held that each human spirit was linked to every other living organism in nature. Therefore, they could accept Christianity, with its Supreme Being, but they did not reject the world of spirits and medicine men. American Indian religious culture also rejected the idea of individual land ownership, because they believed the soil, like the sky, belonged to everyone. Europeans found this idea totally alien. Almost equally alien to Europeans was the matrilineal system—family unity based exclusively on the mother's line—that existed among some groups when the whites arrived. This practice persisted, even when Europeans tried to introduce the patrilineal system of inheritance. The powerful Iroquois League that dominated most of New York, Penn-

The Navajo of the Southwest integrated components of European life-styles into their culture. Sheep, for example, were introduced by the Spanish, and today sheep grazing remains a primary economic activity. The Navajo retain their clan identities and are the largest Native American group in the United States. They inhabit parts of Arizona, Utah, and New Mexico, including Monument Valley, shown here.

sylvania, and Ohio was matrilineal.

Neolithic life, despite its simplicity, was not always peaceful. Food shortages that resulted from population growth, rites of passage to manhood that required demonstrations of bravery, or revenge for insults and damages could lead to warfare. Indian conflict could be almost symbolic or brutal. Warlike tribes tortured prisoners, burned them at the stake, and in some instances engaged in cannibalism. Hostility between the Iroquois and the Algonquin existed long before the Europeans arrived. When whites settled in a region, they often found themselves allied to one tribe or another strictly by accident. Native Americans viewed them as merely another tribe, albeit one with superior weapons.

Anthropologists, ethnographers, and historians have created maps outlining the cultural, tribal, and linguistic boundaries of the Indian groups of North America. These boundaries are far from well defined. To superimpose one of these maps upon another demonstrates the complexities and differences among American Indians. A map of Europe attempting to show all of the ethnic, linguistic, and national differences would look equally as complex.

New World Agriculture
One of the first American Indian customs to be adopted by Europeans was the cultivation of certain crops. Many of the plants Indians grew—such as corn, beans, potatoes, tomatoes, and squashes—had previously existed nowhere else. There have been many other important agricultural contributions. Shown here is an early corn, or maize, plant.

There was great diversity in Native American religious and social organization. The potlatch, peculiar to the Northwest Coast Indians, was a ritual to assume inherited status. Possessions were given away; the more impressive the giving, the higher the status of the donor. Like many other American Indian traditions, Europeans found this custom alien. Shown here are Tlingit men at a potlatch in Alaska in 1901.

Europe Encounters America

Christopher Columbus's voyage to America in 1492 effectively opened the Western Hemisphere to exploration and exploitation by the seafaring nations of Europe. Along with Spanish *conquistadores*, English and French navigators cruised the coasts of both North and South America in search of American Indians who could supply them with furs or gold or precious stones while they looked for sites for future colonies.

The European nations did not compete on equal footing at first. Religious wars between Roman Catholics and Protestants limited English activity during the 1500s.

Although the French did try to follow up on the initial discoveries of Jacques Cartier in 1534, the Spanish, under King Philip II, beat back their advances. For the first century of European conquest, the Spanish dominated the Americas. Spanish seamen successfully mapped most of the coastline of South and Central America, while Spanish soldiers mounted expeditions of conquest against the Aztecs and the Incas, and Spanish-led Roman Catholic priests began establishing missions to consolidate Spain's empire in America.

The French and the English returned to active exploration at the beginning of the seventeenth century. French explorers, soldiers,

Christopher Columbus triggered a chain reaction of maritime exploration. For more than a century, there were four main participants—Spain, Portugal, England, and France—who concentrated on the Americas.

The Age of Discovery

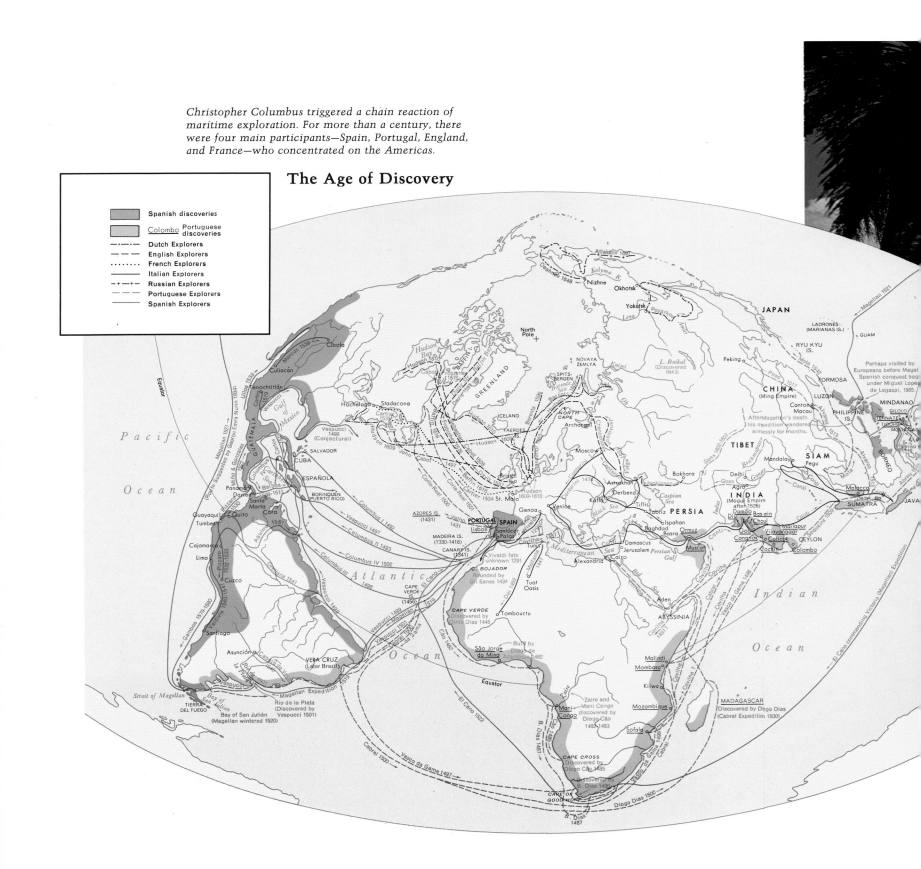

Spanish discoveries
Colombo Portuguese discoveries
Dutch Explorers
English Explorers
French Explorers
Italian Explorers
Russian Explorers
Portuguese Explorers
Spanish Explorers

Roman Catholic missionaries, fur traders, and *coureurs de bois* quickly cast a wide net of empire along the St. Lawrence River, the Great Lakes, and the Mississippi Valley. The English proved dogged. Many of their seamen were actually pirates who plundered Spanish towns and treasure ships; the most famous was Sir Francis Drake. Others founded colonies whose early settlers eventually pushed into the interior regions of the North American seaboard. The history of the struggle for the continent is a dramatic story of exploration and war in the seventeenth century.

Spain's sixteenth-century domination of the New World began in the Caribbean. The islands quickly became producers of sugar, coffee, spices, and tropical fruits. The Native Americans of the region, principally the Arawaks and Caribs, were absorbed or wiped out. Today, part of St. John in the Virgin Islands, shown here, is a United States national park.

Early European Explorers

The Spanish in 1513 were the first Europeans to reach Florida. Several parties struggled for decades to establish colonies on the eastern coast. Inland, Europeans were met with what is now called the Everglades, a mysterious wetland of grass that only Native Americans of the region knew how to effectively navigate. The Everglades is now a national park.

Pirates in the Caribbean
Small, swift ships like this one were popular in the fifteenth and sixteenth centuries. Christopher Columbus and many other navigators of the New World crossed the Atlantic in such vessels. As the Spanish hold on the Americas increased, cargoes of riches bound for Spain required larger ships. Known as galleons, the larger, slower boats, virtually laden with wealth, regularly crossed the Caribbean, where they were easy prey for pirates from other European nations. The pirates, or buccaneers, could lay in wait among the islands, grab their booty, and dart back to their island hideouts. For several centuries, England, France, Spain, Holland—and pirates—fought over control of the Caribbean.

In 1609, an English sea captain named Henry Hudson, employed by the Dutch, explored what is now the Hudson River. His voyage led the Dutch to establish the colony of New Netherland and to purchase Manhattan Island from the Indians.

SEEKING THE FOUNTAIN OF YOUTH.

This depiction of Juan Ponce de León and his men in Florida might give the impression that they were a company of Spanish gentlemen, on a picnic, in search of the fabled fountain of youth. In reality, they were conquistadors in quest of rich Indian societies that might be subdued and looted.

Cultural Collision and Competition

While the Old World collided with the "New World," Spain capitalized on its powerful hold on North America. Many of Spain's sixteenth-century explorers were hard-bitten soldiers, fresh from having driven the Moors out of Spain and familiar with deprivation, war, and death. The swashbuckling generations that followed them likewise knew neither fear nor pity. A fitting example was Juan Ponce de León, who fought the Moors, enlisted for Columbus's second voyage, conquered Puerto Rico—by murdering or enslaving the natives—and in 1513 explored the Florida coast. In 1565, Don Pedro Menéndez established St. Augustine, the first enduring white settlement in what was to be the United States. Meanwhile, Spanish navigators mapped the east coast from Florida as far north as Virginia. At first the Spanish had less knowledge of the Pacific Coast, although in 1542 Juan Cabrillo explored the California coastline. Then, in 1578, Francis Drake's daring raids on Spanish treasure ships in the Pacific, for which Queen Elizabeth made him a knight, forced the wary Spanish to map the Pacific Coast as far north as Alaska.

The Spanish also explored and claimed much of the southwestern interior of North America and the Pacific Coast. Lured on by rumors of cities of gold, American Indian empires as wealthy as that of the Aztec, and the fear that Drake had found the fabled Straits of Anian—the so-called Northwest Passage—the Spanish invaded the Southwest and

California. An expedition led by Francisco Coronado proved disastrous. Instead of finding the legendary Seven Cities of Cibola—Cities of Gold—Coronado encountered the baked-clay villages of the Zuni Indians. His continued quest took him north and east to the Kansas River where he gave up and turned back. His golden cities of the plains were the grass huts of the Wichita Indians.

Later, the Spanish returned to the Rio Grande Valley to establish Santa Fe and to gain control over the Native Americans of New Mexico. Settlers, soldiers, and missionaries eventually occupied the valley. They introduced sheep culture, turning the Indians into a dependent people by making them a part of the world market economy. The mission system was the linchpin of Spanish conquest. It proved less successful in Texas where nomadic Native Americans were more resistant to settlement. In California, however, the missionary efforts of Father Kino and Father Serra established Spanish hegemony.

Despite their early failures, the French never lost interest in the Americas. In 1565, the Spanish under Captain Menéndez had slaughtered French Huguenots in their colony forty miles north of St. Augustine. Even after the massacre, French sailors regularly continued to visit America to fish and trade with American Indians. In 1603, led by thirty-six-year-old Samuel de Champlain, the French returned to Canada. In 1608, Champlain founded a fur-trading post in the St. Lawrence River valley. From there, the frontiersmen of

This depiction of the explorers Louis Joliet and Father Jacques Marquette entering the Mississippi River masks the dangers and hardships faced by the two Frenchmen on a voyage that took them across Wisconsin on the Fox and Wisconsin rivers to the Mississippi.

Despite warnings to the contrary, they encountered only peaceful Native Americans along the way. They turned back after they learned that the river did not lead to the Pacific Ocean.

Europe Seeks a Northwest Passage

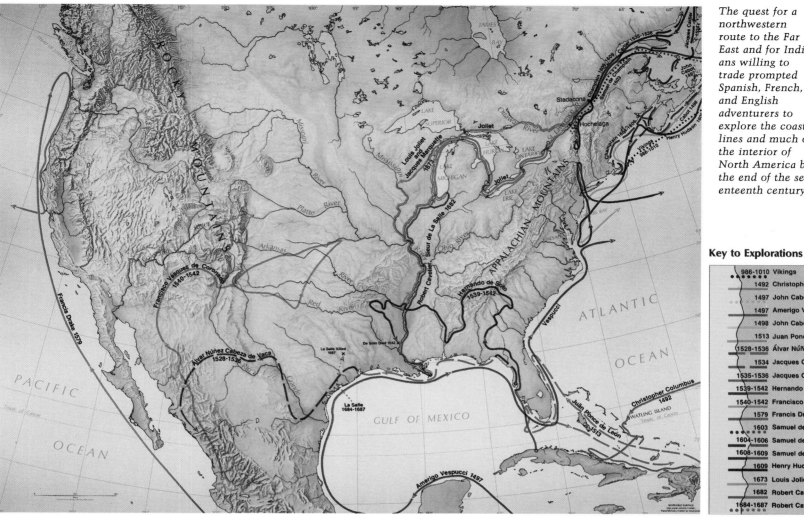

The quest for a northwestern route to the Far East and for Indians willing to trade prompted Spanish, French, and English adventurers to explore the coastlines and much of the interior of North America by the end of the seventeenth century.

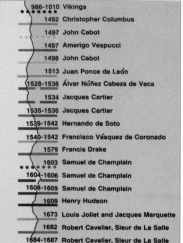

Key to Explorations

986-1010	Vikings
1492	Christopher Columbus
1497	John Cabot
1497	Amerigo Vespucci
1498	John Cabot
1513	Juan Ponce de León
1528-1536	Álvar Núñez Cabeza de Vaca
1534	Jacques Cartier
1535-1536	Jacques Cartier
1539-1542	Hernando de Soto
1540-1542	Francisco Vásquez de Coronado
1579	Francis Drake
1603	Samuel de Champlain
1604-1606	Samuel de Champlain
1608-1609	Samuel de Champlain
1609	Henry Hudson
1673	Louis Joliet and Jacques Marquette
1682	Robert Cavelier, Sieur de La Salle
1684-1687	Robert Cavelier, Sieur de La Salle

The Chippewa originally inhabited the upper Great Lakes region. The French came to this land of lakes and forests in the seventeenth century, at first crossing lakes such as this one, Kabetogama Lake in Minnesota, with the birchbark canoes invented by Native Americans.

Cultural Collision and Competition *(continued)*

New France swept westward with remarkable speed, until the interior of the continent drained by the Mississippi River system and the Great Lakes was in French hands.

From that point on, France moved quickly to strengthen its hold on the New World. Marquette and Joliet explored the upper Mississippi Valley, while the eccentric La Salle traveled the river's length. He died later trying to found a colony at its mouth. But within a century, despite a very small population, the French had encircled the English coastal colonies and were struggling with the Spanish for dominance over the Native Americans on the Texas plains.

While the Spanish tightened their grip on North America and the French challenged it, England's changing fortunes made it possible to begin English colonization in the New World. The Elizabethan sea dogs, led by Francis Drake, not only defeated the Spanish Armada but also gained control of the North Atlantic seaways. Bad economic times in England had created a turbulent, landless labor force; religious dissenters feared repression; and investors eagerly hoped to emulate Spain's success in America. New World colonies could offer England's surplus population a chance to make a new life. Religious dissenters could escape a hostile church, and investors could find outlets for their risk capital. Finally, such colonies could provide bases for English pirates to prey on Spanish treasure ships in the event of war.

In this spirit, the English launched their American enterprise. Protestant dissenters established independent colonies in New England. Virginia and New York became royal British colonies—the first to escape bankruptcy and the second when the English captured it from the Dutch. Pennsylvania, the Carolinas, and Georgia were proprietary colonies, where owners tried to achieve social goals and still make a profit. In time, increasing population, land monopolies, religious dissent, thirst for adventure, and dreams of economic opportunity sparked a movement westward, sometimes in the face of opposition not only from the colonial government but also from the English crown.

In 1564, the French built Fort Caroline near what is now Jacksonville, Florida. The Spanish, in an attempt to maintain their hold on Florida, promptly destroyed the settlement and massacred the French Huguenot inhabitants. Shown here is an artist's rendition of what was probably a rather more primitive fortification.

In the sixteenth century, English adventurers, who were little more than pirates, were known to attack Spanish cities in the Caribbean. Shown here is Sir Walter Raleigh defeating the Spanish on Trinidad in 1595. Raleigh secured a charter from Queen Elizabeth that gave him the right to discover, settle, and govern new lands. The colony he attempted to found in the 1580s at Roanoke Island, North Carolina, failed.

PART TWO

The Early Frontiers

The Early Frontiers

The English colonists in America were fortunate to settle in regions that boasted a moderate climate, adequate rainfall, and good soil. This unexpected bounty meant that many could retain their traditional life-style. Their crops and domesticated animals also flourished in this temperate region. Small grains and grasses—wheat, rye, barley, and timothy—grew splendidly on the eastern seaboard. Over time, European plant and animal life began to drive out less hardy indigenous flora and fauna. Swine, sheep, and cattle thrived, while deer, turkey, and other animals once abundant in the East were hunted to near extinction or found their environments so drastically altered they could not survive. When settlers fenced in their fields, for example, deer were forced away from open pasture land. When people drained swamps, beaver could no longer build dams and lodges. In many ways, European farmers as well as town dwellers drastically altered the American landscape.

The population of the English coastal colonies grew steadily as religious dissenters sought sanctuary in America, other people who found little chance to succeed at home were beckoned by economic opportunity, and Africans were brought in chains to be sold into slavery. This expanding population created greater demand for land, which in turn placed increasing pressure on Native Americans. Almost from the outset, English settlements sparked a series of wars not only with American Indians but also with the French and Spanish, who had claims in the Americas. This pattern continued well after the United States was formed following the American Revolution.

The westward movement of colonists, new immigrants, and slaves was spurred by a remarkable revolution in commerce, transportation, and communication. Although territorial expansion in this period was slow and painstaking, these newcomers to the continent soon populated the region as far west as the Appalachian Mountains. After the American Revolution, improved transportation and communication allowed for the rapid settlement of the area east of the Mississippi River. This period of expansion was due largely to improved roads, extensive railroad construction, and a network of canals. By 1860, the region east of the Mississippi—which had once been the domain of the eastern woodland Native Americans and the wild creatures of the forest—had been converted by white settlers into farms, plantations, and cities.

New England and Virginia were early targets for English settlement. The earliest colonies tended to cluster along the Atlantic coast, in part because the Appalachians prevented easy advance. Shown at right is the mountainous northwestern corner of what is now Massachusetts.

John Smith is well known for his role in founding Jamestown, Virginia, and less well known for his skill as a cartographer. This map of Virginia, drawn in 1612, demonstrates his abilities. The ornamentation was added to the original design. Smith also made one of the earliest and best maps of New England.

Daniel Boone leading settlers through the Cumberland Gap

Coastal Pioneers

The first English frontier settlers had to learn painful lessons before they could succeed in America. Their earliest efforts failed; in fact, the settlers in Sir Walter Raleigh's colony at Roanoke Island simply vanished. The settlement at Jamestown, the first permanent English colony in America, suffered terrible losses from starvation, disease, and exposure until the pioneers learned to adjust to their new environment. The English quest for land to grow food and tobacco for export brought about bitter conflicts between whites and Native Americans. In time, American Indians were either displaced or exterminated. Moreover, investors in the Virginia Company learned the hard way that the cost of colonization was so great that even joint stock companies could not sustain it.

Finally, Jamestown was taken over by the English king. Immigration to America subsequently increased, despite extremely high mortality rates, when individuals saw the opportunity to work for themselves and become landowners. The expanding tobacco frontier resulted in dispersing settlers along the rivers of the tidewater. Like all frontier people, the Virginians demanded self-govern-ment and laws appropriate to their needs rather than those of the home country. Ironically, the Virginia frontier, the first to clamor for representative government, was the first to institute slavery in English North America. The settlers in the southern frontier colonies learned from the Virginia experience that hard work rather than quick profits awaited them in America.

Unlike the earliest settlers in the South, the Puritans in New England came to stay, not to make money and return home. They sought a new and orderly society. In the South, the "head right" system of land grants (which gave fifty acres to each settler or to each person who brought another person over to America) led to law suits over claims, rampant speculation in head rights, and the creation of huge estates. In contrast, the settlers in Massachusetts Bay tried to establish an orderly frontier with organized towns and carefully surveyed lands to avoid both speculation and extreme inequalities in property ownership.

This compact frontier broke down quickly. Religious dissenters and others who chafed under harsh Puritan rule went off to found their own colonies, while many other

Three English ships brought 120 people to Virginia in May 1607; thus began Jamestown, the first permanent English settlement in the Americas. Though told to avoid moist places, the colonists built Jamestown in a mosquito-infested swamp. By January 1608, only 38 people remained. One Englishman described the colonists' plight: "There were never English-men left in a foreign country in such miserie as we were in this new discovered Virginia....If there were a conscience in men, it would make their hearts bleed to heare the pitiful murmurings of our sick men without relief, every night and day; in the morning their bodies being trailed out of their cabines like Dogges to be buried."

people hungered for more land. Conflicts between early and later settlers over towns gradually eroded the original social ideal. Nevertheless, the practice of land surveying in New England eliminated the often bitter litigation that characterized the southern frontier.

Although Puritans regarded American Indians on one level as "nature's children," their underlying attitudes toward Native Americans differed little from those of the Virginians. When the New England Indians had suffered a catastrophic small-pox epidemic in 1617 that killed off many of them, the disaster was viewed as a sign that Providence approved of European settlement. The Puritans took over abandoned Indian fields, and as their population increased, forced the Native Americans out. The Pequot, who not only occupied lands that Massachusetts settlers wanted but also boasted that their religion was more powerful than Puritanism, were exterminated in a bloody war. The Puritan frontier people, despite conflicting moral claims, saw the American Indian as both a threat to the safety of the colony and a competitor for land. The expansion of New England was characterized by incessant conflict with Native American neighbors as well as with the French and their Indian allies to the north in Canada.

The Transplanting of Europe

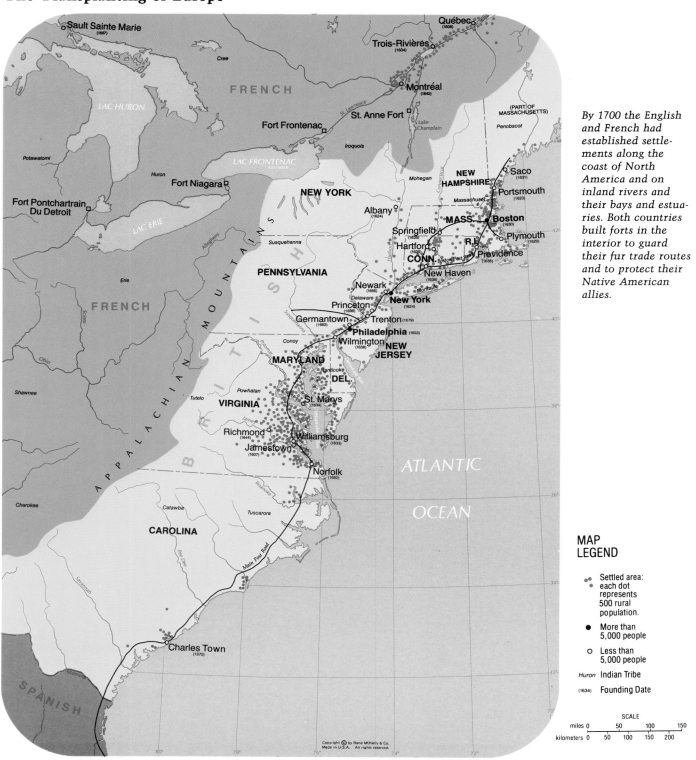

By 1700 the English and French had established settlements along the coast of North America and on inland rivers and their bays and estuaries. Both countries built forts in the interior to guard their fur trade routes and to protect their Native American allies.

MAP
LEGEND

Settled area: each dot represents 500 rural population.

● More than 5,000 people

○ Less than 5,000 people

Huron Indian Tribe

(1634) Founding Date

SCALE

miles 0   50   100   150
kilometers 0   50   100   150   200

Settlement Moves Inland

The earliest English frontier advanced slowly for several reasons. In New England, for example, the Appalachian Mountains blocked any easy advance into the West. Instead, the frontier moved along the narrow coastal plain and up rivers. Even this advance was checked in part by river rapids and falls. Moving above the Fall Line meant carrying exports around this barrier, and this portaging was difficult until good roads were built.

South of New England, the problem was less pressing. The Hudson and the rivers emptying into Chesapeake Bay opened a vast region for frontier settlement. Even so, from Georgia to New England the frontier had to bridge the Fall Line and advance into the up-country, the Piedmont. The first men to explore the Piedmont were land speculators in search of investment opportunities and traders looking to acquire deer skins and beaver pelts that brought high prices in the European fur market.

This expanding English frontier posed immediate and long-range problems for both the French, who saw it as a threat to the fur trade, and for the American Indians, who recognized that the English constituted a menace to their way of life. The English not only upset the environmental balance by cutting down forests and displacing native plants and animals, but they also tipped the military balance by supplying other Native Americans with firearms. The American Indians sought to delay the European advance by playing the French and the English off against each other, but in the inevitable conflict, Native Americans would be the losers.

At first, the river system was the primary means of transportation and communication on the frontier. When waterways became unnavigable, travelers had to portage, or carry all of their possessions as well as their canoes. French voyageurs, English hunters, and American Indians passing through the dense forests all relied on muscle power when it came to portages. Little wonder that trade on the early frontier was both dangerous and exhausting.

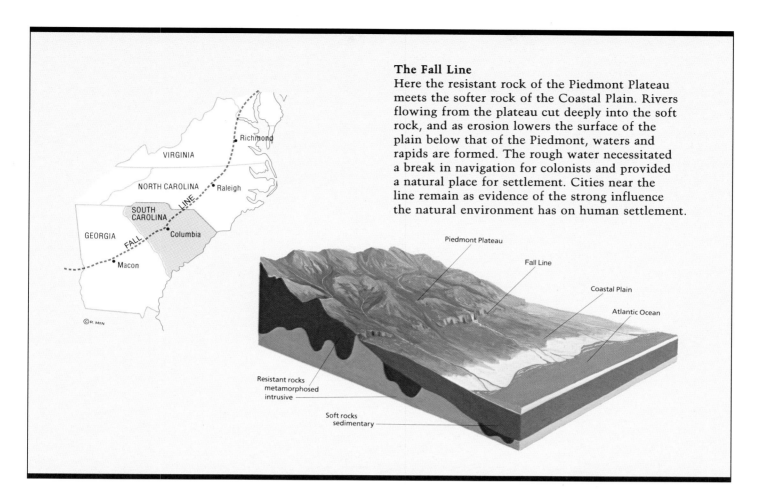

The Fall Line

Here the resistant rock of the Piedmont Plateau meets the softer rock of the Coastal Plain. Rivers flowing from the plateau cut deeply into the soft rock, and as erosion lowers the surface of the plain below that of the Piedmont, waters and rapids are formed. The rough water necessitated a break in navigation for colonists and provided a natural place for settlement. Cities near the line remain as evidence of the strong influence the natural environment has on human settlement.

Though not as imposing as the mountains of the American West, the Appalachians nonetheless proved a barrier to early westward expansion. These ancient mountains extend from what is now Newfoundland in Canada to Alabama and are separated from the Coastal Plain by the Fall Line. Many distinct ranges make up the Appalachians; one of the most prominent is the Great Smoky Mountains, shown here.

Inland Forts

Fort James, built in the spring of 1607, shows the typical palisade structure of an early fort. Surrounding trenches provide additional fortification. At the three corners are bulwarks outfitted with cannons. The site on the James River of Virginia was selected mainly for its strategic location.

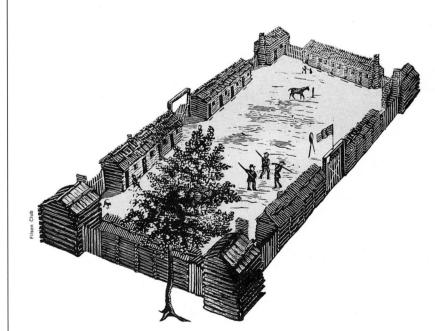

Forts: Symbols of Authority

As British and then American sovereignty moved westward, settlers called for protection from Native Americans, the French, the Spanish, and any other potential threats. The military made its presence known along the frontier in the small installations known as forts. They were mostly built in strategic sites, or in places of disturbance. They were frequently no more than log fences with blockhouses at the corners, and they were actually seldom attacked. Their importance lay in the presence of the troops, who were symbols of authority in the region. The history of the frontier could be recognized as the history of successive lines of forts as the frontier advanced. Often towns and cities grew up on the site of former forts; this fort eventually became Boonesboro, Kentucky.

Fort Ticonderoga was a stone structure in a critical location between
Lake Champlain and Lake George. The fort was a point of contention in
both the French and Indian War and the American Revolution. Shown
here is a depiction, from a Frederic Remington print, of British general
Abercrombie suffering a terrible loss in his unsuccessful attempt to take
Ticonderoga from the French in 1758. It is easy to see how the fortification gave the French advantage in the battle.

Town and Country

With east-west expansion blocked by mountain ranges, the New England frontier gradually spread along the north-south river valleys, such as the Connecticut. Continued immigration from England increased pressure to build new towns farther from Boston. Everywhere in New England good farmland was at a premium. The need for elbow room resulted as much from increased population as it did from the constraints of geography. As Cotton Mather observed of Thomas Hooker's congregation at New Town (now Cambridge, Massachusetts), ". . . such multitudes flocked over to New England after them, that the plantation of New Town became [too] strait for them; and . . . they removed a hundred miles to the westward, with a purpose to settle upon the delightful banks of the Connecticut River."

Although New England's new towns differed in size and layout, almost all of them had a common "green" for military training, a meetinghouse, a graveyard, and a parsonage. A Massachusetts law in 1635 decreed that no dwelling be built more than half a mile from a town meetinghouse. The law was flagrantly ignored, however, as frontier settlers moved to the edge of the forest where they could cut timber for export to England and ship grain and wood to plantation owners in the Caribbean.

Each New England village was responsible for its own roads, and very few towns extended roads beyond village boundaries. Often unnamed paths radiated from the village meetinghouse and dead-ended at the forest's edge. The wilderness pressed in around each of these frontier communities. Travel to adjoining towns was difficult and dangerous; only the daring settler wandered off the beaten paths between towns. Thus, the geography of New England settlement reinforced Puritan religious values of sticking to "the straight and narrow." Moreover, because neighbors were close at hand, the New Englanders relied on each other, not only during times of war against the Indians and the French but also for community projects such as roads, bridges, mills, and other public works.

In the South, tobacco culture virtually dictated the contours of the Virginia frontier. As individuals, these farmers sought out the best land to grow the "weed." Aside from seeking easy access to rivers for shipping their product to England, they used their head right to settle where they pleased. Unlike New Englanders, most Virginians, as tobacco growers, had little use for town life. They lived on isolated plantations, which relied on slave labor, rather than in towns. Therefore, as tobacco culture spread throughout the tidewater, it had centrifugal effect on settlement. Planters distributed themselves along waterways, and the lure of good land was powerful enough to convince a planter to sell out and move west even if his land was still productive.

Carolinians and Georgians, on the other hand, found that raising livestock was profitable, and they established America's first English cattle frontier. Georgia had an official "open-range" policy that required farmers to fence in their crops rather than making livestock raisers fence in their stock. In Carolina, the cattle frontier was more orderly, and English-style cow pens, along with barns and zigzag split-rail fences, became the rule. The plantation system, livestock farming, and the head right created a culture in which most families lived in relative isolation. The tightly knit community with common meetinghouses, schools, and greens that characterized the New England frontier was absent in the South, where the courthouse or crossroads store became the center of community life.

As subjects of the British Empire, the American colonists actively traded with American Indians in the interior and with England and the West Indies overseas. The colonists' diverse production gave them entrance into many English markets.

Colonial Commerce

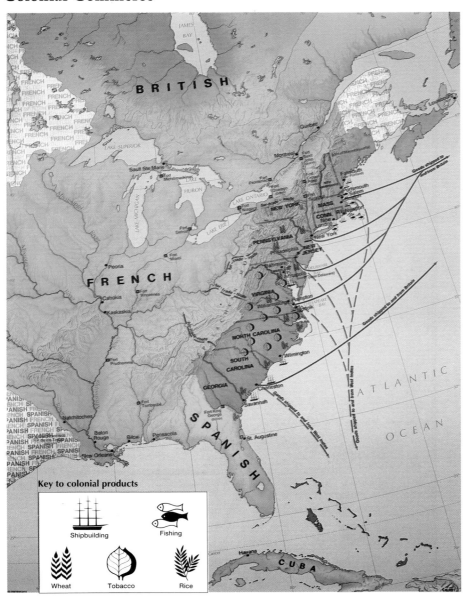

Key to colonial products

Shipbuilding   Fishing

Wheat   Tobacco   Rice

Shown here is a depiction of an early American settlement in the eighteenth century. In the eastern woodlands, clearing the land of trees was difficult. The lumber the forests yielded often went to make zigzag split-rail fences.

By the close of the eighteenth century, Americans who did not live in cities settled along rivers, especially in the South. Rivers were natural highways, and settlers who lived away from them inevitably suffered economic hardship because roads were poor. Ocean-going vessels could navigate many eastern rivers in the tidewater. Above the Fall Line, settlers relied on canoes. Shown here is the Allegheny River in Pennsylvania.

On the Eve of Independence

Events Leading to Revolution
In 1763, the king of England proclaimed that white settlement west of the Appalachian Mountains was closed, thereby angering the colonists who had already begun to settle there. The Sugar Act of 1764, passed in Britain, created taxation without representation for the American colonists, and subsequent taxing of legal documents, newspapers, playing cards, glass, lead, paint, and tea further antagonized them. In 1768, British troops landed in Boston to keep order in the increasingly restless colonies. Colonists smuggled goods to avoid taxes, while British troops carried out searches and seizures. Violence broke out when five colonists were killed by British troops in 1770; two years later, Americans burned an armed English schooner. The Boston Tea party, shown here, occurred in 1773, when a group of colonists disguised themselves, boarded ships docked at Boston, and dumped 340 cases of taxed tea into the harbor. The Intolerable Acts, as they came to be called by Americans, swiftly followed as punishment. The First Continental Congress in 1774 drew up a declaration of colonial rights and grievances to be sent to Parliament.

Abel Buell's map, published in 1783, was "the first ever compiled, engraved and finished by one man, and an American." It was the first map engraved by an American to display an American flag, and it was among the first to use the name "United States." Owners of the map had an accurate view of the newly independent nation after the Revolutionary War.

The British retained control of Maine until well after the war; statehood was gained in 1820. Maine has remained the boundary of the American frontier in the northeast. Shown here is Mount Katahdin, the highest point in the state.

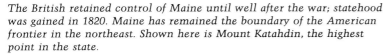

The American Revolution

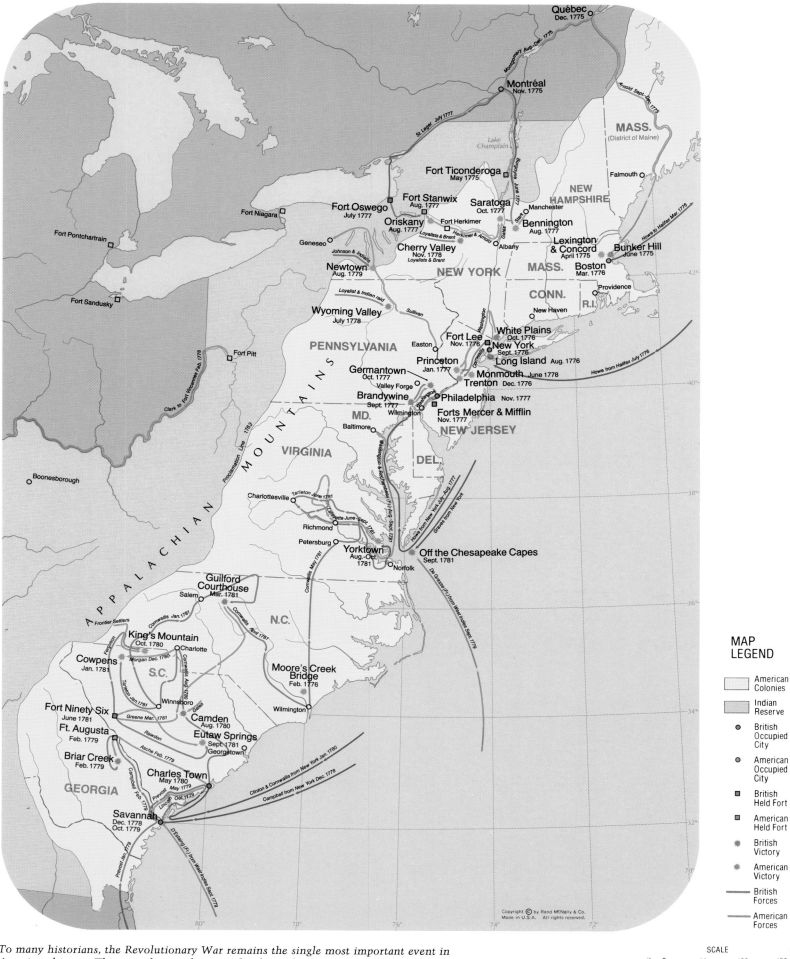

MAP LEGEND

- American Colonies
- Indian Reserve
- British Occupied City
- American Occupied City
- British Held Fort
- American Held Fort
- British Victory
- American Victory
- British Forces
- American Forces

To many historians, the Revolutionary War remains the single most important event in American history. This map depicts the major battles and strategies of the war. The peace treaty of 1783 recognized American independence and more than doubled the size of the former territory.

SCALE

| miles | 0 | 50 | 100 | 150 |
| kilometers | 0 | 50 | 100 | 150 | 200 |

Through the Cumberland Gap

As English settlers pushed their way westward to the foothills of the Appalachian Mountains, English traders found passes through the range and began to challenge the French hold on the interior. The Anglo-French struggle for dominance over America came to a head in the Last Great War for Empire (the so-called French and Indian War). The conflict began in 1754 and ended with an English victory culminating in the Treaty of Paris in 1763. With French power broken, American investors like George Washington and Benjamin Franklin joined land companies in an attempt to acquire hundreds of thousands of acres in the Ohio and Mississippi river valleys. Many farmers and small investors also sought to take advantage of what they saw as a chance to get cheap land. Their efforts came to nothing.

The English government had reserved the land for Native Americans, mostly because the crown opposed the creation of inland colonies, but also because it wanted to maintain peace with local American Indians. Colonel Henry Bouquet, who hated Indians so much he once offered to spread small pox among them or hunt them down with dogs, was ordered to prevent further white encroachment in the West. He failed on both accounts.

The Native Americans in the Ohio Valley, aware that they could no longer play England against France, feared for their future. Led by a spiritual leader named the Prophet, who preached that the abandonment of the white man's way would restore the Indians' power, and an Ottawa Indian chief, Pontiac, they launched a surprise attack on several forts and wiped out dozens of settlers. Although initially successful, Pontiac's uprising failed, and his supporters were ruthlessly suppressed by General Sir Jeffery Amherst.

The English government, hopeful of preventing a wild land rush into the West, had issued the Proclamation of 1763 prohibiting settlement west of a line along the crest of the Appalachian Mountains. This effort was both halfhearted and too late. Even a Pennsylvania law threatening the death penalty for anyone who violated the proclamation line proved fruitless. Frontier settlers simply ignored the laws. By 1768, the English government had virtually given up and decided to draw a line at the Ohio River.

The stream of settlers swelled to a flood-tide along the roads that stretched across Pennsylvania toward Fort Pitt at the fork of the Ohio River. "All spring and summer," wrote colonial land speculator George Croghan, "the roads have been lined with waggons moving to the Ohio." By 1771, an estimated ten thousand families were living in western Pennsylvania. In alarm, General Thomas Gage warned settlers to keep out of Ohio.

This painting by George Caleb Bingham depicts Daniel Boone leading settlers through the Cumberland Gap. Classical in structure and romantic in form, Bingham's work dramatized the strength, courage, and triumph of white settlers over the raw environment. Despite criticism of this interpretation of history, this painting remains one of the most popular American historical images.

Although the Cumberland Gap became the main pass to the west, other gaps were located. Shown here is Newfound Gap in what is now Great Smoky Mountains National Park, at the border of North Carolina and Tennessee.

Farther south, even before the Anglo-French war, English traders had found the Cumberland Gap, a point common to Virginia, Kentucky, and Tennessee. After the war, hunters trekked through this natural pass to harvest a bonanza of furs and hides. Soon Virginia and Carolina land speculators were hiring hunters familiar with the wilderness, like Daniel Boone (made legendary by John Filson's overblown biography), to find the best lands for settlement and to lead pioneers through the Cumberland Gap into Kentucky and Tennessee. Bloody conflict with American Indians followed, as hunters and settlers invaded prime Indian hunting grounds. Although Native Americans could do little more than slow the tide of settlers, they carried on their struggle for more than a decade. By 1800, nearly 300,000 people had moved through the Cumberland Gap. This strategic point virtually governed the course of early westward settlement.

Into the Ohio Valley

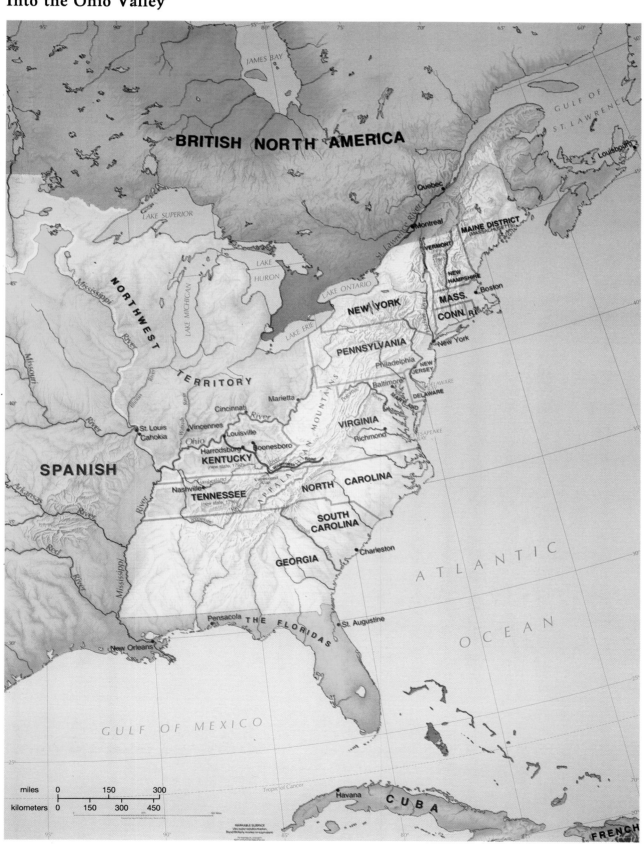

Shortly after the American Revolution, pioneers built stations in Kentucky and Tennessee and established towns along the Ohio River. They also assumed control of the old French villages in Indiana and Illinois. The Wilderness Road, which ran through the Cumberland Gap, became a main route for westward migration.

The Old Northwest Territory

The American Revolution had a profound impact on the expanding frontier. The newly formed United States claimed all western lands as far as the Mississippi River, excluding Canada and Florida. While the Americans under the Articles of Confederation passed ordinances to control the distribution of public land in the Old Northwest and provided for government, the English in Canada continued to occupy the trading posts at Detroit, Niagara, and Mackinac—all on American soil. The English maintained the posts both to profit from trade and to keep the Native Americans quiet.

Unscrupulous English traders, eager to control the Ohio fur trade, misled American Indians into believing that the English would support them in a war against the Americans. In the Indian uprising that followed, the Americans suffered ignominious defeats at the hands of the Ohio Indians. The armies of Generals Josiah Harmer and Arthur St. Clair were so badly mauled that the frontier line was stalled at the Ohio River.

President George Washington sent General Anthony Wayne to drive out the English and crush Indian opposition. A seasoned frontier fighter, Wayne routed the Native Americans at the Battle of Fallen Timbers in 1794. At the signing of the Treaty of Greenville, Wayne told the American Indians, "Let us try to agree upon such fair & equitable terms of Peace as shall be for the true interest and happiness of both white & red people; that you may in the future plant your Corn, & hunt in peace and safety. . . ." Then he compelled them to sign away southern Ohio to the Americans. In 1796, Wayne watched with grim satisfaction as the English withdrew from the fur-trading posts of the Old Northwest.

Wilderness Becomes Farmland
Shown here is an artist's view of farmland in what is now Ohio. Forests gave way to the farmers' determined axes. Wood fences were erected to keep farm animals out of the fields. Early settlers in the Ohio Valley found that land might be rolling or hilly and that streams were plentiful.

Largely a land of dense, quiet forests, like this one in Ohio, the Northwest Territory was established by a U.S. ordinance in 1787. Later called the Old Northwest, the territory was eventually divided into the states of Ohio, Indiana, Illinois, Michigan, Wisconsin, and part of Minnesota.

Initially, trade between American Indians and whites was mutually beneficial. White traders sought furs that were highly prized for clothing; Native Americans came to value the traders' tools, utensils, and ornaments. The trade balance gradually became upset, however, leading the Indians into a ruthless assault on the fur-bearing animals they needed for trade. Artists have frequently idealized interactions between whites and native peoples.

Tecumseh and the War of 1812

Following the crushing defeat of the American Indians at the hands of General Anthony Wayne, thousands of settlers swarmed into southern Ohio, Indiana, Illinois, and Michigan. The government, under heavy pressure from pioneers and popularity-seeking politicians, repeatedly sanctioned land-grabbing treaties that compelled the Native Americans of the Old Northwest to surrender millions of acres of land. The American Indians faced a desperate situation. They could not survive on smaller land bases, and they were increasingly dependent on whites for knives, guns, and metal household goods. Their forced migrations to the west brought them into conflict with other tribes over resources. Little wonder that violent incidents were common along the frontier as frustrated Native Americans and land-hungry whites clashed.

American Indians of the Old Northwest finally found a leader in Tecumseh, a Shawnee chief and implacable enemy of the Americans. Together with his brother, a prophet, Tecumseh began forming a confederation of tribes pledged to make no further land cessions without the consent of all the Indian groups. Tecumseh established a base at Prophetstown, his brother's village on the upper Wabash River. Although he distrusted all white men, including the English, Tecumseh went to Canada to seek aid against the Americans. Rebuffed by the English, Tecumseh realized he was on his own and journeyed south to enlist the Cherokee and other tribes in the confederation.

During Tecumseh's absence in 1811, Governor William Henry Harrison of Indiana, with one thousand men, struck the first blow. He routed Tecumseh's warriors at the Battle of Tippecanoe, sacked Prophetstown, and scattered the Native Americans. If Harrison had hoped to avoid a major Indian uprising, his actions had the opposite effect. Tecumseh rallied his followers, and when war broke between England and the United States in 1812, he joined the English side as a brigadier general. As the war turned against them, the English began withdrawing from central Canada. Tecumseh insisted they make a stand. In the Battle of Thames, Tecumseh and hundreds of his warriors fought to the death in a heroic final battle.

Tecumseh ranks as one of the great Indian leaders in American history. Charismatic and practical, had he succeeded in forging a strong confederation, Tecumseh would no doubt have thwarted, at least for a generation, the relentless drive for land that characterized the American occupation of the Old Northwest.

At the close of the War of 1812, the government refurbished old forts and established garrisons throughout the Northwest to control any Indian rebellion. Fort Snelling at the confluence of the Mississippi and Minnesota rivers was one of the new posts, while Fort Dearborn at Chicago and Fort Mackinac at the head of Lake Michigan were regarrisoned. Although other American Indian tribes, like the Sauk and the Fox, tried to hold out against American pressure, within a quarter of a century whites were firmly established east of the Mississippi River. The remaining Native Americans had been pushed onto marginal lands. By 1821 virtually all of Illinois, Indiana, and Michigan were in white hands. The consolidation of the Old Northwest frontier was under way.

From the end of the seventeenth century, Mackinac Island, at the junction of Lakes Michigan and Huron, was of strategic importance to control of the fur trade. When the English drove the French from North America, they fortified the island. The English continued to hold the post even after American independence, but it was turned over to the United States following the War of 1812.

The Shawnee chief Tecumseh distrusted whites. In this engraving, made from a life sketch done about 1808, Tecumseh is shown in partial western dress and wearing a peace medal. These medals, awarded by the United States, bore the face of the president on the front and peace pipes on the back to symbolize amity between peoples. They were given to American Indian leaders to demonstrate to their followers that they were accepted by whites as spokespersons.

Inspiring Words

The young American nation was ill prepared for war in 1812, and it did not fare well initially. In the summer of 1814, the British seemed positioned for victory. Much military action took place at sea, with British naval power far superior to American. It was during British shelling in 1814 that Francis Scott Key wrote the words to "The Star-Spangled Banner." The words of an American captain who served in the War of 1812 appear together with an American eagle in a wooden carving that once adorned the prow of an American ship.

The Trail of Tears

Just as Americans after the Revolution began moving into the Old Northwest, they also moved west from the tidewater settlements of Virginia, the Carolinas, and Georgia. Unlike the Native Americans of the Old Northwest, the Indian groups in the south were larger, better organized, and often led by men of mixed blood who knew how to deal with Americans. Unfortunately, some of these chiefs, such as Chief Alexander McGillivray of the Creeks (whose father was a Scot and mother a mixed-blood Creek), used their positions of trust for private gain. McGillivray signed the unfavorable Treaty of New York, surrendering a large strip of Creek land in Georgia and Carolina. At the same time, he secured for himself the rank and salary of a brigadier general in the Army of the United States. McGillivray's fellow Creeks rejected the treaty's terms and compelled McGillivray to repudiate it.

The settlement of the Old Southwest might have been slower but for Eli Whitney's invention of the cotton gin. The gin made cotton production highly profitable almost everywhere in the South. Small farmers, as well as plantation owners, quickly recognized that the rich lands owned by the southern American Indians were a potential bonanza. The cotton craze led land-hungry planters to demand that Indian lands be opened for white settlement.

The Creeks were especially threatened. Their land base was barely adequate and their leadership sharply divided about how to deal with demands by the American government. Tecumseh's visit in 1811 inspired many younger Indian men to fight. In 1813, some of them went to Pensacola, Florida, to secure arms and supplies from the Spanish. On their way home, the Creeks were attacked by Americans. The Creeks retaliated by assaulting Fort Mims, a poorly defended militia post, killing more than five hundred settlers. Enraged Tennessee frontiersmen led by Andrew Jackson attacked the Creek

The Cherokee were among the most advanced of the Native American peoples in the Southeast. Most were forced to participate in the terrible journey the Cherokee called the Trail of Tears and were driven to Indian Territory (Oklahoma). Some Cherokee escaped into the mountains, however, and their descendants make up the modern Cherokee community in North Carolina.

stronghold at the Horseshoe Bend of the Tallapoosa River and slaughtered more than eight hundred Native Americans. Broken, the Creek were forced to yield over twenty million acres of land.

The Creek defeat did not mean that the southern Indians were a vanquished people. The Cherokee in Georgia and the Choctaw and Chickasaw in Mississippi were quickly modernizing. Many accepted white dress, white weapons and tools, and farming. In particular, the Cherokee, many of whom were cotton-raising slave holders, had a highly stable political and social community as well as a written language and newspaper press. Therefore, the full tragedy of the Creek debacle was not felt until the 1830s, when the state of Georgia determined to force the Cherokees to leave their lands. Although the Cherokees won their case before the United States Supreme Court, which recognized their existence as a separate nation, President Andrew Jackson refused to abide by the court's ruling.

He is reputed to have said, "John Marshall [the Chief Justice] has made his decision, now let him enforce it." The Cherokees, at the mercy of the Georgia frontiersmen who wanted their land, had no choice but to make the best deal they could with the government.

The federal government now began to plan for the forced removal of all Eastern Indian tribes beyond the Mississippi River into Oklahoma. The Native Americans were promised fair treatment, but the outcome remains one of the more sordid episodes in American history. Driven from their homes like animals, mistreated and misled along the trail west, thousands of Cherokees died. The forced migration of other groups followed, with equally horrifying results. Known as the Trail of Tears, the story of this tragic exodus marks the end of the Indian frontier in the Old Southwest.

The Creeks were one of the so-called Five Civilized Tribes. They successfully opposed the United States until the Battle of Horseshoe Bend, when General Andrew Jackson defeated a group of Creek warriors. Like the Cherokee, the Creek were forced to move to Oklahoma.

The name Seminole, from a Creek word meaning "runaway," was given to a varied group of fugitive slaves, Creeks, and other Native Americans who pushed farther and farther into the swampy woodlands of the Florida Everglades in the face of increasing white encroachment. The Seminoles fought repeated wars and skirmishes with the United States until most of them were forced to become one of the so-called Five Civilized Tribes, along with the Cherokee, Creek, Choctaw, and Chickasaw. A few managed to remain in the Everglades, however, and retain some of their traditional ways.

A Network of Roads

The defeat of the Native Americans east of the Mississippi River after the War of 1812 resulted in millions of acres of fertile land open for white settlement. Pioneers on this trans-Appalachian frontier demanded protection from American Indians and the construction of federal posts and military roads in the newly opened territories. As the white population of these areas increased, settlers clamored for statehood and insisted that their states build roads to encourage further immigration, improve communication, and make transporting goods easier.

The first rush of wagon-road construction took place before 1830. The National Road, a major well-constructed highway stretching from Cumberland, Maryland, to Wheeling on the Ohio River, was completed in 1818 by the Army Corps of Engineers. By 1833 the National Road was extended to Columbus, Ohio. When the modern federal highway system was built, the Old National Road became US 40. A rather crude road extending from Richmond, Virginia, to the Kanawha River in Kentucky was built on an old trail through Ward's Gap in the Blue Ridge Mountains. The Old Wilderness Road crossing the Cumberland Gap remained important for people who traveled through Kentucky to Louisville, and cutoffs from the trail led to Cincinnati, Ohio, and Maysville, Kentucky. By 1830, territorial roads extended from Louisville, Kentucky, to Vincennes, Indiana, and on to Vandalia, Illinois, and the old French towns of Kaskaskia and Cahokia.

By 1850, the northern wagon-road system was virtually complete. The National Road now reached through Indianapolis, Indiana, to Vandalia. The Genesee Turnpike extended from the Hudson River Valley through Buffalo to Cleveland in Ohio. Detroit was connected to Chicago, and the latter city, founded only two decades earlier, was already linked to Green Bay, Wisconsin, through Milwaukee in the north and to Galena, Illinois, in the west.

The southern road-building program kept pace with progress in the North. The old road along the Fall Line of the Appalachians was extended from Virginia to Augusta, Georgia, and west to Montgomery, Alabama. A cutoff of this road passed along the interior from Washington, D.C., to Montgomery, Alabama, through Athens, Georgia. The Great Valley Road, perhaps the most heavily traveled because it led Pennsylvania's pioneers south into the interior, passed through the Virginia back country, across Tennessee into Knoxville, and then on to Huntsville and Florence, Alabama. The famous Natchez Trace led north from Natchez to Nashville, Tennessee, on the Cumberland River.

A map of the eastern United States showing the major wagon roads at this time might give the impression that the nation had an effective highway system. Although many of these roads had been surveyed by the Army Corps of Engineers, they were often "roads" only in name. Many were merely trails slashed through the forest. Others were paths, with tree stumps still in place, that turned into muddy trenches when it rained.

Nevertheless, these early roads still proved useful. Although tavern keepers along the right of way provided shelter and safety to travelers, some routes had a reputation for being dangerous. The Natchez Trace, for example, became infamous for the highwaymen who robbed wealthy travelers returning north from New Orleans after selling cargoes they had shipped down the Mississippi River. Legend has it that one gang, the Masons, beheaded the leader of a rival gang, the Harpes, and tried to claim a reward. Captured later, the Mason gang member was himself executed. More than likely, however, there was no more violence along the southern trails than on any of the other roads.

As use of these early highways increased, they were gradually improved. By the 1840s heavy wagons known as Conestogas were a frequent sight on the major routes as pioneers from the east headed for Oregon and California. "Old America," one traveler noted, "seems to be breaking up and moving westward."

Early Turnpikes
Here a carriage stops to pay a toll on an early American road. A pole, or pike, across the road stopped travelers until they paid the toll. When the toll keeper lifted the pike or turned it aside, the people could go on with their trip. Americans took to calling such roads "turnpikes."

New Stars in the American Flag

By 1821, lands east of the Mississippi had achieved statehood, and Americans were beginning to cross the river. With the Louisiana Purchase, the United States laid claim to a region extending from the northern Great Plains to the far northwest of Oregon and Washington.

This early photograph captured westward-moving settlers in Conestoga wagons. Before the construction of the nation's railroad system, between 1820 and 1850, use of the Conestoga, "the wagon of the empire," was at its peak. These settlers are crossing under telegraph wires; wagons were not the only thing to follow the new network of roads. Samuel Morse perfected the telegraph in 1844, and telegraph lines were subsequently built along major routes. American transportation and communication networks grew together.

Canal and Railroad Fever

The wave of wagon-road construction that followed the War of 1812 was scarcely under way when New York authorized $7,000,000 to build the Erie Canal. Governor De Witt Clinton, who had planned the canal, had the satisfaction of being in office when it opened in 1825. Within a decade, it had not only paid for itself but also earned such huge profits that freight rates fell by almost 90 percent. Tolls were collected by weight. Jacob Schramm, a German traveler, explained how the boats were weighed: "The boat is taken into a lock. . . . When the boat is at the right spot the lock is opened on the other side so that the water runs out. When it is out the boat rests on a scaffold connected with big scales, and in five minutes the weighing is finished. . . .The lock is again opened so that the water can rush back."

The success of the Erie Canal touched off an era of massive spending on internal improvements. All the states in the Old Northwest began building canals or financing railroads to connect inland cities to canals and rivers. Canal and railroad fever swept the nation as state after state sold bonds to eager investors, many of them foreigners who did not understand that these frontier states had few assets to back the bonds.

The giddy financial spree ended in the Panic of 1837, and by 1842, nine states had defaulted on their bonds. English investors alone lost $100,000,000. However, this business depression neither ended the migration of people westward nor stopped the steady increase in agricultural production. Farmers and merchants in the interior states and traders in the coastal cities of New York, Boston, Philadelphia, and Baltimore recognized that improved transportation was an economic necessity if they were to survive and grow.

The railroad construction that began anew in the 1840s differed from that of pre-Panic days. The new lines were built from major marketing cities to capture the trade of the hinterland. The railroads were not seen as adjuncts to the waterway system but as a powerful network in their own right. Moreover, railroad technology was so improved that rail

The earliest United States rail lines reflected the primitive technology of the era. Construction involved almost no machinery, and the wood-burning engines, faulty rails, and semiskilled labor created hazards. Nevertheless, many lines were built, and American railroad technology was not behind that of any other nation.

traffic was able to compete with shipment by water. States financed these new lines with private capital rather than with state bonds, which foreign investors shunned and taxpayers resented.

The first major rail lines were built from east to west by capitalists in Philadelphia and Baltimore who had lost trade to New York because of the Erie Canal. New York merchants soon realized they needed rail connections or their trade would wane when winter ice prevented water travel. By the late 1850s, rails connected most of the large eastern cities with Pittsburgh, Cincinnati, Cleveland, Columbus, Indianapolis, Chicago, and even St. Louis. By 1860, 350 railroad companies had invested more than $1 billion in the construction of 31,000 miles of track. Henry David Thoreau believed that trains had changed America: "They come and go with such regularity and precision, and their whistles can be heard so far, that the farmers set their clocks by them, and thus one well-regulated institution regulates a whole country."

First the Erie Canal and then railroads spurred development in upper New York State. What was once a quiet backwoods area was suddenly a main artery of the nation. Shown here is the Mohawk River near Schenectady.

The Erie Canal connected New York City, by way of the Hudson River, with Lake Erie, at Buffalo, New York. The canal contributed to the success of New York City as a port as well as to immigration to the upper Great Lakes region. The canal was not only a significant engineering feat but also a highly profitable financial venture. This bucolic image does not do justice to the remarkable industrial and agricultural revolution that took place along its route.

The Rise of Urban America

The movement westward, so often depicted as farmers and planters seeking land, must also include the rapid spread of urbanization. Frontier communities founded at the critical intersections of wagon roads, canals, rail lines, and natural waterways such as the Ohio-Mississippi River system and the Great Lakes often grew rapidly into large cities.

Some, like Louisville, at the falls of the Ohio River, became a trans-shipment point for farm products; others, like New Orleans, became great seaports that stored and exported the products of the entire lower Mississippi River region. Regardless of their primary function, the communities grew up simultaneously with the development of the surrounding farmland. In some instances, when enterprising entrepreneurs saw a chance to preempt a market, the cities grew even before most of the rural areas were settled.

Western cities vied with each other for economic advantage, offering free lots to those who would build hotels and factories.

Railroads received special treatment, including free land, tax exemptions, and even promises of financial aid. The business leaders of St. Louis, New Orleans, Memphis, Chicago, and Vicksburg all hoped their city would emerge as the eastern terminus of the transcontinental railroad.

St. Louis, established by French and Spanish settlers in the 1760s, had long dominated the western fur trade because of its strategic location on the Mississippi River. However, it eventually lost out to Chicago as the lakeside city became a main rail hub. To the east, Cincinnati acquired the nickname "Porkopolis" because of its slaughterhouses and significant shipments of meat to the eastern seaboard. These western cities were "new" on the national scene, and throughout the 1800s, their populations grew at remarkable rates. In terms of plan and architecture, they tried to emulate leading eastern cities, even to the extent of building neoclassical Greek and Roman structures on the open prairie.

Westward Expansion

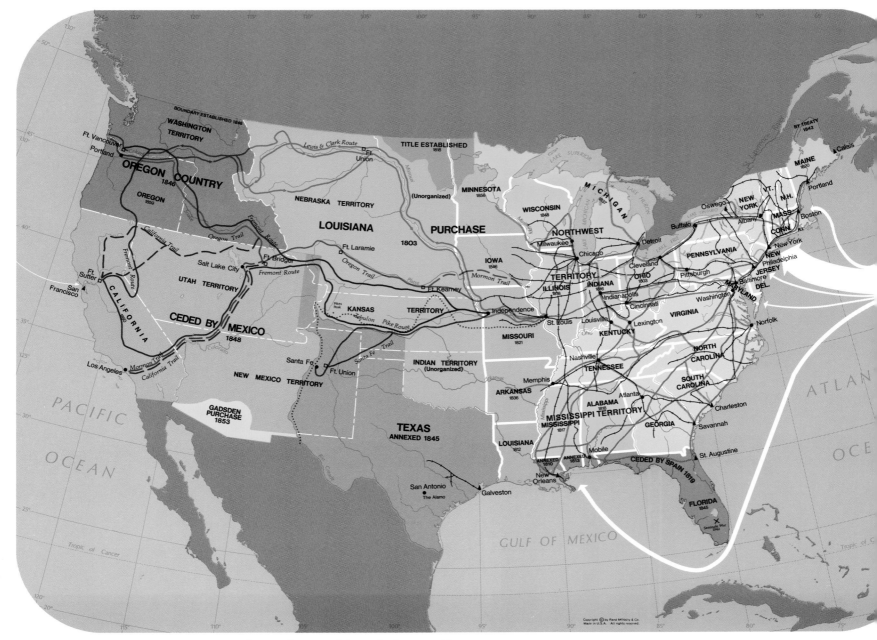

Between 1803 and 1860, the United States had acquired by treaty, purchase, or war all the land that was to make up the nation's contiguous territory. Moreover, primary communication and transportation routes were clearly established.

Before the expansion of the railroad system, St. Louis was the main gateway to the West. It had long been the transshipment point for goods going both up and down the Mississippi and Ohio rivers. French merchants who crossed the Mississippi to escape English rule after the French and Indian Wars founded the town in 1764.

MAP
LEGEND

▲ Port Cities
● Other Cities
▢ States
   as of 1803
— Roads
— Canals
→ Railroads
   Width of flow lines
   are proportional
   to actual numbers
   of immigrants
   entering the
   United States through
   the ports indicated
   during the period
   1840-1855.

SCALE

miles 0   100   200   300   400
kilometers 0   200   400   600

New York City emerged as the nation's major banking and commercial center with the development of the Erie Canal. For years, New York entrepreneurs had invested in western lands, the China-Pacific trade, and internal improvements. Before the Civil War, New York was the primary source of domestic investment capital as well as the location of a vital commercial and manufacturing community.

The Rise of Urban America (continued)

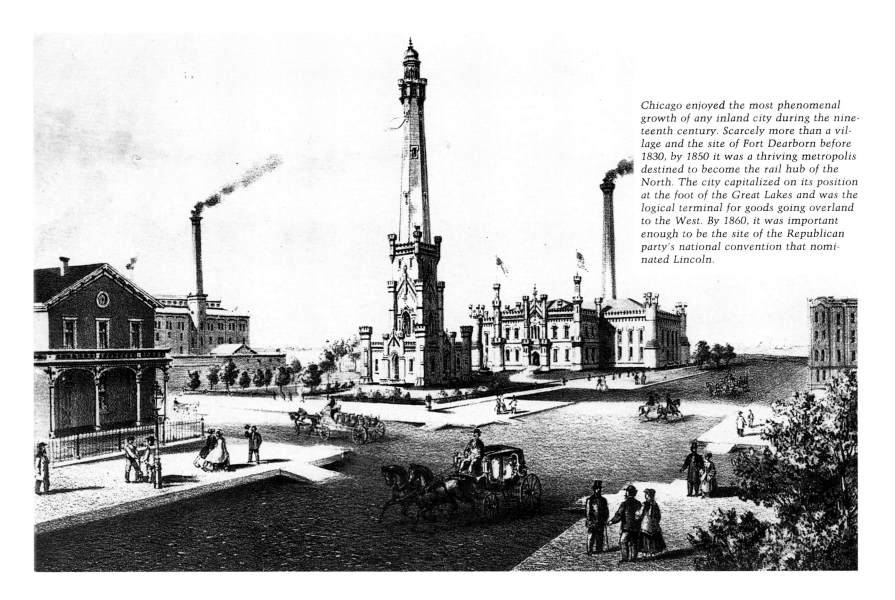

Chicago enjoyed the most phenomenal growth of any inland city during the nineteenth century. Scarcely more than a village and the site of Fort Dearborn before 1830, by 1850 it was a thriving metropolis destined to become the rail hub of the North. The city capitalized on its position at the foot of the Great Lakes and was the logical terminal for goods going overland to the West. By 1860, it was important enough to be the site of the Republican party's national convention that nominated Lincoln.

From its founding in 1718, New Orleans had been a principal city of the South and the primary transshipment point for the goods that were transported down the Mississippi River system. Even after the growth of railroads, New Orleans retained its hold on most of the inland trade.

The Frontier Across the Mississippi

The Frontier Across the Mississippi

Although there had been an American frontier from the time Europeans landed on the continent, in the minds of many modern Americans, the American West—the trans-Mississippi region—remains the real frontier. Movies, television, novels, and advertising have perpetuated the mythic images of the western frontier, among them the rugged cowboy, the horse-mounted American Indian, the smoke-filled saloon, and the gun-slinging outlaw. These icons sprang from the everyday life of a time that spanned only a quarter of a century and in which life was difficult at best.

Public attitudes toward foreign nations, native people, economic development, and the use of land had been well established by the time President Thomas Jefferson's agents bargained for the Louisiana Purchase in 1803—long before the era of the Wild West. Nonetheless, the mid-1800s saw great territorial expansion by the United States, as Texas, Oregon, California, and the Southwest were acquired. As whites moved into the trans-Mississippi region, the demographic makeup of this part of the American frontier was, at first, primarily one of single males of European descent, just as it had been east of the Mississippi.

The fate of Native Americans on the trans-Mississippi frontier did not differ significantly from that of the eastern Indians. First, as whites advanced, so did their diseases. More American Indians fell to smallpox, measles, and cholera than to any weapon. Then, major battlegrounds between whites and Indians crossed the Mississippi around 1850 and continued as groups such as the Cheyenne, Comanche, Sioux, Apache, and Navajo were subdued. One major difference on the trans-Mississippi frontier was that the Great Plains had long been thought to be the refuge of the American Indian. What is now Oklahoma, for instance, had been designated a permanent home for the Native Americans of the Southeast, the so-called Five Civilized Tribes. Later, Plains Indians were also forced into Indian Territory, and by 1885, fifty different groups were relocated to the territory.

Recently, many have begun to question the meaning and morality of the American West. Was the "winning of the West" a heroic struggle in the name of progress, or was it racist, sexist, and environmentally disastrous? Today, more and more people see both sides to these questions. The moods, motives, and rationalizations of manifest destiny have appeared elsewhere in the histories of powerful nations and empires; thus the self-confident conquest of the North American continent by Europeans was not completely unprecedented. Nonetheless, as Americans continue to be fascinated by their own history, they also continue to decipher it.

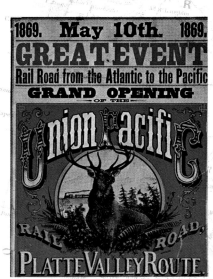

Historic poster

By the time this map was made, in 1856, the United States was a transcontinental nation. Vast areas west of the Mississippi River, however, remained territorial in status. Wagon roads and railroads were already beginning to form transportation and communication networks in the East, and there was intense competition between the North and South over the location of the first transcontinental railroad.

Perhaps more than any other place, Monument Valley, at the border of
Utah and Arizona, has come to symbolize the western frontier. Caused by
erosion, the red sandstone buttes, mesas, and arches show up again and
again in the media as icons of the American West. The valley is part of
the Navajo Indian Reservation.

American bison

Onward Across the Mississippi

Even before the United States purchased the Louisiana Territory, many Americans recognized the economic opportunities that existed beyond the Mississippi. As early as 1788, George Morgan, a Philadelphia businessman and western land speculator, established the town of New Madrid in southern Missouri when the area was still under Spanish rule. Another Philadelphian, Moses Austin, moved to Potosi, Missouri, in 1798 to open a lead mine.

The Spanish required Americans to accept Roman Catholicism and Spanish citizenship before they could settle in their territory. Austin became a Spanish citizen and later planned to establish an American colony in Texas. Other French and Spanish cities such as New Orleans and St. Louis also attracted American settlers and enterprising businessmen.

Americans knew of the intense competition between the English and Spanish for control of the American Indian trade on the upper Missouri River. In the 1780s, agents of the Hudson's Bay Company and the Northwest Fur Company struck out from their bases in Prairie du Chien, Wisconsin, and Mackinac Island to trade with the Plains Indians as far west as the Mandan villages on the Missouri River. Well supplied with cheap goods and fiercely competitive among themselves, the fur traders' motto was a parody taken from the Book of Job, "a skin for a skin," meaning the life of a trader for the skin of a beaver.

The English fur trappers proved more than a match for the Spanish. When Spain feared that it would lose control of northern Louisiana to the English, it recruited the support of the French merchants in St. Louis. Long experienced in dealing with Native Americans, the French, led by the veteran trader Auguste Chouteau, began to organize expeditions to reach American Indians on the upper Missouri.

The English enjoyed the advantage of operating out of bases that were actually on United States territory. Initially, the Americans lacked the military strength to drive them out. The English, in turn, claimed their traders at Mackinac and Prairie du Chien kept the Native Americans from attacking settlers by providing them with goods. Then, in one stroke, Jefferson's purchase of Louisiana changed the international equation. The United States now laid claim to all the land that France had possessed in the trans-Mississippi West. Although a clash between the English fur companies and the Americans seemed inevitable, the Spanish had more to

This view of life at a rustic trading post offers a benign image of what had ceased to be an equal exchange. Increasingly, American Indians lived in a society of mixed material goods, and they were in many instances reduced to marginal status.

The Land of the Bison
The grasslands from the Mississippi River to the Rocky Mountains were the grazing lands of an estimated thirty million bison when whites first arrived. These wild cattle, inaccurately known as buffalo, were a primary resource for the Plains Indians. The influx of white settlers west of the Mississippi proved devastating to both the Plains Indians and the bison; by the end of the nineteenth century, only about five hundred bison survived.

fear. Weakened by years of bitter European warfare, Spain confronted a dangerously expansionist democratic society to the north of Mexico with an insatiably land-hungry population.

The Lewis and Clark expedition to Oregon, commissioned by Jefferson, was a harbinger of American plans and dreams. It opened the way for Americans to challenge English fur traders on the upper Missouri and in the central Rocky Mountains. The expedition clearly indicated that American pioneers would soon begin to settle the west bank of the Mississippi River. These settlers were not simply after the fur trade and dominance over Native Americans but also wanted to claim the land for farms.

The northern Great Plains was home to many Plains Indian groups. The Blackfeet, Assiniboin, Sioux, Hidatsa, Mandan, Crow, and Cheyenne were all part of the thriving Plains community, which was largely dependent on the great herds of bison that roamed freely. Shown here is part of the northern plains, near the Little Missouri River, North Dakota.

This photograph of a Cheyenne camp illustrates in part how the Great Plains life-style was drastically altered by contact and trade with whites. Native Americans became dependent on white society for wagons, guns, and cooking utensils, yet the quality of their lives had suffered because they were in what was becoming the white man's world, but they were not of it.

Lewis and Clark

The Explorers of the West

The overland expeditions of Lewis and Clark and Zebulon Pike were essential to President Thomas Jefferson's plan to map the nation's boundaries, locate the headwaters of rivers, and survey the resources of the United States. The Spanish were already well established in the Southwest.

Meriwether Lewis and William Clark led the first United States expedition that crossed the western half of the continent and returned. Along the way, the men learned about the languages and customs of the Native Americans they encountered, and except for one episode, their contacts with Indians were peaceful.

Among the discoveries of Lewis and Clark was the Snake River, which, with its tributaries, is one of the largest river systems in North America. Later, the Oregon Trail followed part of the Snake. Shown here is the river at Grand Teton National Park, Wyoming.

Surveyors of the West

No sooner had the United States acquired Louisiana than President Thomas Jefferson decided it must be thoroughly explored. He prepared detailed instructions for the U.S. Army's exploring parties, beginning with Meriwether Lewis and William Clark. When he sent William Dunbar and George Hunter to explore the Red River, the two men, fearful of the Spanish, ignored his instructions and traveled only as far as the Ouachita River in Arkansas. Thomas Freeman, also recruited by Jefferson, was even less successful in seeking the headwaters of the Red River. Jefferson had better luck when he sent twenty-six-year-old Lieutenant Zebulon Montgomery Pike to search for the headwaters of the Mississippi River. Pike mistakenly assumed that Leech Lake was the river's source, but he managed to convince the Canadian fur trappers he found in Minnesota to haul down the Union Jack and raise the Stars and Stripes.

Pike is better known for leading an expedition up the Missouri River to explore the central and southern Great Plains. When the pro-Spanish Pawnee Indians tried to stop him, Pike warned that the "warriors of [the] Great American Father were not. . .to be turned back by words" and pressed on. His trail took him to Colorado, where he reported that his men, on seeing the Rockies, "gave three cheers to the Mexican Mountains." He unsuccessfully tried to climb what may have been Pikes Peak.

Moving south into Mexican territory, Pike was captured by Mexican soldiers and taken to Chihuahua. He carefully noted all that he saw along the way. His report, reconstructed from memory, earned him recognition as an explorer. Pike pointed out that parts of the Great Plains were too arid to be farmed and likened them to desert regions: "These vast plains of the hemisphere may become in time as celebrated as the sandy deserts of Africa. . . ." Jefferson never fulfilled his hope that military expeditions would unlock all the geographic secrets of the trans-Mississippi West.

Where the army failed, however, fur traders succeeded. Spurred by the lure of wealth, these adventurers crisscrossed the West between 1807 and 1840. Always looking for unsophisticated American Indians who would trade a rich fur harvest for liquor, cheap tools, and traps, they trailed up river valleys, discovered passes through the Rocky Mountains, and made the Native Americans increasingly dependent on the whites for their livelihood. The fur traders contributed directly to the white conquest of the West. Unfortunately, cut-throat competition among the traders caused them to hunt to near extinction the fur-bearing animals that were their victims.

The fur traders came in the wake of the Lewis and Clark expedition. The first, Manuel Lisa, was a St. Louis merchant, who in 1807 explored the upper Missouri and Yellowstone rivers. John Colter, a veteran of the Lewis and Clark expedition, was employed by Lisa. He spent the winter traveling alone over five hundred miles of icy northern Rockies and may have been among the first white explorers to see the thermal geysers of today's Yellowstone Park. William Henry Ashley, entrepreneur and fur trader, led parties to the northern and central Rocky Mountains as well as originating the "rendezvous," a scheme that brought together American Indian and white trappers and hunters for an annual trading fair.

Perhaps the greatest mountain man was Jedediah Strong Smith. Famed for his courage and for his religious convictions—he carried a Bible with him—Smith was once attacked by a grizzly bear that seized his head and ripped off his scalp and one of his ears. Although at death's door, Smith instructed one of his men to sew his head together and his ear back on. In ten days he was again ready to travel, but his maimed features thereafter spoke eloquently of the dangers of life in the wilds. His travels of discovery took him from Missouri to the Mojave Desert of California and as far north as Oregon. He probably knew more about the West than any fur trader other than the Hudson's Bay Company explorer Peter Skene Ogden.

The army never abandoned its role as mapper of the West. John Charles Frémont created one of the most remarkable examples of the army's work. Frémont's well-written accounts, illustrated by the distinguished artists who traveled with him, and his excellent maps gave the American public a superb knowledge of much of the continent's vast interior. He also exhibited a profound sympathy for the plight of Native Americans and once observed: "We have taken from them their property and means of support and are bound to a corresponding obligation." Frémont's expedition was only one of many sponsored by the Bureau of Topographical Engineers. Their work was to prove invaluable not only to the early travelers and settlers but also to later road and railroad builders who began linking eastern cities to the West.

The Grand Canyon, a gigantic chasm that covers 217 miles in northern Arizona, is one of the natural wonders of the continent. The first white man to see the canyon was one of Coronado's soldiers. Because of the rugged terrain, the canyon remained virtually unexplored until 1869. By the 1890s, a few white tourists with a taste for adventure had visited the South Rim. With the construction of the Santa Fe Railroad across the Southwest, however, the Grand Canyon emerged as one of the most popular tourist sites in the nation.

Havasupai Creek joins the Colorado River, the primary river of the Grand Canyon, after a series of waterfalls. Many ruins in and around the canyon reveal part of its human history as home to groups of Native Americans. The Havasupai today occupy Cataract Canyon as they have for over nine hundred years.

The Great American Desert

The military explorers who trailed through the West were often surprised by what they found. Lieutenant Zebulon Pike, when he encountered the semiarid region lying between the 100th meridian and the Rocky Mountains, called that vast expanse the Great Sandy Desert and spoke of it in terms of Africa's Sahara region. His views were echoed fourteen years later in 1820 by Major Stephen H. Long, who described the region as "almost wholly unfit for cultivation, and of course uninhabitable by a people depending upon agriculture for their subsistence." In other words, they saw it as the Great American Desert. The term was used repeatedly on maps of the United States before the Civil War. Today the area is known as the Great Plains.

Both Pike and Long had grown up in the East where rainfall was abundant—often exceeding thirty inches a year. They did not believe it was possible to farm the Great Plains, where, in many places, precipitation was less than twenty inches per year. To some nineteenth-century observers, the soils of the Great Plains seemed sterile: devoid of trees, except for cottonwoods in the river bottoms, with thin vegetation, bitterly cold winters, and hot dry summers. This view echoed the earlier judgments of Pike and Long that the Great Plains stood as a barrier to the farmers'

frontier. Eastern farmers regarded it as a wasteland to be hurriedly crossed. Pike and Long thought the region best left to American Indians whose nomadic life-styles were adapted to the environment.

Then, in 1838, John C. Frémont traveled across the Great Plains and challenged this view. He found he could graze his animals on the native grasses and concluded that agriculture would be possible. He also insisted that America's true desert was in the Great Basin, the plateau between the Rockies and the Sierra Nevada. Frémont's report received attention only after the Civil War, when railroad entrepreneurs, laying track across the West, sought to sell land on the Great Plains. Additionally, the government land office, as well as speculators, encouraged settlement, even in areas believed to be semiarid.

Unfortunately, the early settlers tried farming the plains, despite warnings from officials like Colonel John Wesley Powell. These eastern farmers were misled by pseudoscientists and charlatans who assured them that "rainfall followed the plow." Instead, they found themselves beset by severe droughts, dust storms, and devastating insect infestations. Throughout the frontier era, efforts by farmers to conquer the Great Plains failed. Eventually, the region became the cattle kingdom of the nation.

There was little romance to life for early settlers of the prairie. Everyone, regardless of status, endured an equal amount of discomfort. The landscape itself could be depressing. The horizon in the winter and autumn, virtually without trees or vegetation, often displayed a vast, almost soulless, void. Little wonder that travelers on the Great Plains often described it as a land of nothing but prairie and sky.

"Badlands" are areas of severe erosion, usually found in dry regions that are poorly pro-
tected by vegetation. The term was first used to describe a region of the northern Great
Plains, where the prairie disappears into silent, eerie shale and limestone formations.
Adding to the otherworldy dimension of the Badlands of South Dakota, shown here, were
the visible fossils of long-extinct creatures.

Original Residents of the West

For many Plains Indians groups, the bison was of utmost importance. These Native Americans made use of virtually all of the bison: they derived food, clothing, shelter, and tools from slain animals. The bison, too, was an integral part of their religious practices. But before they secured horses from Europeans, many Plains Indians groups lived marginally on the vast grassland and relied on dog power. Their effectiveness in hunting the bison herds, and even in following them across the plains, was limited, and agriculture was important. In the seventeenth and eighteenth centuries, the horse revolutionized the life-styles of many of the Plains Indians. Horses and bison became the focal points of their cultures. The horse not only allowed these American Indians to follow the herds more closely, but it also made killing the animals easier.

Western Wildlife

Lands that appeared to be uninhabitable desert to some humans were anything but to other creatures. The Great Plains, Rocky Mountains, and beyond were the rich habitats of multitudes of large mammals. The cougar, grizzly bear, and mountain goat thrived in the American West, as did the coyote, prairie dog, pronghorn, and bison. Many other unique mammals, insects, reptiles, and plants were found on the Great Plains and beyond. With the advance of white civilization, especially agriculture, much of the wildlife of the West has been relegated to a few remaining refuges.

As was the case east of the river, west of the Mississippi were many Native American cultures of amazing diversity. The Hopi of the Southwest, a Pueblo group, remained for many years the most isolated of North American peoples. Known for their kachina masks and dramas and for their pueblos, they have preserved a distinctive culture. When the Spanish entered the Southwest, the Hopi, probably descended from the Anasazi, were essentially sedentary farmers and small-scale hunter-gatherers. The Hopi life-style included religious practices, monogamy, and the matrilineal clan system (inheritance was through the female line). Each clan "owned," or exercised control over, secret worship practices. Among the unique religious dramas of the Hopi was the flute ceremony of the Walpi, captured in this 1900 photograph. The flute ceremony, like many religious practices, had sacred and secret meanings.

The Navajo, who are today the largest Native American group in the United States, are believed to have migrated to the Southwest from what is now Canada about five hundred years ago. Once in the Southwest, Navajo contact with Pueblo Indians, such as the Hopi and Zuni, as well as the vastly different environment, brought about changes, and the traditional Navajo way of life evolved. One aspect of daily life that became uniquely Navajo was the dwelling known as the hogan. Shown here is a hogan today in Monument Valley.

The Overland Trail

By the 1840s, even while good land was still available in the Mississippi Valley, some restless Americans—spurred on by religion, adventure, profit, and patriotism—headed for Oregon and California. Jesse A. Applegate, who made the trip as a small boy, recalled how he and his cousins looked into coffee cups to see the future. "We thought we could see covered wagons and Indians scalping women and children. How little we guessed of what the future held in store for those wagons of courageous people. Little did we dream of the weary days and weeks and months of that long and toilsome march towards the land of the setting sun, a test of courage of soul." Few who made the trip anticipated that they would be forced to jettison furniture, stoves, and other reminders of home because their worn-out animals and wagons could not haul them farther.

Their trip across the continent followed what historians now call the Overland Trail. The route to Oregon was familiar to fur traders, some of whom became the first Americans to settle in the Northwest. The trail began at Independence, Missouri, turned north to the Platte River, followed the river west to the Sweetwater, pursued the Sweetwater to South Pass, turned south to Fort Bridger, and then north to Soda Springs. There the California-bound wagon trains turned south to the Humboldt River and followed it

Along the Westward Trails

Before the Civil War, settlers moving to Oregon and California traveled westward along the trail that followed the Platte River and crossed the Rockies at South Pass. Beyond the pass, the trails divided to cross the harshest part of the route. The term "overland trail" is used in reference to all the old trails westward from the Missouri to the Pacific.

to the foot of the Sierra Nevada, where several passes over the mountains opened onto the Sacramento Valley. Oregon-bound emigrants turned north from Soda Springs to Fort Hall, then followed the Snake River to a cutoff that reached the Columbia River, which was then rafted to Fort Vancouver and the Willamette Valley. The Oregon Trail, two thousand miles in length, proved to be the greatest emigrant trek in recorded history.

Among the earliest Americans to settle in Oregon were Presbyterian missionaries. An 1836 party of missionaries included two women—Narcissa Whitman and Eliza Spalding, who were the first white women to travel overland to Oregon. Guided to the annual fur traders' rendezvous, where they were shocked by the behavior of the mountain men, the missionaries later established stations among Oregon's Native Americans. Narcissa Whitman and her physician husband died tragically during an Indian uprising.

Large-scale emigration began in 1841 when the Bidwell-Bartleson party left Missouri. Guided by the experienced mountain man Thomas Fitzpatrick, the group went as far as Soda Springs, where it divided roughly in half. One group went on to Oregon. Bidwell's party struck out for California and suffered incredible hardships as it wandered through deserts and scaled icy mountains. Forced to abandon their wagons, the would-be settlers were later compelled to eat their pack animals or starve. In early November, they finally arrived in California, the first emigrant train to make the trip all the way from Missouri.

Although many emigrants traveled successfully along the trail, disaster awaited any group that took a misstep. The most grisly example was the Donner party from Illinois, who started west too late in the summer, squabbled about leadership en route, and was caught in an early Sierra Nevada snowfall. Confronted with starvation, members of the party turned to cannibalism to survive.

The California Trail was less popular than the Oregon branch, and most observers believed that the Oregon-bound travelers were of a "better sort." That is, until the California gold rush in 1849. With the gold rush, the character of travel on the Overland Trail changed. Bridges replaced river fords, stores and stations opened along the route selling goods and services to travelers. Although the trip was still a test of endurance and courage, the travelers now could rely on money to overcome most of the journey's hardships.

The changing number of people who followed the trail west reveal an interesting story. Prior to 1848, perhaps 2,000 people journeyed to California and 10,000 to Oregon. In 1850, the numbers jumped: 6,000 went to Oregon and 44,000 moved to California. Between 1849 and 1860, during the gold-rush years, more than 50,000 went to Oregon, but over 200,000 traveled to California. By that time, the Overland Trail had become many roads that paralleled the routes of the early pioneers.

Even after the rail lines were built, travel by wagon was still necessary at times. Isolated farmers had to haul all their possessions and purchases from towns out to the countryside. People made their way slowly along the rutted roads of the West.

Scotts Bluff, Nebraska, was known as a landmark along the Oregon Trail. The site is now a national monument. Shown here is Mitchell Pass, another nearby landmark on the old trail.

Mormons in Utah

The Mormon Vision

Among the earliest settlers to cross the Mississippi and venture into the West were the Mormons. Members of the Church of Jesus Christ of Latter-day Saints, founded in 1830 in upstate New York, Mormons encountered religious and social hostility in several states when they attempted to found colonies. Their response was to move farther west. After violence and hostility forced them from the town of Nauvoo, Illinois, the bulk of the Mormons, led by church president Brigham Young, decided to move to an unsettled area of the West where, in isolation, they could practice their religion in peace.

The Mormon refugees from Nauvoo regathered, and they numbered more than ten thousand. Preparation for the migration to the West required careful planning. Aware of the explorer John C. Frémont's account of the Great Basin, Brigham Young and other Mormon leaders decided to settle near the Great Salt Lake. In 1847 Young led the initial expedition of 148 volunteers west along the Oregon-California Trail.

When they reached the Salt Lake Valley, Young is reputed to have said, "This is the place." This painting depicts the Mormons' first vision of Salt Lake City.

In the years that followed, thousands of Mormons made their way to the valleys of the Great Basin. Most traveled along the north side of the Platte River to avoid contact with other parties that were headed west. The north side of the Platte is sometimes called the Mormon Trail.

The Mormon community was successful. Salt Lake City became a commercial center as well as a main station along the road to California. The Mormons made the desert bloom as they pioneered irrigation and applied strict conservation rules regarding water and other natural resources. Within thirty years, the Mormon population had increased so markedly that Mormons were moving into Idaho, Wyoming, and even southern California. The Mormons did not escape hostility and prejudice until after 1890, however, when the church ceased the sanction of polygamous marriages.

The region centered on Salt Lake City receives the most precipitation in Utah and remains the state's most populous area. Much of the rest of the state is desert. Shown here are scenes from two of Utah's national parks, Canyonlands left and Bryce Canyon above, in desolate but beautiful sectors of the state.

The Republic of Texas

The Louisiana Purchase had given the United States a dubious claim to Texas, one which Secretary of State John Quincy Adams surrendered to Spain in 1819. But American frontier people paid scant attention to national boundaries and began to move across the Mississippi. Moses Austin, who had mined lead in Missouri, negotiated first with the Spanish and later the Mexican government to found an American colony in Texas. When he died, his son, Stephen, not only became one of the leading colonizers in Texas but also contributed a section to the Mexican Constitution of 1824 that encouraged further colonization.

Under the generous Mexican policy, men like Austin were to receive enormous land grants if they settled 100 families within their colonies in six years. The colonists themselves were granted 4,428 acres for $30, a far better offer than the United States land law, which granted 80 acres for $100. Little wonder that Texas appealed to poor farmers in the Southwest and to European immigrants. The colonists took advantage of the policy and engaged in land-speculation schemes. Almost immediately this corrupt practice created a conflict between Mexican authorities and American settlers.

As thousands of Americans moved into Texas, they insisted on speaking their own language, building their own schools, owning slaves, and trading with the United States. Alarmed by this Americanization of Texas, the Mexican government sought to end immigration from the United States. The Texans revolted. In February 1836, the Mexican general Antonio Santa Anna laid siege to a mission called the Alamo in San Antonio. Mexico ultimately captured the Alamo, and its defenders—many of whom were Mexicans, not Americans—were killed. Nonetheless, the Texans declared their independence, and in April, the Mexican army was routed by Gen-

Toward the Pacific Shore

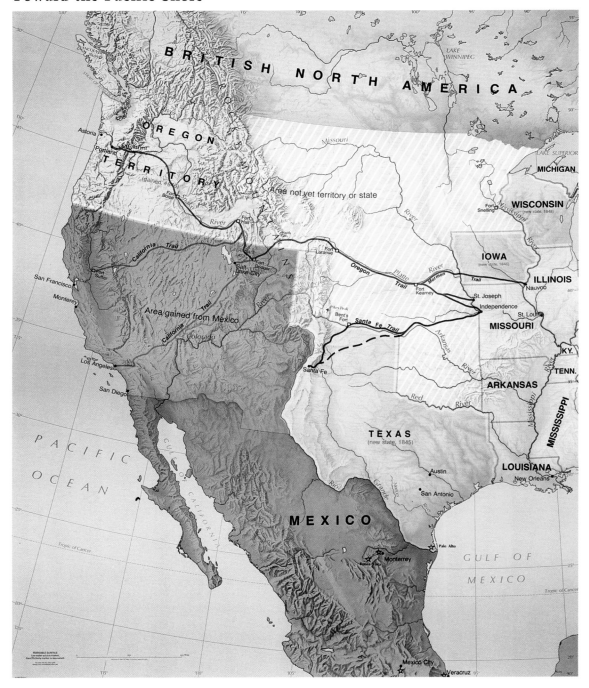

During the presidency of James K. Polk (1845-49), U.S. territory reached the Pacific. Polk peacefully negotiated a northwest boundary treaty between the United States and Canada, and the Oregon Territory was organized. He then waged a war against Mexico that brought most of the Southwest and California into the Union.

eral Sam Houston. Santa Anna was captured, and Texas became an independent republic.

Although Texas sought immediate admission into the United States, the territory did not become a state until 1845. War with Mexico followed in 1846, when President James K. Polk used a border dispute with Mexico to justify an invasion. The Americans defeated Mexico's armies and occupied Mexico City. The federal government brought Santa Anna back into power to sign a peace treaty that gave the United States the entire Spanish-speaking Southwest.

The population along the Texas frontier grew rapidly. Between 1836 and 1860 the state grew from 135,000 to 600,000 people. By 1900, the population had reached three million. As people moved into west Texas, bison herds were slaughtered and replaced with cattle. Indians defeated in battle were moved to the Indian Territory of Oklahoma. Within slightly more than half a century, a sleepy Mexican province had become the largest and one of the wealthiest states in the Union. Even though large portions of Texas remained sparsely populated, its frontier days had ended.

The Alamo, a mission turned into a fort in San Antonio, was the site of the bloodiest battle in the Texas Revolution. A small force of freedom-minded Texans of both American and Mexican ancestry were besieged by five thousand Mexican soldiers, who eventually breached the walls and captured or killed almost all of the defenders on March 6, 1836.

The Rio Grande, the fifth longest river in North America, is not navigable for commerce. Its major role in the settling of the frontier commenced when it became the border between Texas and Mexico. Shown here is Big Bend National Park, Texas, situated at the point where the river takes a giant turn from southeast to northeast.

Of Mines and Cattle

Miners and Cattle Drivers

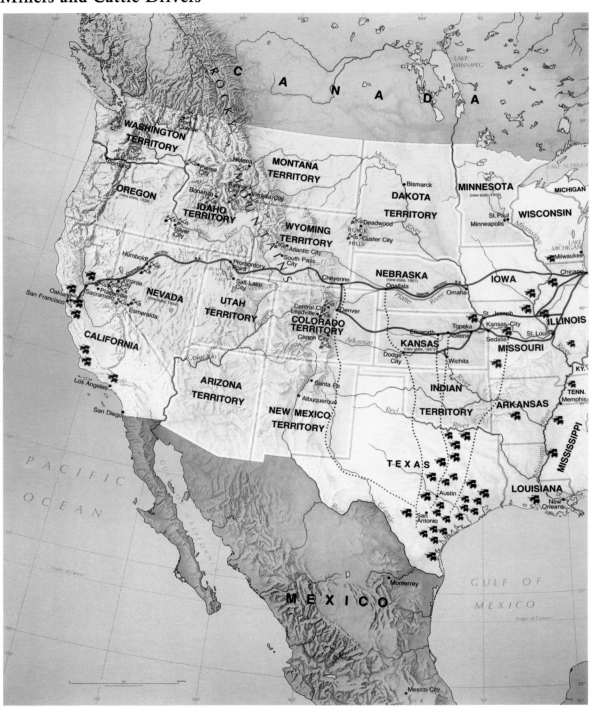

Cattle raising

Gold Mining

Silver Mining

•••••••••••• Cattle trail

Distribution of gold fields throughout the West lacked a formal pattern; the mining frontier was determined by the deposits of precious metals. The cattle industry, which spread west from the Mississippi River states and north from Texas, extended across the Great Plains. Cattle trails reveal the northward and westward expansion of the cattle frontier from Texas.

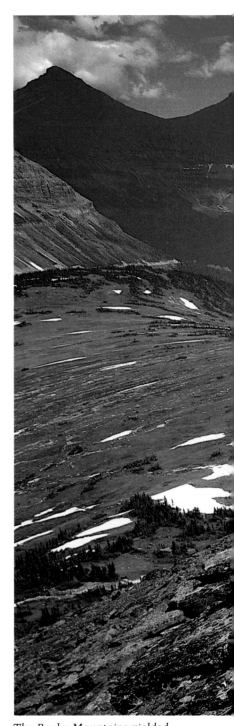

The Rocky Mountains yielded much to the eager miners of the nineteenth century. Significant deposits of copper, gold, lead, silver, coal, natural gas, and petroleum have been located in the rugged Rockies. Shown here is part of the Continental Divide, in Glacier National Park, Montana. East of the divide, rivers flow to the Gulf of Mexico; to the west, they flow to the Pacific Ocean.

to New Mexico to help Canby, fighting between Union and rebel forces was virtually over along the frontier.

Most of the western troops went on to guard against Indian attacks or to prevent pro-southern elements from fomenting dissension. Because the Mormons were suspected of being pro-Confederate, federal Colonel Patrick Connor and one thousand Californians established Fort Douglas outside Salt Lake City to keep an eye on them. The Mormons remained neutral, however, and President Lincoln left them in the charge of their own leaders.

The federal cause fared less well in Oklahoma among the Five Civilized Tribes that had been forced out of the Old Southwest. As slaveholders, these Native Americans sympathized with the Confederates. The Choctaw, Seminole, and Chickasaw joined the Confederacy. The Cherokee tried at first to be neutral but eventually went with the South as well. Stand Watie, a mixed-blood slaveowner, organized the First Cherokee Mounted Rifles and was the last Confederate general to surrender. The Creeks broke into both pro- and anti-Union groups. The pro-southern American Indians were forced to make major land concessions at the war's end.

Most conflicts with Native Americans that took place during this time were not related to Civil War issues. In 1862, corrupt officials and traders provoked the Minnesota Sioux into attacking when they told the starving Indians to eat grass. In a rampage, the American Indians murdered hundreds of whites and stuffed dung into the mouths of dead traders. Many Sioux were captured and eventually hanged, but the bulk of them retreated westward and remained hostile.

In Colorado, white volunteers under Colonel John Chivington, a fanatical Indian hater, attacked a village of sleeping Cheyenne, who were actually under government protection. The whites murdered more than two hundred Native Americans, mostly women and children. The crazed Colorado militiamen returned to Denver to display the body parts of their tragic victims. This, the Sand Creek Massacre, remains one of the most disgraceful episodes in frontier history.

The enraged Sioux retaliated by virtually stopping cross-plains travel. Fighting also occurred in the Southwest where General James Carleton and Kit Carson achieved some victories against the Apache and Navajo but little against the Comanche. As far as American Indians were concerned, the Civil War era was merely another phase in their continuing struggle for survival against encroaching whites.

Throughout the West, volunteers were recruited to serve for the Union. Most remained in the West, however, to do garrison duty or to combat American Indians. They were notoriously brutal in their treatment of Native Americans. The Colorado Volunteers helped to thwart the Confederate advance into New Mexico. Shown here is a group of Colorado recruits in 1862.

African Americans were first recruited into the Army of the United States during the Civil War. More than 200,000 served during the war. After the war, two cavalry regiments and two infantry regiments were composed of black soldiers and noncommissioned officers. These regiments fought American Indians, hunted desperadoes, and guarded the Mexico border for more than a quarter of a century. Between 1870 and 1890, fourteen African-American soldiers won the Congressional Medal of Honor.

Twilight of the Native American

For the American Indian, the three decades following the Civil War brought rapid and destructive change. The United States government embarked on a policy of "civilizing" Native Americans, turning them into farmers, and moving them out of the path of white occupation. American Indians had no voice in this decision. To them, white civilization meant the end of their own identity and way of life. Many knew, however, that those who failed to accept white culture and move onto reservations would be forced into submission or eliminated.

President Ulysses S. Grant summarized this position clearly: "All Indians disposed to peace will find the new policy a peace policy," but "those who do not accept this policy will find the new administration ready for a sharp and severe war policy." From the white viewpoint, Grant's policy simply perpetuated Native American conquest and assimilation, a process that had been going on since the first European settlers arrived. At this point, however, there was a major difference: the northern Great Plains, the frontier now under contention, had been promised in treaty to the American Indian as a permanent homeland.

When the United States government became willing to violate those treaties, the Indians' fate was sealed. The army was handed the job of fighting these last frontier battles. Equipped with the weapons and tools of modern technology and backed by a nation with millions of potential soldiers, the United States military was restricted only by bureaucratic infighting, Congressional frugality and humanitarian sentiment, its own faulty leadership, and Indian reformers who pressured the government to honor its promises. Time served the army. The brutal nature of frontier warfare led to demands for enforced peaceful solutions. One by one, Indian leaders were killed or exiled and recalcitrant groups were rounded up and put on marginal lands.

Some of the conflicts—such as the Modoc War (1872-73)—involved only a handful of participants, while small skirmishes were almost annual affairs. Other engagements had a more drastic effect on public opinion. General George Armstrong Custer's disastrous attack on a large Sioux village at the Little Bighorn in 1876 resulted not only in white losses but also in the demand of the nation that the Indian "problem" be solved.

In the wake of the Battle of Little Bighorn, the army adopted a scorched-earth policy. The Plains Indians were already suffering because the bison herds—their major source of food—had been sharply reduced. Civil War hero General Philip Sheridan now hunted Native Americans during the winter, burned their villages, and destroyed their food supplies. As hungry Indians began surrendering, they were dismounted, disarmed, and placed under guard on reservations or exiled far from their homelands.

Small American Indian groups that sought to live outside of the white establishment were compelled to surrender or be destroyed. This was true of the Nez Percé in 1877 under Chief Joseph; the northern Cheyenne under Dull Knife and Little Wolf in 1878-79; and the Apache under Geronimo in 1885. Guerrilla attacks produced a few Indian victories, but the wars usually ended tragically for the bands involved.

The nation still lives in the shadow of one of the more ghastly episodes in Indian-white contact. Native Americans on the Pine Ridge Reservation in South Dakota were caught up in the Ghost Dance, a religious revival promising an end to the white presence. Soldiers tried to disarm some of the Indians, and in the fight that followed, the troops, armed with machine guns, slaughtered men, women, and children. This, the Wounded Knee Massacre (1890), left both whites and Indians embittered and disillusioned. Although the actual battles for the frontier were over by 1890, in the aftermath of Wounded Knee, whites and Indians alike have continued to wrestle with the moral issues of the conquest of the continent.

The Ghost Dance movement on the northern Great Plains was inspired by the American Indian prophet Wovoka. Educated in a school where Native American children were taught to live like white people, Wovoka was caught between two cultures. He regained his identity as an Indian during an illness, when he had a vision that told him that a ceremonial dance, the Ghost Dance, would eventually drive the white man from America. Shown here is a group of Arapaho engaged in the Ghost Dance.

On reservations, traditional Native American dress became in large part ceremonial, worn for special events and holidays. These staged demonstrations of American Indian attire unfortunately contributed to the stereotyping of Native Americans. Shown here are Plains Indians on a Montana reservation.

The First National Park
The first of its kind, Yellowstone National Park was established in 1872. Protecting this wilderness, which lies mostly in northwestern Wyoming, was at the time a revolutionary idea. The original plan was to ensure public ownership of a spectacular scenic resource. Then other values emerged. The last significant herd of bison on the Great Plains found refuge in the park. Yellowstone held the largest elk herds in the United States, and beaver were still common in its waters. Outside the park's boundaries, these species had been nearly exterminated. Yellowstone shortly demonstrated value far beyond its scenic delights, and it led to other forest, wildlife, and nature preserves in the United States and around the world. Shown here is the falls of the Yellowstone River.

The Cattle Kingdom

After the Civil War, the United States conquered the Great Plains. The American Indians were put on reservations, the railroad system grew throughout the West, and the great American bison herds were virtually wiped out. A gargantuan meadow that extended from Canada to Mexico in a belt almost three hundred miles wide, the semiarid Great Plains became an empire of vast cattle ranches.

Originally, the Spanish and English brought cattle to America. Northward from Mexico into Texas came thriving herds of bellowing longhorns, a tough breed of cattle well suited to the warm Southwest. Southerners brought English Hereford cattle as they migrated west. Spanish and English cattle and ranching styles met and mixed on the Great Plains.

As public domain, grass was free on the Great Plains. The earliest ranchers sought to stock the open range as fully as possible to keep out competitors. They drove longhorn cattle north from Texas by the thousands, to Colorado, Wyoming, and Montana, and west into New Mexico and Arizona. They shipped eastern whiteface cattle into Kansas, Nebraska, and the Dakotas. Free grass, new major slaughterhouses in Chicago, high beef prices in the East, and low railroad rates made the cattle industry lucrative.

Cowboys drove cattle from the open range to cow towns along the railroads for shipment East. Abilene, Kansas, was the first cow town. Such railroad towns as Bismarck, North Dakota; Cheyenne, Wyoming; and Dodge City, Kansas, each had a heyday. Although later glorified in the movies—with dance halls, gambling dens, brothels, saloons, and assorted sheriffs and outlaws—most of the cow towns were really quite tame. Locals were quick to demand churches, schools, and good government. The hard-working cowboys were allowed a certain amount of rowdyism after they brought cattle in from the range, but the local police chief generally kept the peace.

Capitalists in the East and Europe clamored to invest in the highly profitable cattle kingdom. By the mid-1880s, however,

Much ranch work was solitary. Looking after small herds of cattle widely dispersed over the plains where grass was sparse required long hours in the saddle. The job mostly involved protecting the livestock from predatory animals and keeping them from stampeding during storms or from simply wandering away. Cowhands were often said to sleep in winter to make up for the long hours they worked in summer.

the open range was dangerously overstocked, and efforts to regulate land use and keep new ranchers out proved unsuccessful. Disaster came first with collapsing beef prices, higher rail rates, and more discriminating packing houses. Then in 1885 came a cycle of summer droughts, bitterly cold winters, and numbing blizzards. Surviving ranchers realized that they could no longer prosper on the open range. They began to buy up large tracts of land, and the government passed legislation that allowed the ranchers to secure thousands of acres at almost no cost.

After 1890, new ranching practices appeared. Cattlemen raised hay to feed stock and protect themselves from drought, erected windmills to assure their water supply, and introduced fences to keep other livestock off their land. Better breeds of cattle also appeared, and the day of the longhorn maverick bull was over. Ranchers who tried to operate as was common before the collapse of the 1880s were unwelcome in any community.

Cowhands drove large herds of animals to the railways. Keeping animals safe and healthy became increasingly important when meatpackers paid top prices only for pure-bred healthy animals. Here a herd crosses the Milk River in Montana.

The Cowboy Artist
The work of Charles M. Russell has contributed much to perceptions of the American West. Russell, a self-taught artist, began as an itinerant cowboy before he turned to art. His western images, both in sculpture and painting, depicted cowboys, Indians, animals, and western life as he knew it. Although usually focused on dramatic episodes and often quite humorous or stylized, Russell's work captured for his and subsequent generations a sense of the West that remains unrivaled. Shown here is Russell's *Bronc to Breakfast.*

Cowboys: Knights of the Cattle Barons

The working ranch hands of the cattle kingdom had little in common with the cowboy heroes of movies and myth. The life of the real cowhand held little romance; cowboys were laborers who worked on horseback. They rode alone, ate and slept on the open range, and suffered in adapting to the extremes of the Great Plains climate. Ranch owners might call on a cowboy to serve as "hired gun," although the legendary pistol was more ornament than tool. Rounding up, roping, and branding cattle were dangerous jobs. Some cowhands became so disenchanted with their working conditions that they went out on strike during a roundup in 1884.

Cowboys came from many walks of life and ethnic groups. They were black, white, Mexican. Some earned their living by breaking wild horses; others worked as cowhands for a few years and then drifted off to other jobs or became ranch owners. Some maintained family life while working at one ranch for years. Women frequently owned ranches but generally were not employed as ranch hands.

The cowboy's work changed after the financial collapse of the 1880s. They began to ride fences rather than herd on the open range. They raised hay, helped with breeding, and worked like farmhands year-round. Even the length of the drives became shorter to save the cattle from weight loss. The work remained dangerous, however, and the clothing and tools remained unique. For the real cowboy, much of the romance was just ordinary life. In reality, he spent much of his time out in the elements on a ten-dollar horse and a forty-dollar saddle.

On the open range, branding was essential. Each breeding season, young unmarked animals could be claimed by anyone. These mavericks, as the unmarked were termed, were rounded up from the open range and branded. This was hard and dangerous work—perhaps the most difficult part of ranching.

Frederic Remington was among the best-known artists of the American West. An illustrator, writer, painter, and sculptor, Remington traveled widely throughout the West. He achieved his lasting reputation with his depictions of cowhands, Indians, and soldiers. His images contributed to the persistent themes of courage, power, and masculinity on the frontier.

A HARD TRAIL.

The rolling plains of eastern Montana proved to be prime grazing lands for cattle and sheep. Creeks and small rivers, like the Judith shown here, ensure the water supply, and large-scale ranching still dominates this portion of the Great Plains.

The Wild West

Robert Leroy Parker, alias Butch Cassidy, was one of the West's more notorious outlaws. He was lured into a life of crime by a cattle rustler named Mike Cassidy and took his mentor's name. He earned the name Butch when, in 1892, he worked in a Wyoming butcher shop. Cassidy emerged as the leader of a group of desperadoes who robbed trains and banks from Montana to New Mexico and from Colorado to Nevada.

Train, bank, and stagecoach robbers Jesse and Frank James became legendary as bandits who stole from the rich and gave to the poor. In 1882, Jesse was killed by a member of his own gang who claimed a reward; on his death he was declared a hero in some of the popular press. Frank James claimed so much public sympathy and support that he escaped criminal conviction even after three trials.

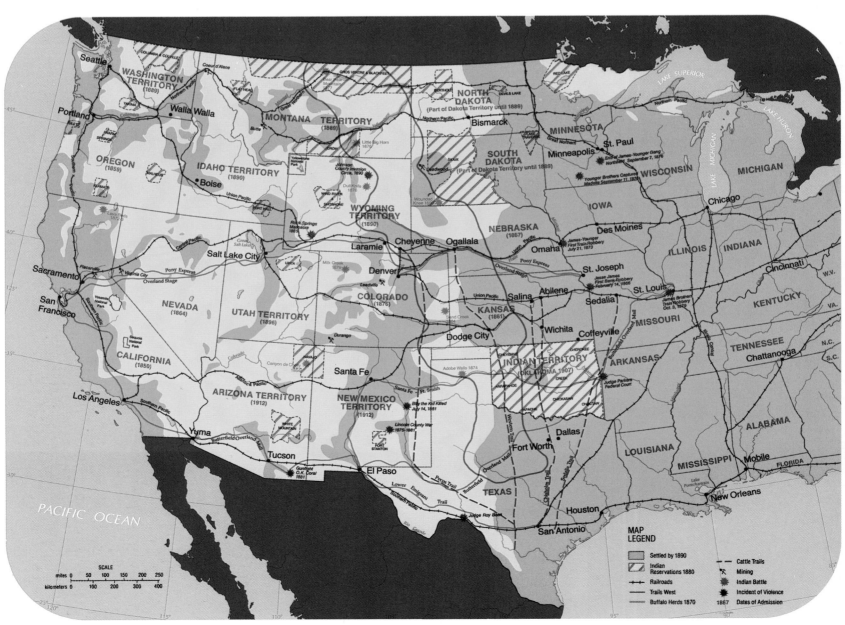

On Western Frontiers   *The period recalled as the Wild West occurred between about 1860 and 1890. Near extermination of the bison, extension of the railroad system, growth of the mining industry, and the spread of the cattle empire forced the Native Americans of the West off their homelands and onto reservations.*

Canyon de Chelly National Monument, Arizona, lies within the Navajo Indian Reservation and contains numerous remains of ancient Native American civilization. In 1864, the canyon was the site of a battle between the Navajo and the U.S. Cavalry, under the command of frontiersman Kit Carson.

The Pony Express, a swift mail service between St. Joseph, Missouri, and Sacramento, California, was inaugurated in April, 1860, and terminated in October, 1861. Young men riding ponies between stations fifteen miles apart covered the route in eighteen days (later thirteen days because of extended telegraph lines). Despite a $1 million-per-year subsidy from the government, the venture proved a financial loss. It was doomed from the outset because the telegraph was both cheaper and more efficient. Nevertheless, the story of the express and the young men who rode the route, including Buffalo Bill Cody, is a dramatic episode in the history of the West.

Boomtowns and Ghost Towns

Like the Spanish before them, prospectors searching for precious minerals explored some of the most desolate parts of the West. Rich veins of gold and silver often were discovered in almost inaccessible mountain sites buffeted by high winds and heavy snowfall in winter and droughts in summer. The land around mining towns was quickly stripped of forest for wood to burn in smelters, brace mine shafts, and build homes. Desert mining towns were even bleaker, as mining operations destroyed the fragile environment around them.

Most of these boomtowns were as short-lived as the prospectors' dreams of great wealth. These settlements had a cyclical existence: rapid growth, when a few sturdy brick or stone buildings were raised; rapid abandonment, when surface veins of ore were exhausted; and slow decay, when new technology extracted the last of the ore. In the end, most mining towns were abandoned unless the settlers found another source of wealth. The boomtowns turned to ghost towns.

Such towns have raised questions about how the West was settled. For some, the ghost town is a symbol of the rape of the land. The stark towns are surrounded by slag heaps, while only weather-worn buildings and abandoned cemeteries remain. But while these towns flourished, they offered people higher wages than they could make elsewhere, unusual opportunities for profits, and the chance to make a fortune. In this light, ghost towns offer a testimony to the dreams of wealth harbored by nineteenth-century Americans and to the opportunities the West symbolized.

Even in well-established mining camps, men vastly outnumbered women. Saloons like the one shown here became a primary source of recreation, though their patronage often reflected the ethnic biases of their owners.

Hostility toward Chinese and Mexican miners led to segregation and limited access to skilled jobs by the Cornish- and Welsh-controlled unions. Most Chinese miners were contract laborers, who worked under a patron who brought them to America, controlled their wages, and looked after their housing. Chinese were not allowed to own mines, and they were often denied legal rights. Anti-Chinese riots were not unusual.

Early mining camps, such as this gold-mine camp in Arizona, were often little more than a collection of tents and shacks. The need for wood both to buttress mine shafts and to fuel the smelters meant the land was quickly denuded.

Pioneers on the Great Plains

Toward the close of the nineteenth century, settlers in Kansas, Texas, and Arkansas began eyeing the Indian Territory hungrily. They began to take up Indian lands illegally, and government efforts to force violators off proved almost impossible. Squatters defied arresting officers, and public opinion was staunchly behind the white intruders. Pressure to open Indian lands to white settlement had been a pattern since the earliest days of the republic. Now the pressure was even greater because federal policy since the Civil War had encouraged Americans to take up land.

Congressional legislation paved the way for whites to occupy the Indian Territory. In 1885, Congress passed laws allowing the government to purchase "unoccupied" Indian lands for further white settlement. The Dawes Severalty Act was a measure that broke Indian tribal lands into individual holdings and released millions of acres of Indian land for white settlement. Then, in 1889, President Benjamin Harrison formally opened Indian Territory, or Oklahoma, for settlement.

Preparations for a land rush began. Thousands of homesteaders, town-site speculators, and expectant capitalists lined the boundaries of the Territory. A few days before the rush, 100,000 people jammed the roads and even

Beginning in the late 1880s, millions of acres of land in what is now Oklahoma were thrown open to homesteaders. Several land rushes occurred in 1889. The greatest land rush in history took place in 1893 when six million acres of land were claimed in little over one day. By 1905, all the "unoccupied" Indian land was gone. Shown here are scenes from the 1893 rush. ▶

slipped passed soldiers to identify the sites they planned to occupy. Federal troops were stationed along the boundary to hold back these Sooners.

At high noon on April 22, soldiers fired the signal to start, letting loose a pandemonium of horses, wagons, bicycles, and trains carrying people into Oklahoma. Land was taken up at incredible speed; within a few hours, almost two million acres were claimed. Oklahoma City, population ten thousand, and Guthrie, population fifteen thousand, sprung up virtually overnight. Tents, cabins, and a variety of shelters dotted the landscape as settlers staked out their holdings. And in September 1893, another rush occurred when 100,000 settlers invaded six million acres of newly opened land.

The dramatic land rushes in Oklahoma were only one result of constant pressure to open land throughout the West to white settlers. The Dawes Act, which was intended to help or force Native Americans to adjust to modern capitalist society, made millions of acres available for white settlement. At the same time, railroads made efforts to bring people west to create western markets for goods and to raise produce for export back East. Millions of Americans moved westward to take up land and to realize their own part of the American dream.

This image of the Oklahoma land rush was painted by American artist John Steuart Curry. It hangs in the Department of the Interior building in Washington, D.C.

The Desert is Cultivated

The Grain Growers

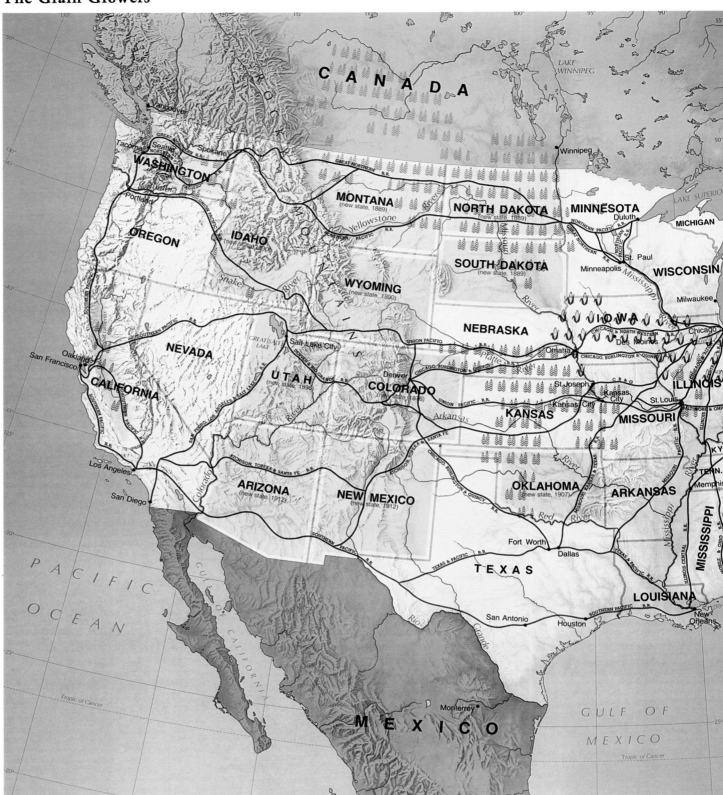

Rapid extension of the railroad system and the lure of relatively cheap or free homestead land brought farmers into the semiarid Great Plains. Wheat became the major cash crop, although other grains were produced as animal feed. In many regions, the cattleman's range lands gave way to the wheat farmer's plow.

Key to grain growing

Corn growing area

Wheat growing area

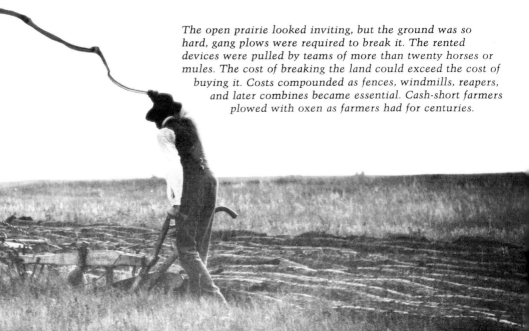

The open prairie looked inviting, but the ground was so hard, gang plows were required to break it. The rented devices were pulled by teams of more than twenty horses or mules. The cost of breaking the land could exceed the cost of buying it. Costs compounded as fences, windmills, reapers, and later combines became essential. Cash-short farmers plowed with oxen as farmers had for centuries.

Homesteading was hard for women, who not only did the usual household chores but often joined men in the field when other labor was unavailable. It was almost impossible for a farm to be self-sufficient, but farm women limited expenses by making do with as little as possible from the outside. Lacking wood for fuel, for example, they gathered buffalo chips, twisted prairie hay into bundles, and burned whatever else was accessible. Children became workers at an early age.

The Farmer's Frontier
In a sense, after the Civil War, the Great Plains—a vast, virtually flat, semiarid region—became the last frontier. Settlers were lured onto the Great Plains by governmental policies that encouraged settlement. The Homestead Act made land almost free to people who would live on it; the Timber Culture Act added to a settler's holding if he planted trees; and other measures also stimulated settlement. Moreover, many of the transcontinental railroads offered land at very favorable prices to encourage settlement along their routes.

Some farmers built frame houses, but those who lived far from transportation or who lacked cash often lived in dugouts or sod houses. "Nebraska Marble," as someone once called sod, was cheap, and houses made of it were warm in the winter and cool in the summer. Even with whitewashed interior walls and careful housekeeping, however, sod houses were dusty and far from leakproof in heavy storms.

Immigrants on the Frontier

The United States has long been known as a nation of immigrants, and the western frontier received its share. Just as thousands of immigrants settled in eastern coastal cities and in the emerging industrial centers of the Middle West, thousands more found work in mines, on ranches, and in lumber camps on the trans-Mississippi frontier. An estimated one-third of the population in the West in 1870 was foreign born—a full 60 percent in Arizona, and perhaps as many of the adult males in Utah, Idaho, and Nevada. In California, fully one-fourth of the population was Irish by birth in 1870.

Although the extraordinary flood of people arriving from Europe after 1800 settled mostly in the eastern industrial and mining states, large numbers continued on to the West. Of San Francisco's 233,000 people in 1880, almost 105,000 were immigrants. Virtually every western city had its "Chinatown" or "Little Italy" or "Irish Town." The mining towns in the Rocky Mountains or along the transcontinental rail lines were homesites for the foreign-born laborers who dug the mines, built the lines, and kept the communities going.

The Mormon church played a large role in bringing immigrants to the Great Basin region. Mormons believed that "the faithful should gather" and launched a spirited campaign encouraging European converts to leave Europe and come to Utah. Support for immigration lasted until church leaders felt that there was a shortage of farmland. By that time, however, Mormon immigrants had settled in Idaho, Wyoming, and northern Arizona.

Although the Mormons were perhaps the best organized group, German, Dutch, and Scandinavian sects also established communities in the West. The completed transcontinental railroad system and accompanying pro-

Immigration's Impact

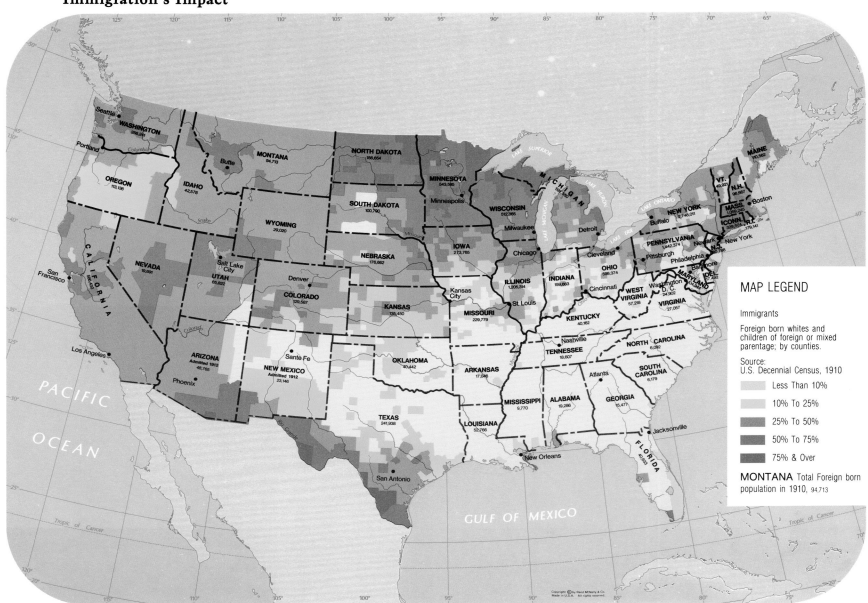

MAP LEGEND

Immigrants

Foreign born whites and children of foreign or mixed parentage; by counties.

Source:
U.S. Decennial Census, 1910

Less Than 10%

10% To 25%

25% To 50%

50% To 75%

75% & Over

MONTANA Total Foreign born population in 1910, 94,713

miles   0 100 200 300 400
kilometers 0   200   400   600

War, famine, and oppression drove millions of people from their motherlands to American shores. This map depicts where these immigrants and the children of mixed or foreign parentage had settled by 1910.

motions to sell land proved highly effective. Thousands of Scandinavian settlers went to Oregon and Washington to take up land, while others found employment in fishing and lumbering. By the closing decade of the nineteenth century there was a widely dispersed immigrant population across the West.

In the early 1900s, millions of eastern and southern Europeans made the arduous journey across the Atlantic. Most of these immigrants crowded into ethnically insulated sections of large industrial cities. They filled America's growing demand for labor in factories, mills, and stockyards. On the West Coast, immigration laws first passed in 1882 restricted entry for the growing tide of Asian and Latin American immigrants. The South lacked both heavy industry and available land, so immigrants tended to bypass the region and head to the North and West.

During the final years of the nineteenth century, immigration to the United States accelerated. Economic opportunity, political and religious freedom, and the absence of a military draft encouraged continued migration, especially from southern and eastern Europe. For many immigrants, such as these Jewish refugees from Russia, the Statue of Liberty became a symbol of a new frontier and a new life.

Settlers in the Rocky Mountains had access to wood, but they were often so isolated that living conditions were primitive. The cost of a log cabin, aside from sweat labor, was in windowpanes and perhaps an iron stove and pipe. This was the life that greeted many immigrants, such as these early homesteaders in western Colorado.

A Land of Commerce

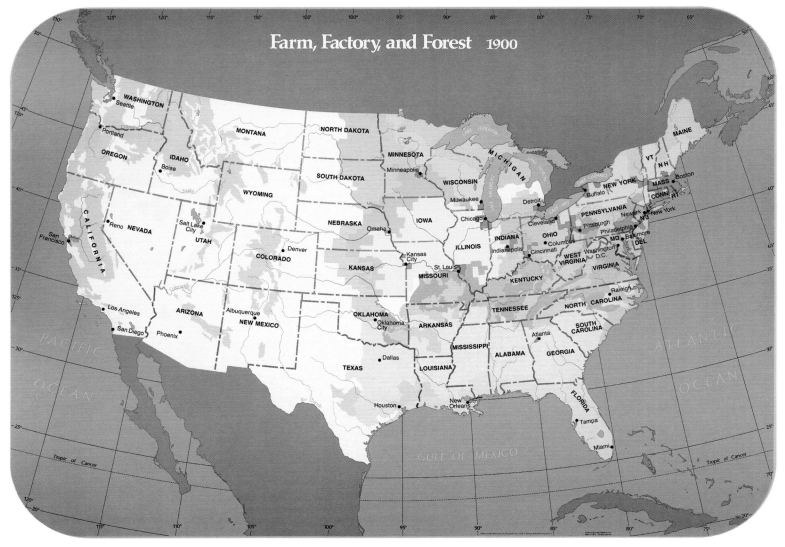

Farm, Factory, and Forest   1900

By 1900, the United States was a modern nation with a balanced economy and an abundance of agricultural and industrial products to export. Although cheap land was still available for farming, most required irrigation or better transportation to make it productive.

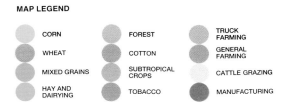

MAP LEGEND

- CORN
- WHEAT
- MIXED GRAINS
- HAY AND DAIRYING
- FOREST
- COTTON
- SUBTROPICAL CROPS
- TOBACCO
- TRUCK FARMING
- GENERAL FARMING
- CATTLE GRAZING
- MANUFACTURING

During the last three decades of the nineteenth century, the area of land under cultivation in the United States more than doubled, increasing to 414 million acres. Crop production nearly tripled. Farming techniques were more efficient in terms of both labor input and crop output. Field-work was still hard labor, however, as evidenced in this photograph of farmers at work in Iowa about 1900.

Many of the trees of Sequoia National Park are more than two thousand years old. By the late 1800s, it became evident that these trees needed to be protected, and in 1890, the park in California was established.

As the United States population grew and settlement moved westward, the center of the lumbering industry shifted to the Northwest. The industry was highly seasonal and usually employed single men without special skills. Mill towns and larger cities filled with loggers after the cutting season. Loggers such as those shown on this train in Oregon in about 1900 were often recent immigrants, many from Scandinavia.

American factories at the turn of the century were highly labor intensive, even the most modern facilities such as the Pullman works just outside of Chicago. Pullman's workers were housed in a model company town; this variety of paternalism failed, however, and the massive Pullman strike of 1894 became an episode in the growing American labor movement.

The End of the Frontier

In the wake of the 1890 census, the superintendent of the United States Census Bureau announced it was no longer possible to draw a line on a map indicating where the frontier began. This did not mean that all land was farmed or that every mineral was extracted; rather that people were so widely distributed across the West, except for pockets in the mountains and deserts, that the entire continent, from the Atlantic to the Pacific, was settled.

The closing of the frontier raised many questions for Americans who had grown accustomed to thinking of the country as boundless. Where would future opportunity exist if there was no new West? Some speculated on the gloomy future of American democracy without the perpetual renewal that the westward movement had offered. Some believed that the frontier had provided an outlet for the young, the restless, the poor, the risk takers, and the fugitives who felt dissatisfied with eastern society. Without this "safety valve," would American society be threatened?

The closing of the frontier did mark the end of an era. In 1893, historian Frederick Jackson Turner observed that the open frontier was already a phenomenon of the past, and that America had to move on to another chapter of history. Other Americans saw the frontier differently; they had earlier looked north to Alaska, which was acquired by the United States from Russia in 1867, and west-

The United States Constitution requires that a census be taken every ten years for the purpose of apportioning representatives in Congress according to population. The first United States census was taken in 1790. Census data can reveal many different population-related facts; in the 1890s, historian Frederick Jackson Turner used census data to support his frontier theory of American history. Shown here is a depiction of the 1870 census being taken from a sketch by Thomas Worth.

Improved roads were only part of the transportation revolution that began at the end of the nineteenth century. The automobile and its increased availability to the American middle-class consumer helped create a new vision of the West: an accessible wilderness ripe for recreational exploration.

Some argue that the geographic frontier did not end at the California coast but extended into the Pacific. The American absorption of Hawaii resembled in some ways the settling of the continental West; for example, the native peoples of the American West and the Hawaiian islands suffered similar fates. Thousands of native Hawaiians died of Europeans diseases to which they had little immunity, and others were confined to reservations. Today, the state of Hawaii has a robust tourist industry, drawing visitors from around the world with its American culture, climate, and scenic beauty. Shown here is the Na Pali coast on Kauai.

The End of the Frontier (continued)

ward across the Pacific to Hawaii, which was acquired when Americans ousted the local monarchy in 1898. Following the Spanish-American War, the American frontier thrust deeply into the Pacific with the acquisition of Wake and Guam (later fortified) as well as a protectorate in the Philippines. To these were added the islands of American Samoa in 1899. Only Alaska among these acquisitions seemed representative of the older frontier of the contiguous states. Gold, and later oil, discoveries in Alaska touched off a mining rush reminiscent of the earlier era. Hawaii, the most racially and ethnically mixed state, became a bastion of American culture in the Pacific.

By the First World War, the American frontier, as it had been known since the days of Daniel Boone, was gone. Some say that a new American frontier emerged; that the frontier had been refined as a symbol of opportunity, ingenuity, invention, skill, and drive.

By the 1890s, larger cities in the West shared in the American consumer culture that came with the steady rise of industrialism and improved transportation. More affluent citizens had access to a variety of manufactured products. General stores offered everything from canned goods to ready-made clothes. The era of frontier self-sufficiency and independence was drawing to a close.

The Legacy of the Frontier

The Legacy of the Frontier

For several centuries, Europeans and their descendants moved steadily into lands occupied by Native Americans. The conquest of the American Indians—through disease, destructive wars, and the reservation system—decimated many groups and nearly erased Native American culture. Native people were not the only group to be pushed aside, however, as the frontier advanced.

When the United States replaced England as the dominant power in North America, French- and Spanish-speaking people, who had long occupied their lands, were also overrun by Americans. Many French, who began to be called Creoles, inhabited Louisiana Territory and saw Americans as intruders. The United States annexed Texas and wrenched away Mexico's northern provinces after the Mexican War. Even the British were humbled by threats of war over the boundary of the Pacific Northwest and forced to yield control of Washington, Oregon, and part of Idaho.

The American frontier experience casts a long shadow. The restless, aggressive march of American pioneers who carried the flag of the United States through the Cumberland Gap, then through the South Pass of the Rocky Mountains, and on to the Pacific Ocean left an indelible imprint on the attitudes and character of the American people. Generation after generation of people shared in the process of moving west, confronted by hardships that defeated some and strengthened others, forging the essential American character. The westering experience, and the values and habits associated with it, were not only part of personal family histories but also formed a national history reported in the popular press, taught in the schools, and glorified in patriotic explanations of the American story.

Americans learned to see themselves from a frontier perspective. Frontier people were described as individualistic, self-sufficient, mobile, aggressive, practical, democratic, socially egalitarian, materialistic, progressive, and optimistic. But of late, many have pointed to the dark side of this portrait. The frontier spirit has also been perceived as racist, wasteful, and violent.

However, this new view of our frontier legacy takes nothing away from the spirit that has illuminated the country's history for over two hundred years and continues to make the United States a symbol of hope for many in the world. In fact, it may be part of the frontier legacy that Americans continue to question and to strive for a more ideal society and world.

This map shows the United States today—a vast and complex nation with a dramatic past and a challenging future. It remains to be seen how the legacy of the frontier serves the nation as it swiftly approaches the twenty-first century.

Suffragettes in New York City

Some see Alaska as a vast land of rich resources, ripe for exploitation. Others see it as one of the few remaining wildernesses, vulnerable and in need of protection. In the frontier era, Alaska's natural riches might have been utilized without question. The large number of Americans who are reevaluating priorities when it comes to environmental issues is a post-frontier phenomenon.

Nat Love, American cowboy

One Nation, Many Voices

In the United States, the frontier ideals of democracy, social equality, and economic opportunity have battled humanity's age-old fears and prejudices. From the first landing of white settlers in the early 1600s to the modern era, Americans have struggled to create a society in which everyone has an equal voice. The sweeping landscapes of the American West seemed to hold the promise of a new start for people, a start that was free of the shackles and burdens of the past. The voices of Native Americans, African Americans, women of all colors, and others have, however, frequently been muted in history as the United States has sought to realize that promise. For many decades, the voice of white males of European descent was regarded as the legitimate American majority.

Discrimination was often a part of the frontier experience. The "Indian problem" was "resolved" by resettling Native Americans onto reservation areas. Some western territories took other measures to keep outsiders at bay. Frontier Oregon barred blacks, free or slave, from settling in the territory, while the miners in California drove out Hispanics and relegated the Chinese to working depleted claims. California laws restricting Japanese land ownership and prohibiting interracial

For more than a century, Custer Battlefield National Monument, Montana, stood as a memorial to the "last stand" of George Armstrong Custer and more than 250 American soldiers who met their death in a fierce battle with Native Americans on June 25, 1876. In 1991, Congress passed legislation to rename the park Little Bighorn Battlefield National Monument. The bill also creates an American Indian memorial, in recognition that the clash was the last major Native American victory against the United States Army.

Regional Voices

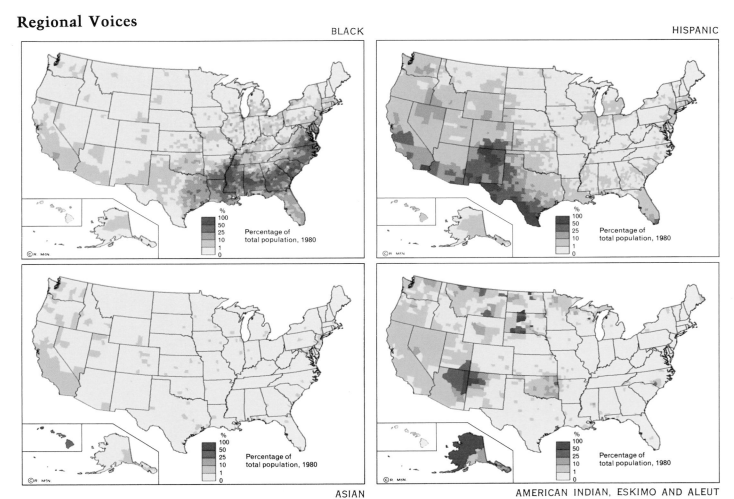

These maps show where portions of the total United States population are located. The black portion, for example, represents approximately 11.7 percent of the total United States population. The vast majority of the total American population is descended from Europeans. The distribution of the minorities makes sense in terms of the specific group's history.

marriages remained on the books for many years. Even today, only in the lands wrenched from Mexico do women enjoy the benefits of community property laws.

Over the years, the voices of diverse peoples have insistently demanded that the country live up to its frontier ideals of full economic opportunity and political equality. In 1869, Wyoming Territory led the nation in granting suffrage to women. The Civil War ended the institution of slavery not only in the South but in the western territories. Even so, many nonwhites were denied equal rights. The restrictive laws against Asians were gradually repealed, and in 1924, Native Americans were granted full citizenship rights in the United States. In the Civil Rights movement of the 1950s and 1960s, the words of Dr. Martin Luther King, Jr., and others helped to recall the image of a frontier president, Abraham Lincoln, who envisioned a nation "united and free."

Nat Love, also known as Deadwood Dick, was born in Tennessee in 1854, and following the Civil War, migrated to the West and became one of its most famous cowboys. Over the years, Love took part in many cattle drives, many of which originated in Texas and ended at such cow towns as Dodge City, Kansas. Love's autobiography was published in 1907.

Preserving the Land

The vastness of the frontier landscape fostered a belief in the pioneers and their descendants that the nation's natural resources were unlimited. When they exhausted land or minerals in one region, settlers simply packed up and moved West to areas equally rich in precious metals, timber, furs, and farmland. Millions of acres of forest land were burned or clear-cut, ranchers overgrazed huge areas of the Great Plains, and hydraulic mining techniques poisoned countless mountain valleys.

Yet even in the midst of the headlong rush to exploit natural resources, conservationists sought to preserve the wild beauty of the western lands and to manage the nation's development more intelligently. Yellowstone National Park was created in 1872, and as early as 1864, the United States government granted Yosemite Valley to California so it could establish a state park (Yosemite was reclaimed by the national government in 1890). The National Park Service was established in 1916. Conservationists like John Wesley Powell and naturalists like John Muir (founder of the Sierra Club) led the way. But the struggle has not been easy. Even today, the clash between conservationists and those who claim the right to develop the natural resources of the West continues in many regions.

Nevertheless, despite a strong tradition of personal economic freedom and a dislike of government regulation, exhaustion of fossil fuels, problems of pollution, increased demand for recreational facilities, and general concern for the environment have forced increased governmental action.

About equally as destructive to the environment as hydraulic mining was a manner of mining shown here: the gold dredge. The dredge floated on an artificial pond and tore up the landscape with an unending chain of buckets. This one was in use in Alaska, but many more were used in California.

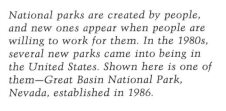

National parks are created by people, and new ones appear when people are willing to work for them. In the 1980s, several new parks came into being in the United States. Shown here is one of them—Great Basin National Park, Nevada, established in 1986.

North American Environments

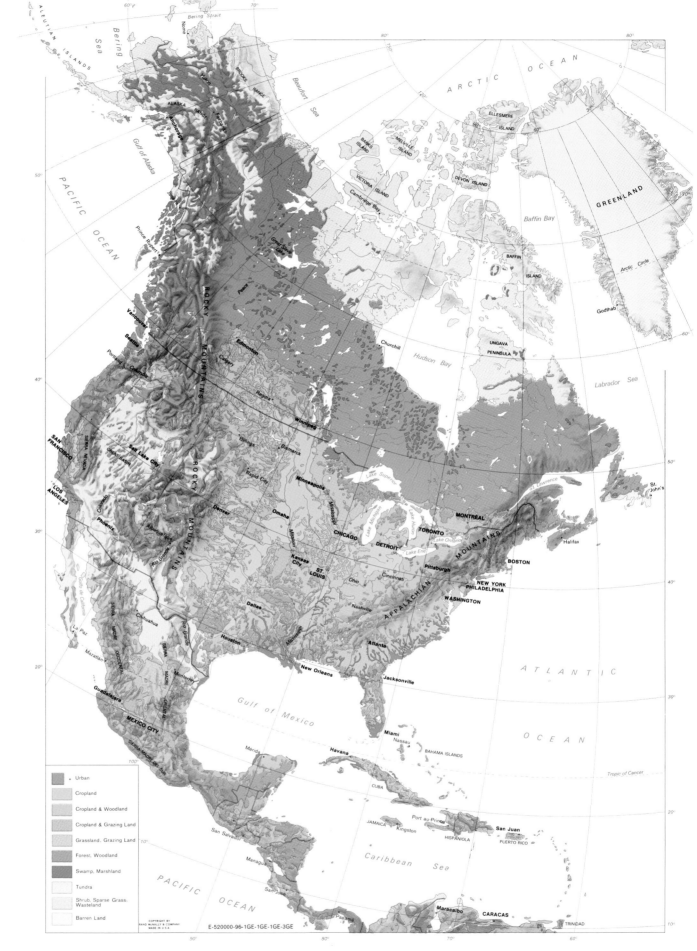

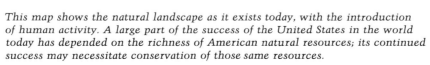

This map shows the natural landscape as it exists today, with the introduction
of human activity. A large part of the success of the United States in the world
today has depended on the richness of American natural resources; its continued
success may necessitate conservation of those same resources.

Reaching Across the Continent

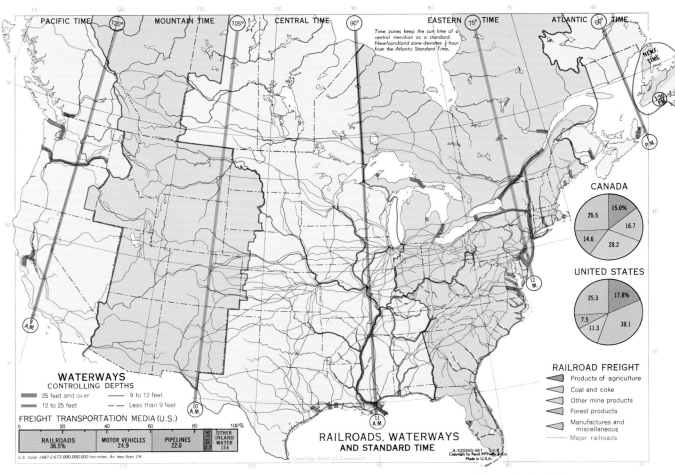

Transportation in the United States

As the size of United States territory increased, so did Americans' desire to conquer the great distances of the continent. Citizens called on the government to increase and improve lines of transportation and communication, and after 1850 both networks grew under a series of subsidies. These maps show contemporary railroads, waterways, major highways, and pipelines.

Today, the United States contains nearly 3.5 million miles of surfaced roads—enough, if they were all strung together, to stretch around the equator about 140 times. The United States Interstate Highway System, authorized in 1944, makes up about 1 percent of total U.S. highway mileage but carries over 20 percent of all traffic. Shown here is a particularly scenic stretch of road in Zion National Park, Utah.

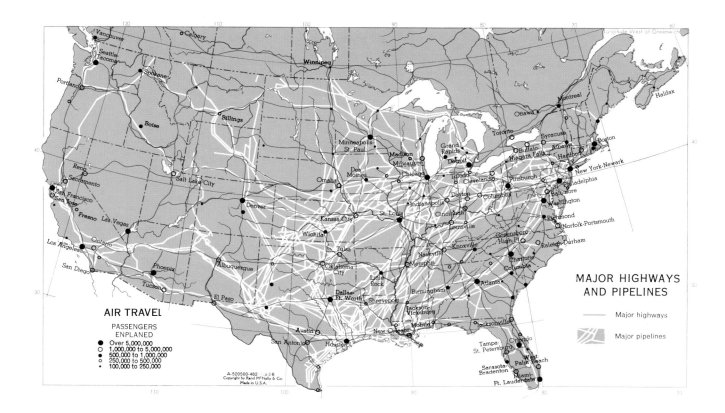

AIR TRAVEL

PASSENGERS ENPLANED

● Over 5,000,000
○ 1,000,000 to 5,000,000
● 500,000 to 1,000,000
○ 250,000 to 500,000
∙ 100,000 to 250,000

A-520500-462   4-26
Copyright by Rand McNally & Co.
Made in U.S.A.

MAJOR HIGHWAYS
AND PIPELINES

Major highways

Major pipelines

It seems only fitting that the United States would be the spawning ground of the airplane. The nation's great distances and rugged terrain created a challenge to such travel innovators as Wilbur and Orville Wright, shown here during their famous flight on December 17, 1903. Transcontinental trips now take a few hours and little effort on the part of the airline passenger.

Early in the nation's history, the Mississippi River, shown here, became a main transportation artery. Its largely navigable course runs well over two thousand miles, and many major tributaries flow into it. After the steamboat came into wide use, by 1830, transport on the river increased substantially. The late 1800s saw the beginning of a rivalry that endures today between river and rail transport. Traffic along the river is still on the rise.

Law and Disorder

ome say that violence was an inescapable part of frontier life—from the Indian wars to the mining towns, and from the bitter range wars to the mythic outlaws and lawmen that seem to have populated the West. Indeed, the Colt revolver and the Winchester rifle are among the most enduring images of the Old West. Yet an equally strong, though perhaps less popular, legacy of the frontier was an enduring respect for law and order. The classic battle between law and disorder is part of our western cultural heritage.

The sheer size of the frontier and the rapid pace of early settlement meant that miners, farmers, townspeople, and ranchers often had to serve as judge, jury, and executioner to maintain order. Federal marshalls and judges acted to enforce the law in the territories of the United States. Vigilance committees administered their own form of rough justice to corrupt officials, thieves, and rustlers when the local legal system proved incapable of dealing with such criminals. Although it may seem that frontier society was ruled by violence, one of the first acts of any organized

Opinion polls and the media suggest that violence and crime are continually on the rise in the United States. Still, the fact remains that millions of Americans live peaceful lives in undisturbed communities such as this quiet town in Maine.

town was to hire a sheriff to take over the job of establishing law and order. Legendary towns such as Dodge City and Abilene were never really the lawless cow towns depicted in the movies, although each went through a brief period when outlaws attempted to coerce the community.

The brief wide-open days of the frontier also gave rise to such folk figures as the outlaws Black Bart, Butch Cassidy, Billy the Kid, Jesse and Frank James, and a host of lesser-known "long riders." But the lawmen who tamed the western towns and hunted down the outlaws—Wyatt Earp, Bat Masterson, Tom Smith, and Pat Garrett—became equally famous. As the frontier era drew to a close, the public romanticized gunslingers and lawmen and created a market for stories of the frontier in magazines, books, and newspapers. Later, the Western became a staple of the movies. The theme of the quiet, resourceful, and solitary hero who suppresses evil and violence and who reluctantly uses force to set things right has found its way into police stories and even into science fiction.

Many experts express a concern that because of our attachment to the legends of the Old West, Americans believe that some problems can be solved only through physical force and violence. They cite as examples the fictional and actual police response to gun-related murders committed and the rise of urban street violence. Many people who own guns and fear criminals feel that the clock has been turned back to an era when everyone went armed for their own protection. They point to the frontier tradition where the average citizen used force in self-defense or to stop a lawbreaker, although historical evidence contradicts their claim.

Their view overlooks the solid legal foundation of most frontier life. Like the settlers in the early towns, people in strife-torn areas look not to the gun but to legally constituted authority to help create a stable community for their children's future. Perhaps we need to remember that despite the West's romantic legacy of extensive violence, it was the law that prevailed in the end.

The now-epic legends of the Wild West are part fact and part fiction. On both sides of the law tales have been told, and heroes and villains alike have achieved mythic stature. Sometime lawman Wyatt Earp, shown here, is one of those surrounded by controversy and opposing views, which only seem to increase public fascination with him and others like him.

A Nation on the Move

The Shifting Population

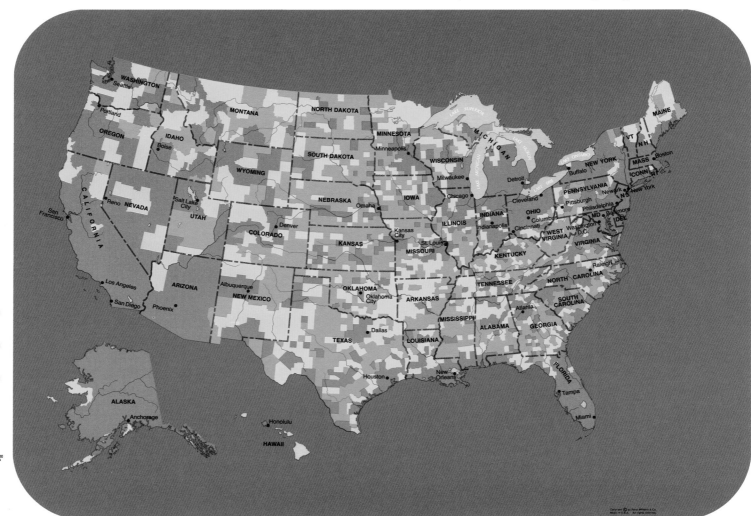

The legacy of the frontier can be found in the restless spirit of the American public. Whenever opportunity has diminished in one region, Americans have pulled out and moved on—traditionally to the West and North where jobs or land seemed more plentiful. Of late, however, more people have been migrating to the suburbs of major cities and to the West and South. This map shows some regional changes for the period 1940 to 1970.

MAP LEGEND

- Population Increased 1940-1970
- Population Decreased 1940-1970
- Population Increased and Decreased 1940-1970

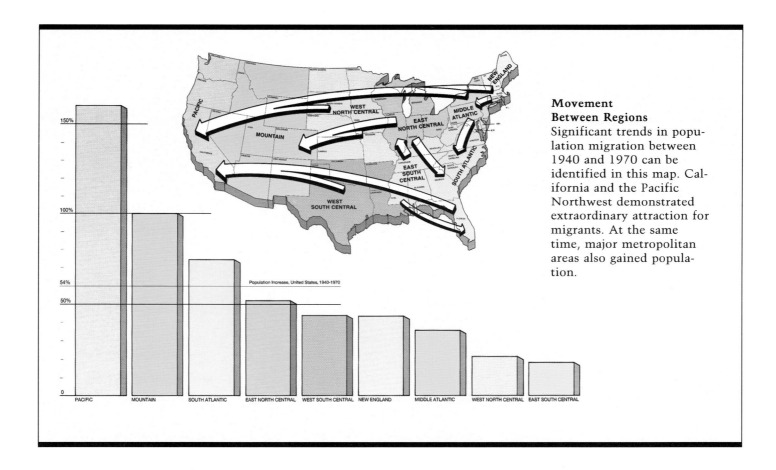

Movement Between Regions

Significant trends in population migration between 1940 and 1970 can be identified in this map. California and the Pacific Northwest demonstrated extraordinary attraction for migrants. At the same time, major metropolitan areas also gained population.

Population Increase, United States, 1940-1970

Although it has become by far the most populous state, California has managed to maintain many wild areas in the form of protected lands. Shown here is Lassen Peak in Lassen Volcanic National Park.

The Necessity of Invention

Whatever challenges the frontier presented, American inventiveness has proved equal to the task. "Yankee ingenuity" has become a legendary part of the American character. Americans came to see obstacles not as dead ends but as opportunities for innovation.

Many innovations had to do with adapting to the new land. To conquer the expanses on the way west, for example, Americans invented the Conestoga wagon, which could hold an entire family and all its possessions. With their white canvas tops, Conestogas and their progeny, the "prairie schooners," moved like ships through tall grass. To farm the tough soil of the Great Plains, settlers had to invent a new kind of plow that could slice through the tangled roots of grass. When there was no wood for houses, the pioneers built homes of prairie sod as shelter against the summer heat and bitter cold in winter.

But frontier inventiveness was not limited to the land; it extended to social and political arenas as well. The newly opened West placed few restrictions on what people could do for a living. Without any formal residency or educational requirements, frontier people could take up any profession they wished or change professions at will. In frontier Illinois, Abraham Lincoln became a successful lawyer with only modest legal training. Many doctors received merely a smattering of medical knowledge before they advertised themselves as physicians, and whoever could afford a printing press could declare themselves journalists.

The more populist spirit of the West also produced its share of innovations that expressed the independence and democratic ideals of the pioneers. Free public higher education available to all was an effort to reject the tradition of European class differences and to promote the democratic experience among the young. Western states also introduced the referendum and the recall. Under these provisions, the people could initiate legislation by popular vote or recall any elected official. Perhaps the most radical innovation occurred when Wyoming and Utah granted women the right to vote years before universal suffrage became a constitutional amendment. In recognition of their part in settling the West, women were also given more control over their property both before and after marriage.

Yankee ingenuity did not stop with the closing of the frontier. The ability to devise new solutions to new problems and the economic freedom to profit from the results produced one of the greatest explosions in human creativity the world has ever seen. From the humble rocking chair to the principles of mass production to the sophisticated electronic technology that has enabled us to explore outer space, Americans have secured more patents for new inventions than any other nation. The frontier tradition of relying on one's ingenuity to survive has instilled in Americans the belief that they can meet any challenge and solve any puzzle. This spirit should serve the nation well as it enters the twenty-first century.

In a strange twist of history, most suffragist activity took place in the East, yet by 1914, women were allowed to vote in every state west of the Rockies (except for New Mexico), and had not yet gained suffrage in any state east of the Rockies (except for Kansas). These suffragettes in New York City in 1912 plainly make their point.

The inventor who creates something useful through ingenious thinking and experimentation is a classic American image. One of the United States' most honored scientific innovators, George Washington Carver, is shown here at the Tuskegee Institute. Carver was both a horticultural experimenter and teacher. The Tuskegee Institute itself was an innovation; it was established in 1881 as a trade school for African Americans.

Frontier doctors often relied on a variety of skills for their livelihoods. They often doubled as preachers, and they sold concoctions to help support their business. Like everyone else on the frontier, doctors had to be robust and resourceful.

The New Mythic Hero

The frontier myth of the rugged individual glorified the young country's confidence in itself and in each person's power to control his or her own destiny. The spirit of western individualism has been captured in many larger-than-life legends.

Some heroes were truly mythic, such as Paul Bunyan, Minnesota's giant logger with his blue ox Babe, and John Henry, the steel-driving railroad man. But others were historical figures like Mike Fink, the riverboat king, and Davy Crockett, "king of the wild frontier," who were transformed by newspaper stories and later by films and television into legendary folk heroes. These men were distinguished by their reputations as fighters and by an unabashed willingness to promote their own myth. Mike Fink described himself as "half horse, half alligator," ready to take on any and all challengers. The personal strength and courage of the frontier Indian fighter, hunter, flatboatman, or range rider established the American model of the hero who overcomes all odds or dies in the attempt, inspiring others to succeed.

This brash, self-confident hero still has great appeal today. Whether the mythic character turns up in the movies or in sports, business, politics, or space travel, behind that modern hero loom the larger-than-life figures of American frontier legends.

The Heroic Frontiersman
This drawing of Meriwether Lewis depicts one vision of the heroic American frontiersman. Clad in animal skins and what is perhaps a raccoon-skin cap, with his gun firmly planted, Lewis exhibits the rugged, self-confident look often associated with heroes of the American frontier.

Shown here is a sight not uncommon to Americans in the 1990s, yet most still find it awe-inspiring. This is the space shuttle Columbia rising from earth on one of its heroic journeys into one of the latest frontiers.

The United States—and, indeed, the rest of the world— loves legendary western heroes. The image of the cowboy hero is one of the most popular and enduring in American history. Even the western landscape itself has become a heroic icon, as vistas of wide-open spaces and red-rock buttes and mesas continue to inspire Americans. Shown here is a place specifically associated with pioneer heroism: Scotts Bluff National Monument, Nebraska, a landmark to travelers along the Overland Trail.

The Frontier Spirit Today

The images, language, and myths of the frontier experience pervade nearly every aspect of American life. Its hallmarks can be seen from the sports arena to the political convention hall, from the classroom to the corporate boardroom. Although other nations regard frontiers as boundaries, to Americans the word calls up wide-open spaces and a promise of unlimited opportunity.

Popular culture displays a wealth of frontier images. Sports teams with names taken from frontier icons take to the field, while sportswriters discuss their games with terms like "shootout" or "showdown." Even in this high-tech era, the Western in novel and movie form can still attract an eager audience. Industry leaders talk about "blazing a trail" in the new economic wilderness and using the "pioneer spirit" that helped to create American industry to fashion a new economic partnership for the future.

Politicians have relied on the frontier experience to gain support for their programs

United States Population in 1990

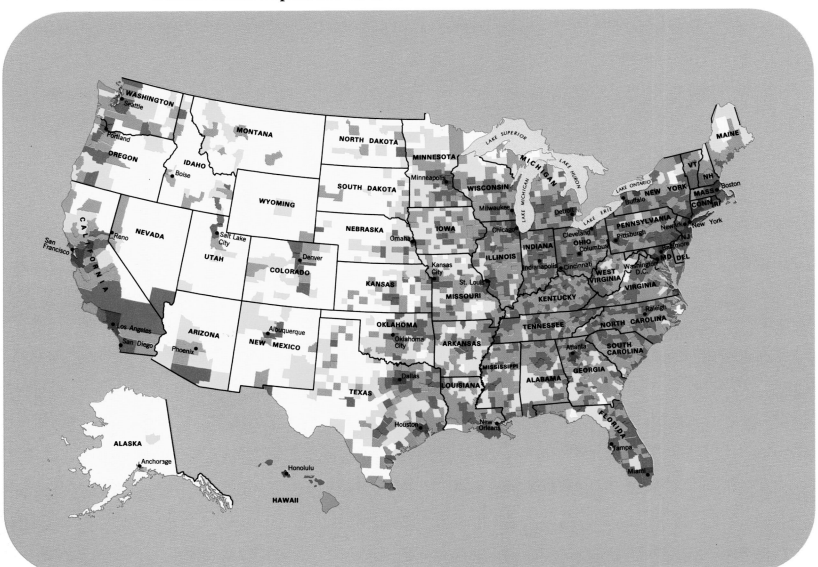

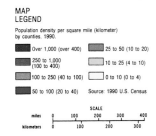

MAP
LEGEND

Population density per square mile (kilometer) by counties, 1990

- Over 1,000 (over 400)
- 250 to 1,000 (100 to 400)
- 100 to 250 (40 to 100)
- 50 to 100 (20 to 40)
- 25 to 50 (10 to 20)
- 10 to 25 (4 to 10)
- 0 to 10 (0 to 4)

Source: 1990 U.S. Census

SCALE

miles   0   100   200   300   400
kilometers   0   100   200   300

Today the West is a battleground for environmentalists, ranchers, loggers, and other groups. Just which interests prevail where remains to be seen. In the meantime, the 1990 census reveals that the American population is increasingly urban and suburban. Some believe a new frontier may be emerging on the wide-open spaces of the American West, as population on the Great Plains has actually decreased in recent years.

and policies. President Theodore Roosevelt, explaining his mild language in foreign policy negotiations, quoted a westernism, "Don't draw unless you intend to shoot." In the 1960s, President John F. Kennedy named his program the New Frontier and called on Americans to venture into unexplored areas of opportunity, especially in space and science.

Throughout the nation's history, Americans have taken the frontier spirit to heart. They tend to regard progress in learning in the arts, health, industry, and science as advancing the frontiers of knowledge. The nation's passionate commitment to and belief in the idea of continuing progress and economic growth is a clear legacy of the frontier tradition of optimism and self-confidence. Despite mounting problems facing the country, there is an underlying belief in our ability to find new solutions.

Nowhere has this spirit been more visible than in the American space program. Although NASA voyages have been far more a

The American landscape itself continues to symbolize the land of the free and the home of the brave. The frontier notion that the wilderness and its resources are unlimited, however, may be changing as Americans become more aware of the human impact on the natural world and that scenes such as this one, which features Mount Shuksan, Washington, are worth preserving.

The Frontier Spirit Today (continued)

group effort than most national undertakings, Americans still view their astronauts as rugged individuals on the frontiers of the known world. The same mythic characteristics—skill, courage, physical endurance, and resourcefulness—are evident in the men and women who have piloted our space craft. The astronauts themselves often have adopted the language of the frontier. When astronaut Gene Cernan landed on the moon in 1972, he surveyed the bleak landscape around him and began to sing, "Oh, bury me not on the lone prairie." The haunting refrain of a cowboy lament coming from 150,000 miles out in space offered a fitting tribute to the original pioneer spirit.

With the settling of most wilderness areas, the concept of the frontier has come to symbolize a state of mind where the human imagination is free to explore and create, unhindered by what has been done in the past. Confronted with the problems of their society and the challenge of living within the limited resources of the earth, Americans are reinterpreting this frontier legacy. Yet its spirit can continue to inspire succeeding generations to meet the future with ingenuity and courage.

Some say the first pictures of the earth taken from the moon had a profound effect on the American public. People saw that the earth was really just a tiny spaceship, floating in empty space. For the first time, perhaps, Americans began to see limits to their world and that they are a part of a larger, quite fragile, whole.

Historical Maps

The American Colonies in 1776

When war in the American colonies broke out, British interest in the lands across the Atlantic heightened. In the days before satellite television and fax machines, one way to inform the public about the world was to issue maps to help people envision the events they heard about. This map, published in early 1776 by R. Sayer and J. Bennett, was entitled "The Theatre of War in North America." It was sold in the streets of London.

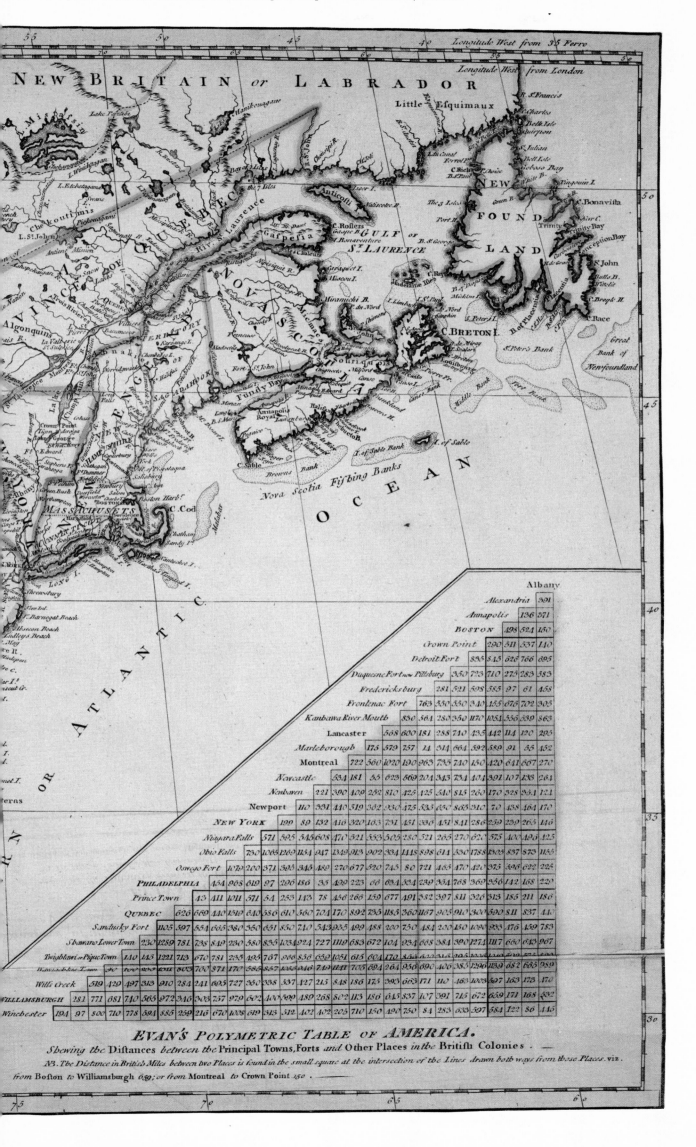

The United States in 1816

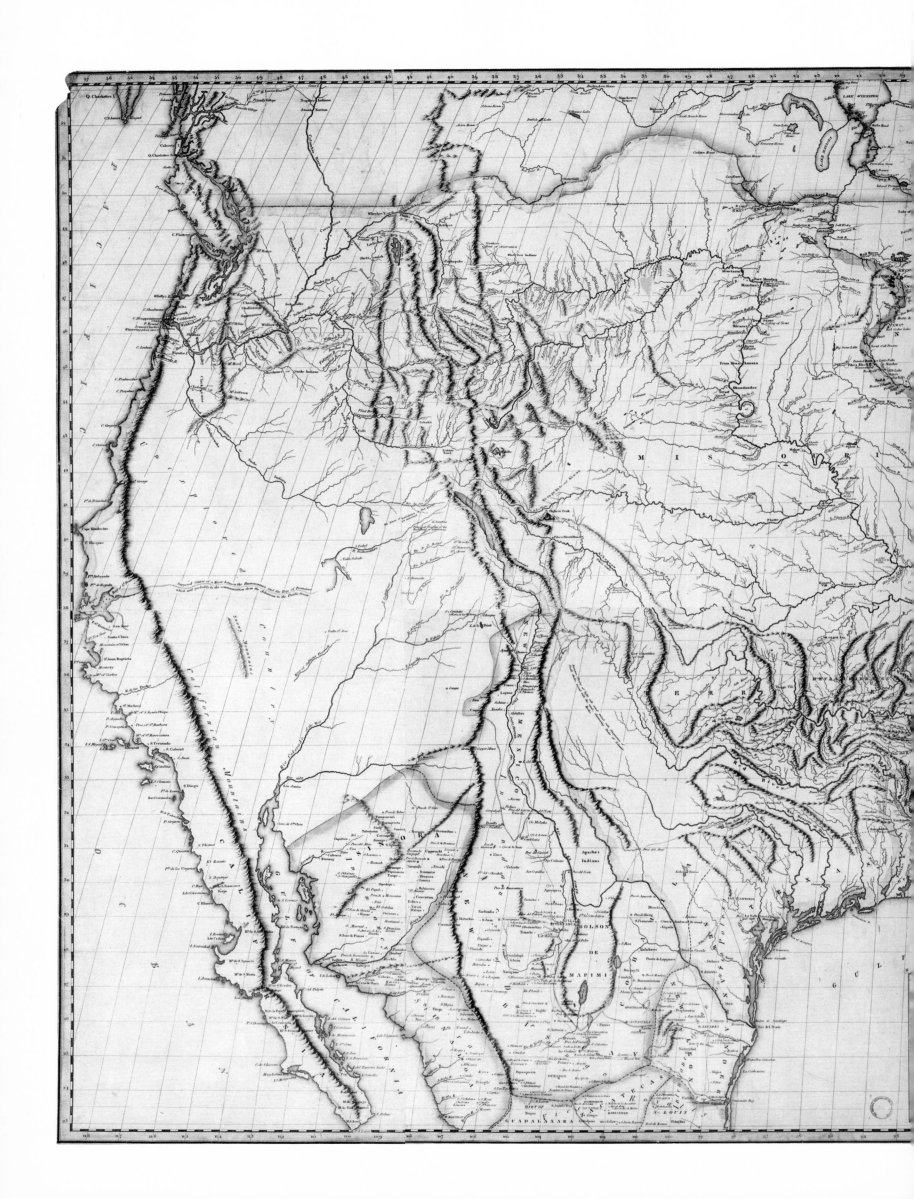

This map, produced by John Melish in 1816, was the first American-produced wall map depicting the country from coast to coast. The geography of the unexplored Southwest remains greatly distorted. Melish incorporated data from state and military maps as they became available and fre- quently revised the map. It is estimated that over twenty revisions of the map were issued between 1816 and 1823. The United States–Mexico boundary was first determined on one of these Melish maps.

The United States in 1856

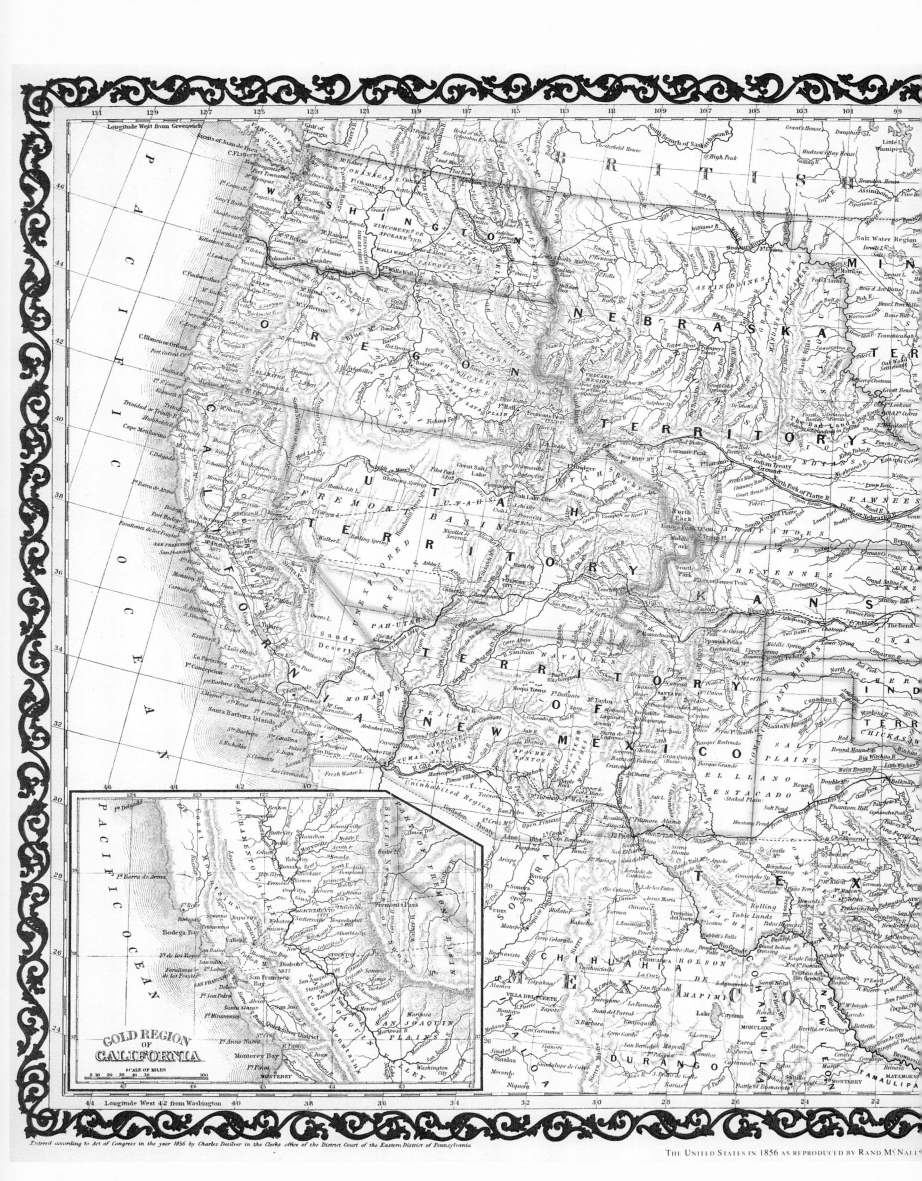

GOLD REGION OF CALIFORNIA

SCALE OF MILES

Entered according to Act of Congress in the year 1856 by Charles Desilver in the Clerk's office of the District Court of the Eastern District of Pennsylvania

THE UNITED STATES IN 1856 AS REPRODUCED BY RAND McNALLY

This map, by J.H. Young, was published in Mitchell's Universal Atlas. Although the territory of the United States reached from coast to coast, only about half of the area had been organized into states. The remainder was contained in vast western territories. Railroads extended as far as the Mississippi River; beyond the river lay the frontier of the American West. The dotted lines west of the Mississippi represent proposed railroad routes to the Pacific Ocean.

A NEW
MAP OF THE
UNITED STATES
of America
BY J.H. YOUNG,
PHILADELPHIA
PUBLISHED BY CHARLES DESILVER 251 MARKET S.T 1857.

RAILROAD ROUTES PROPOSED TO THE PACIFIC OCEAN.

The dotted lines which cross the continent to the west coast of the United States represent the different routes proposed for the GREAT PACIFIC RAILROAD. The northern route will commence probably at Chicago, and extend via. the South Pass, and the Great Salt Lake to San Francisco. The central route will commence at St.Louis, and extend very nearly on a parallel, crossing the Rocky mountains at about Lat. 38° also to San Francisco. The southern route will commence either at Memphis or Vicksburg, and will extend via. El Paso to San Diego The distances from ocean to ocean by these routes in connection with the railroads already made from the Atlantic sea-board will be the northern about 2850, the central 2700, and the southern 2300 miles.

SCALE 1= 8750000

STATUTE MILES 69 TO A DEGREE

EXPLANATION.

Capitals of States and Territories
Principal Cities and Towns
Railroads
Do. Proposed
Common Roads
Battle Fields
Figures attached to Mountains indicate their heights in feet.

Engraved by
J.L.Hazzard & E.Yeager

DISTRICT OF COLUMBIA
SCALE OF MILES

REFERENCE
1 The Capitol
2 Presidents House
3 Department of State
4 War Department
5 Navy
6 Treasury Do.
7 Gen. Post Office
8 Patent Office
9 Smithsonian Institute
10 Navy Yard

Longitude West from Washington   Longitude East from Washington

The United States in 1881

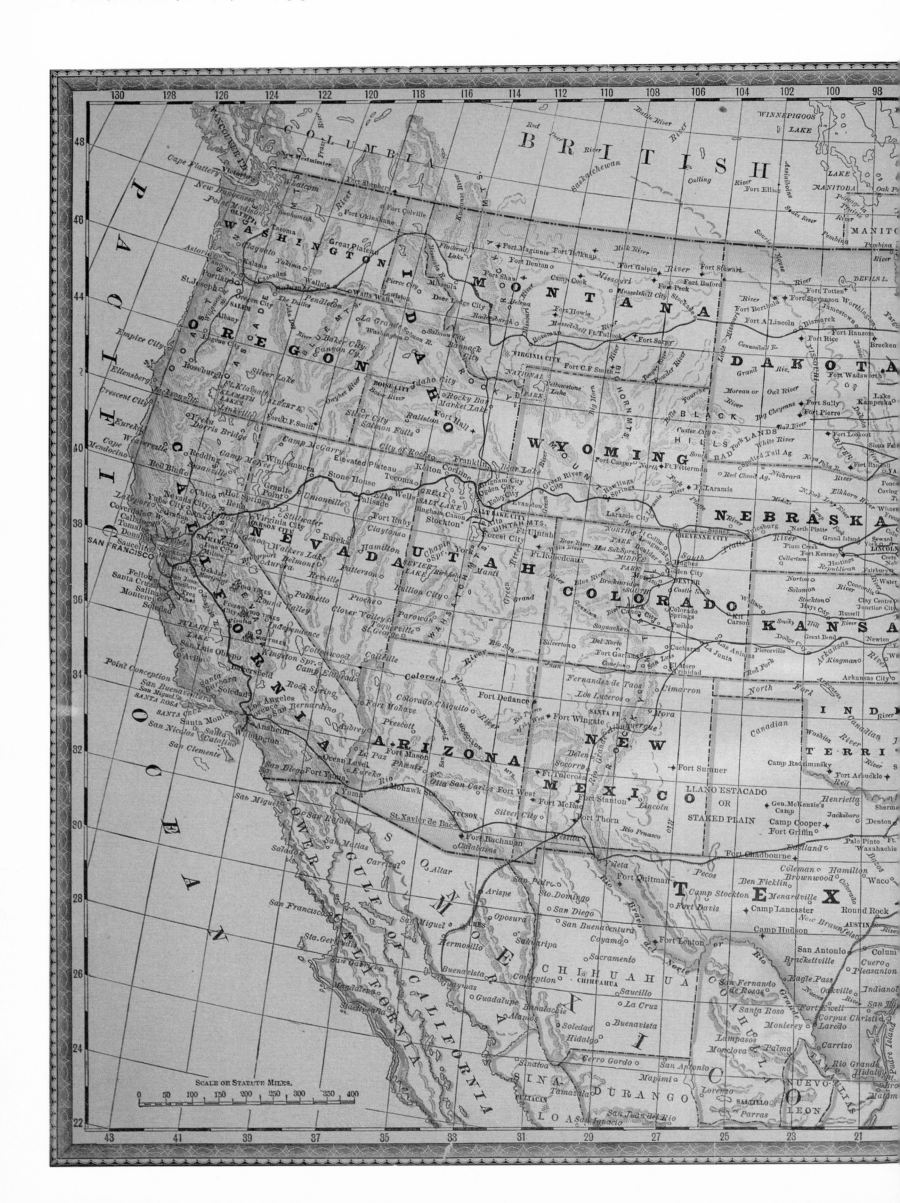

From the Rand McNally Business Atlas of 1881, this map reveals that most of the western territories had by this time been carved into states. Of the continental United States, only Oklahoma retained its territorial name, Indian Territory, and Dakota had yet to be divided into north and south.

The red lines are railroads. East of the Mississippi, the rail lines already formed a complex web. West of the Mississippi, however, the network quickly faded into single tracks, stretching alone across the Great Plains, Rocky Mountains, and Great Basin to the West Coast.

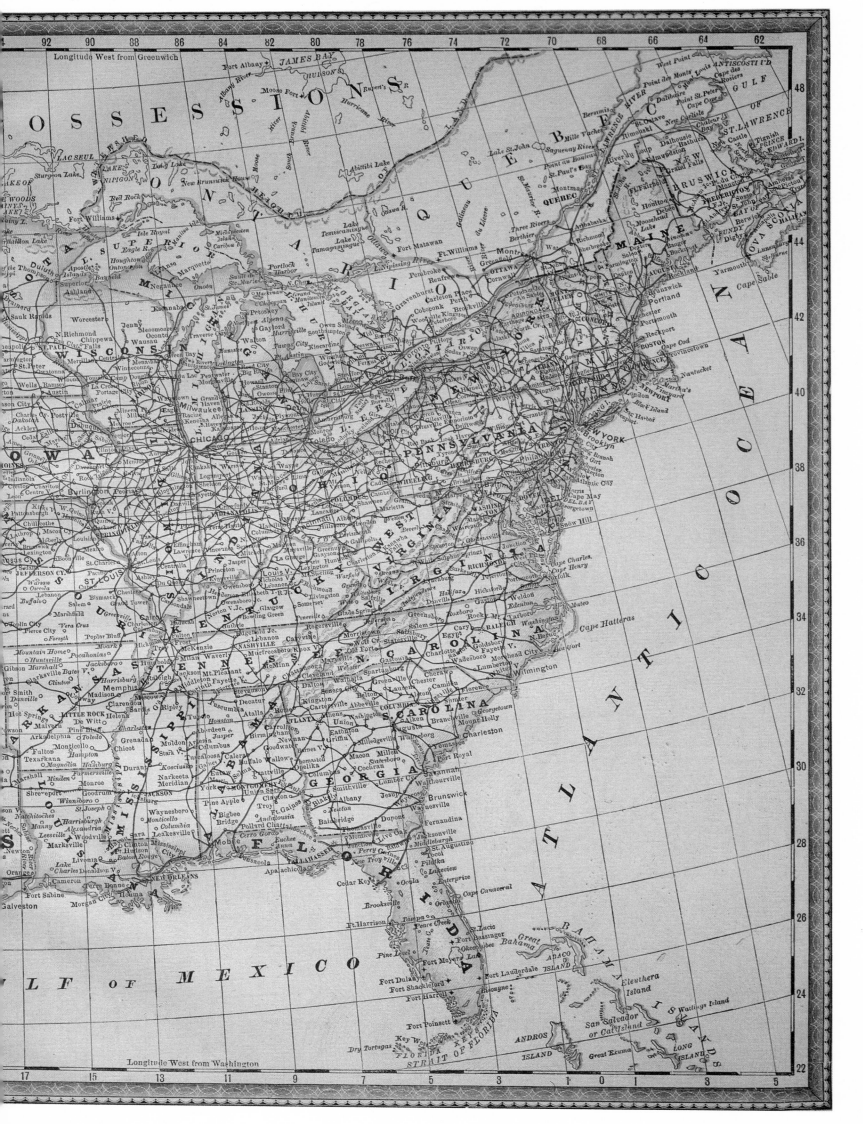

The United States in 1889

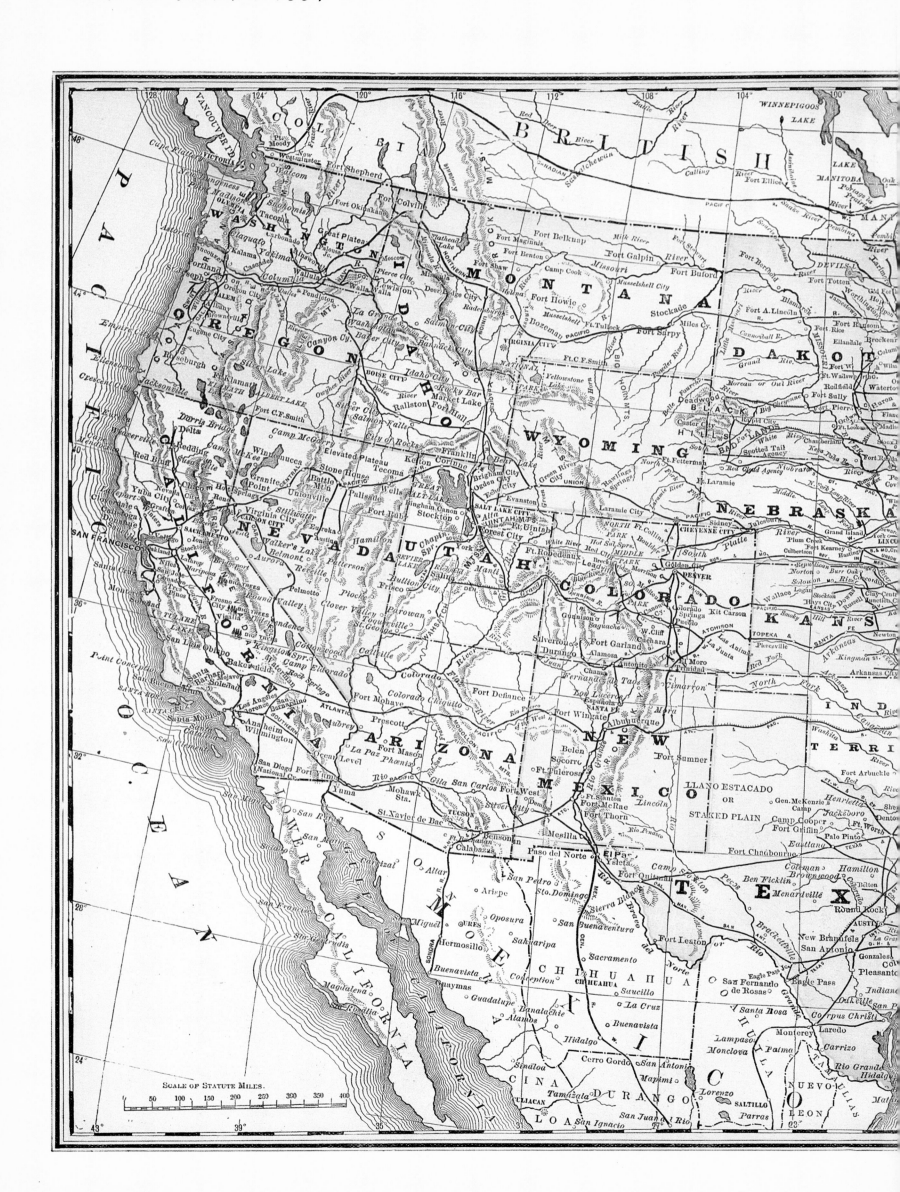

In 1889, Rand McNally's Standard Atlas of the World represented the United States with this map. The contiguous states are tinted with various colors, lending an impression of established permanence to the nation—even to the western states. The population figures reveal the distribution of citizens just before the 1890 census, after which the frontier was declared closed. In a way, this map is the last glimpse of the West as the American frontier.

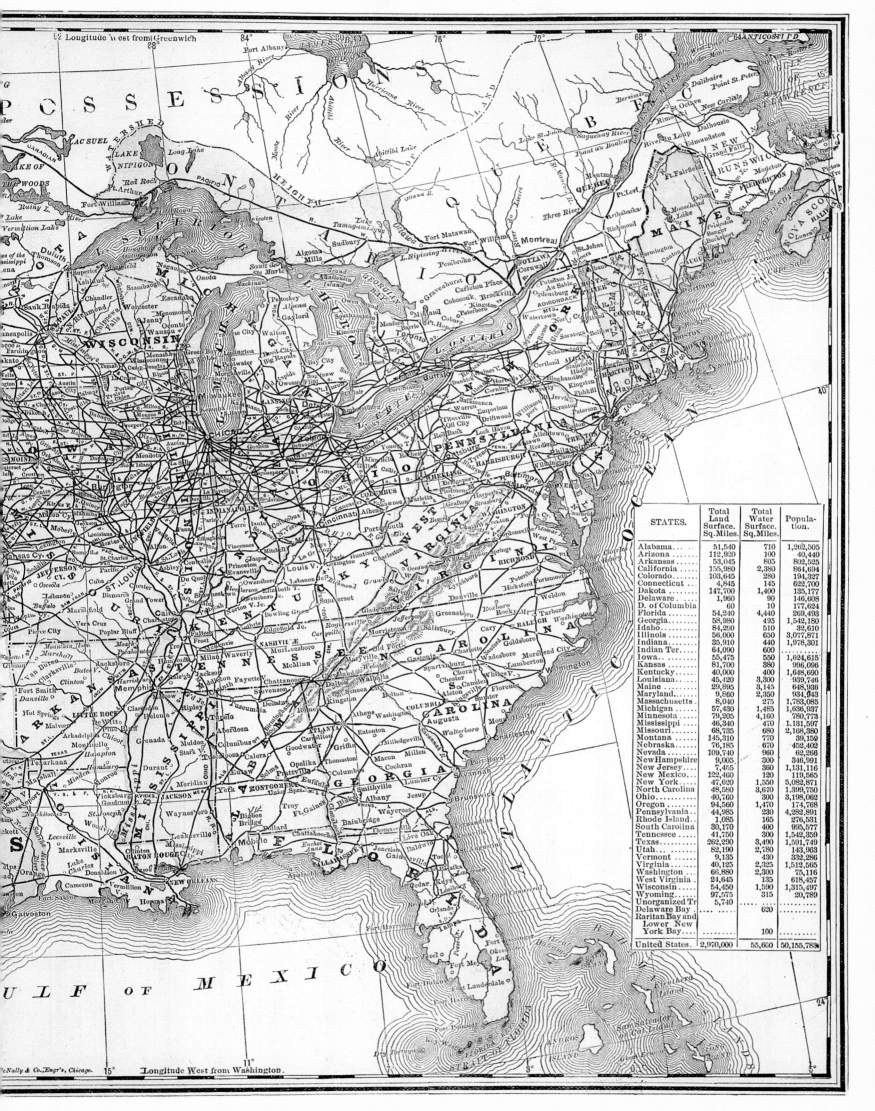

STATES.	Total Land Surface. Sq. Miles.	Total Water Surface. Sq. Miles.	Population.
Alabama......	51,540	710	1,262,505
Arizona	112,920	100	40,440
Arkansas	53,045	805	802,525
California	155,980	2,380	864,694
Colorado......	103,645	280	194,327
Connecticut ...	4,845	145	622,700
Dakota	147,700	1,400	135,177
Delaware	1,960	90	146,608
D. of Columbia	60	10	177,624
Florida	54,240	4,440	269,493
Georgia......	58,980	495	1,542,180
Idaho........	84,290	510	32,610
Illinois	56,000	650	3,077,871
Indiana	35,910	440	1,978,301
Indian Ter....	64,000	600	
Iowa.........	55,475	550	1,624,615
Kansas.......	81,700	380	996,096
Kentucky.....	40,000	400	1,648,690
Louisiana.....	45,420	3,300	939,746
Maine	29,895	3,145	648,936
Maryland.....	9,860	2,350	934,943
Massachusetts .	8,040	275	1,783,085
Michigan	57,430	1,485	1,636,937
Minnesota	79,205	4,160	780,773
Mississippi ...	46,340	470	1,131,597
Missouri	68,735	680	2,168,380
Montana	145,310	770	39,159
Nebraska	76,185	670	452,402
Nevada	109,740	960	62,266
New Hampshire	9,005	300	346,991
New Jersey....	7,455	360	1,131,116
New Mexico....	122,460	120	119,565
New York.....	47,620	1,550	5,082,871
North Carolina	48,580	3,670	1,399,750
Ohio.........	40,760	300	3,198,062
Oregon.......	94,560	1,470	174,768
Pennsylvania .	44,985	230	4,282,891
Rhode Island..	1,085	165	276,531
South Carolina	30,170	400	995,577
Tennessee	41,750	300	1,542,359
Texas........	262,290	3,490	1,591,749
Utah.........	82,190	2,780	143,963
Vermont	9,135	430	332,286
Virginia......	40,125	2,325	1,512,565
Washington ...	66,880	2,300	75,116
West Virginia .	24,645	135	618,457
Wisconsin	54,450	1,590	1,315,497
Wyoming	97,575	315	20,789
Unorganized Tr	5,740		
Delaware Bay..		620	
Raritan Bay and Lower New York Bay....		100	
United States.	2,970,000	55,600	50,155,783

The United States in 1926

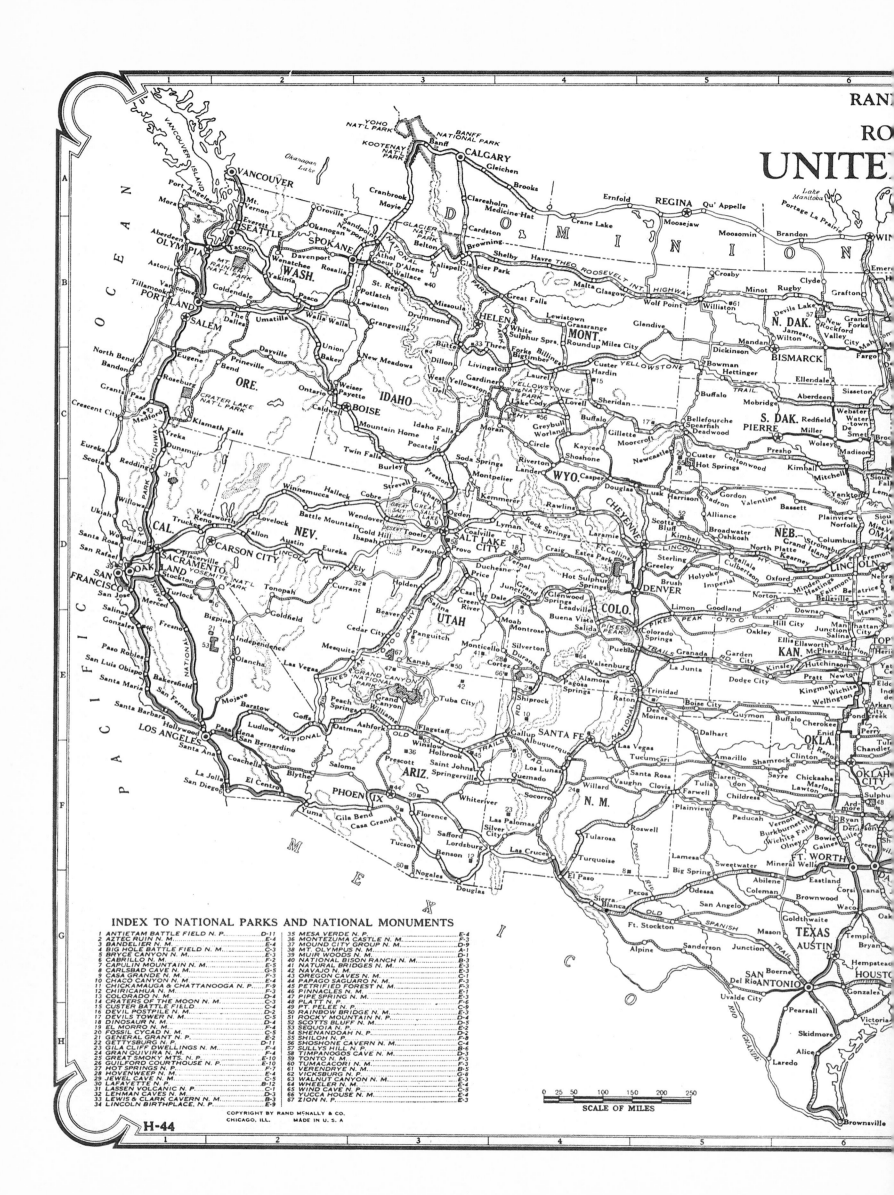

INDEX TO NATIONAL PARKS AND NATIONAL MONUMENTS

1 ANTIETAM BATTLE FIELD N. P.	D-11	35 MESA VERDE N. P.	E-4
2 AZTEC RUIN N. M.	E-4	36 MONTEZUMA CASTLE N. M.	F-3
3 BANDELIER N. M.	E-4	37 MOUND CITY GROUP N. M.	D-9
4 BIG HOLE BATTLE FIELD N. M.	C-3	38 MT. OLYMPUS N. M.	A-1
5 BRYCE CANYON N. M.	E-3	39 MUIR WOODS N. M.	D-1
6 CABRILLO N. M.	F-2	40 NATIONAL BISON RANCH N. M.	B-3
7 CAPULIN MOUNTAIN N. M.	E-5	41 NATURAL BRIDGES N. M.	E-3
8 CARLSBAD CAVE N. M.	F-5	42 NAVAJO N. M.	E-3
9 CASA GRANDE N. M.	F-3	43 OREGON CAVES N. M.	C-1
10 CHACO CANYON N. M.	E-4	44 PAPAGO SAGUARO N. M.	F-3
11 CHICKAMAUGA & CHATTANOOGA N. P.	F-9	45 PETRIFIED FOREST N. M.	F-3
12 CHIRICAHUA N. M.	F-3	46 PINNACLES N. M.	E-1
13 COLORADO N. M.	D-4	47 PIPE SPRING N. M.	E-3
14 CRATERS OF THE MOON N. M.	C-3	48 PLATT N. P.	F-6
15 CUSTER BATTLE FIELD	C-4	49 PT. PELEE N.P.	C-9
16 DEVIL POSTPILE N. M.	D-2	50 RAINBOW BRIDGE N. M.	E-3
17 DEVILS TOWER N. M.	C-5	51 ROCKY MOUNTAIN N. P.	D-5
18 DINOSAUR N. M.	D-4	52 SCOTTS BLUFF N. M.	D-5
19 EL MORRO N. M.	F-4	53 SEQUOIA N. P.	E-2
20 FOSSIL CYCAD N. M.	D-5	54 SHENANDOAH N. P.	D-11
21 GENERAL GRANT N. P.	E-2	55 SHILOH N. P.	F-8
22 GETTYSBURG N. P.	D-11	56 SHOSHONE CAVERN N. M.	C-4
23 GILA CLIFF DWELLINGS N. M.	F-4	57 SULLYS HILL N. P.	B-6
24 GRAN QUIVIRA N. M.	F-4	58 TIMPANOGOS CAVE N. M.	D-3
25 GREAT SMOKY MTS. N. P.	E-10	59 TONTO N. M.	F-3
26 GUILFORD COURTHOUSE N. P.	E-10	60 TUMACACORI N. M.	F-3
27 HOT SPRINGS N. P.	F-7	61 VERENDRYE N. M.	B-5
28 HOVENWEEP N. M.	E-4	62 VICKSBURG N. P.	G-8
29 JEWEL CAVE N. M.	C-5	63 WALNUT CANYON N. M.	F-3
30 LAFAYETTE N. P.	B-12	64 WHEELER N. M.	E-4
31 LASSEN VOLCANIC N. P.	C-1	65 WIND CAVE N. P.	C-5
32 LEHMAN CAVES N. M.	D-3	66 YUCCA HOUSE N. M.	E-4
33 LEWIS & CLARK CAVERN N. M.	B-3	67 ZION N. P.	E-3
34 LINCOLN BIRTHPLACE N. P.	E-9		

COPYRIGHT BY RAND McNALLY & CO.
CHICAGO, ILL.   MADE IN U. S. A.

SCALE OF MILES
0 25 50   100   150   200   250

H-44

By 1917, the reign of the automobile was just beginning. In that year, Rand McNally published the first United States road map to identify highways by number for motorists. The first Rand McNally Road Atlas was published in 1924; shown here is a map of the United States from the 1926 edition. By now, Oklahoma had adopted its contemporary name, and railroads were not alone in the West. Although many of them were not yet paved, United States roads crisscrossed the continent.

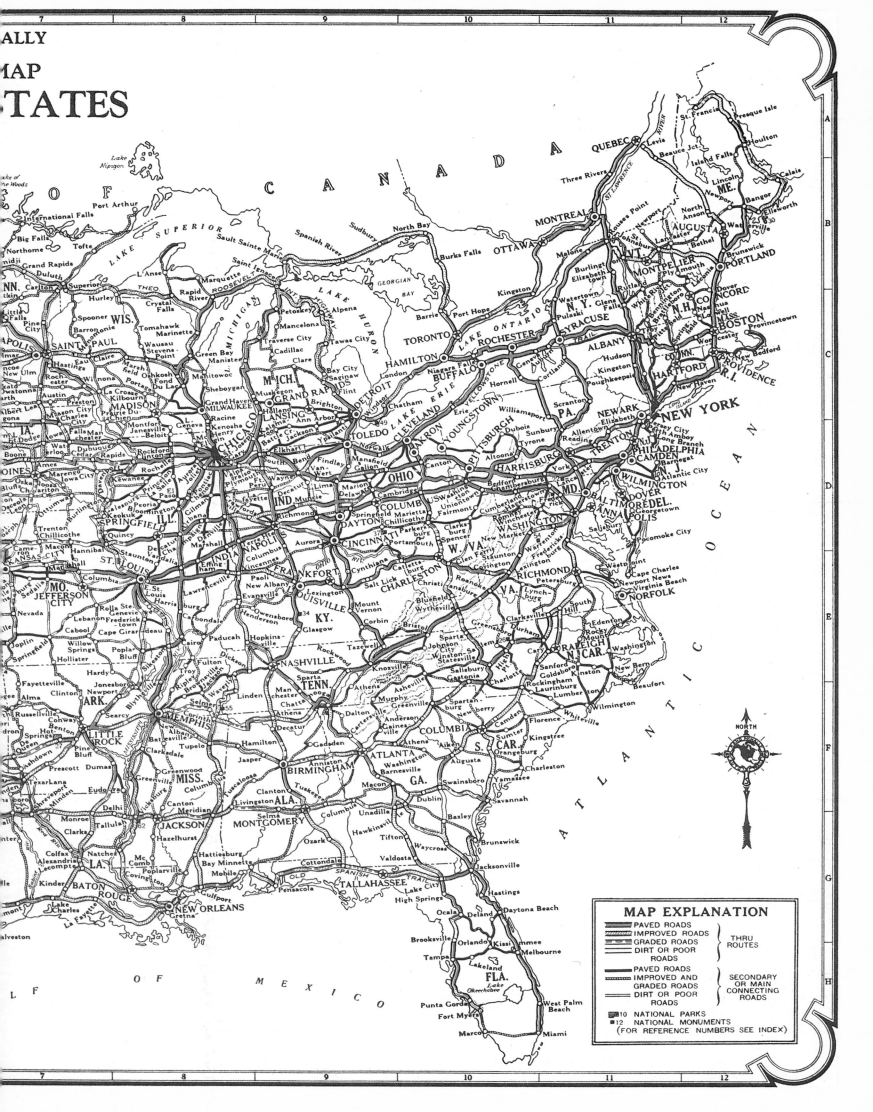

MAP EXPLANATION

PAVED ROADS		
IMPROVED ROADS		THRU
GRADED ROADS		ROUTES
DIRT OR POOR ROADS		
PAVED ROADS		
IMPROVED AND GRADED ROADS		SECONDARY OR MAIN CONNECTING ROADS
DIRT OR POOR ROADS		

10 NATIONAL PARKS
12 NATIONAL MONUMENTS
(FOR REFERENCE NUMBERS SEE INDEX)

P A R T S I X

Reference Maps

MAP LOCATOR

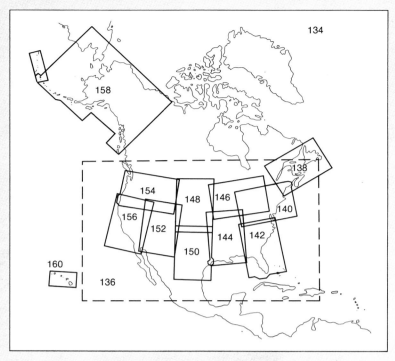

Boxes with page numbers above
show the location of maps in the book.

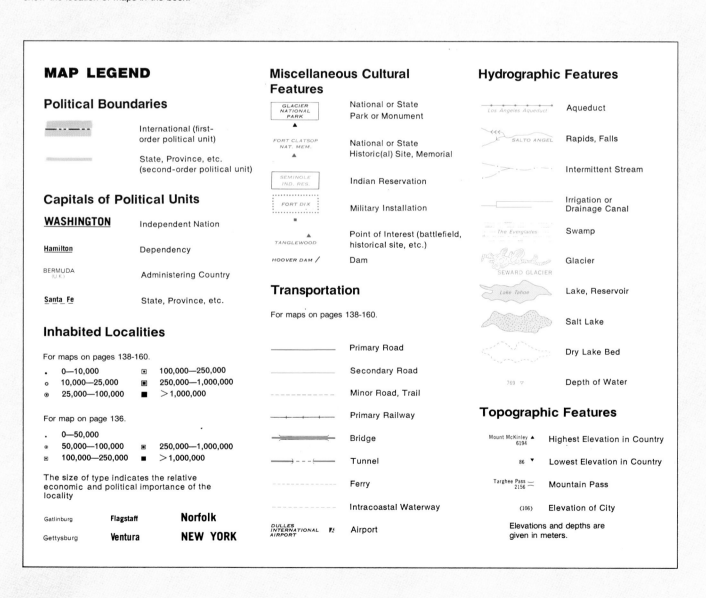

MAP LEGEND

Political Boundaries

International (first-order political unit)

State, Province, etc. (second-order political unit)

Capitals of Political Units

WASHINGTON   Independent Nation

Hamilton   Dependency

BERMUDA (U.K.)   Administering Country

Santa Fe   State, Province, etc.

Inhabited Localities

For maps on pages 138-160.

. 0—10,000   ⊡ 100,000—250,000
o 10,000—25,000   ◉ 250,000—1,000,000
◉ 25,000—100,000   ■ >1,000,000

For map on page 136.

. 0—50,000
◉ 50,000—100,000   ⊡ 250,000—1,000,000
⊡ 100,000—250,000   ■ >1,000,000

The size of type indicates the relative economic and political importance of the locality

Gatlinburg   **Flagstaff**   **Norfolk**

Gettysburg   **Ventura**   **NEW YORK**

Miscellaneous Cultural Features

GLACIER NATIONAL PARK ▲   National or State Park or Monument

FORT CLATSOP NAT. MEM. ▲   National or State Historic(al) Site, Memorial

SEMINOLE IND. RES.   Indian Reservation

FORT DIX ■   Military Installation

TANGLEWOOD ▲   Point of Interest (battlefield, historical site, etc.)

HOOVER DAM /   Dam

Transportation

For maps on pages 138-160.

Primary Road

Secondary Road

Minor Road, Trail

Primary Railway

Bridge

Tunnel

Ferry

Intracoastal Waterway

DULLES INTERNATIONAL AIRPORT ✈   Airport

Hydrographic Features

Los Angeles Aqueduct   Aqueduct

SALTO ANGEL   Rapids, Falls

Intermittent Stream

Irrigation or Drainage Canal

The Everglades   Swamp

SEWARD GLACIER   Glacier

Lake Tahoe   Lake, Reservoir

Salt Lake

Dry Lake Bed

769 ▽   Depth of Water

Topographic Features

Mount McKinley ▲ 6194   Highest Elevation in Country

86 ▼   Lowest Elevation in Country

Targhee Pass — 2156 —   Mountain Pass

(106)   Elevation of City

Elevations and depths are given in meters.

World

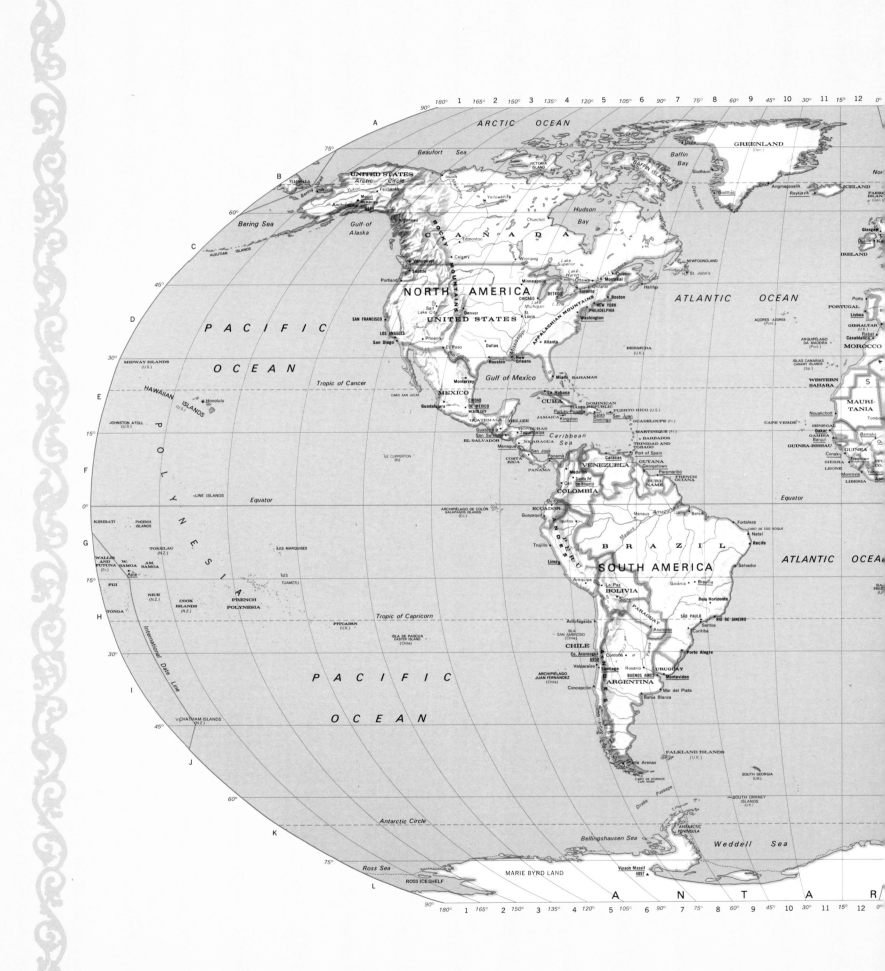

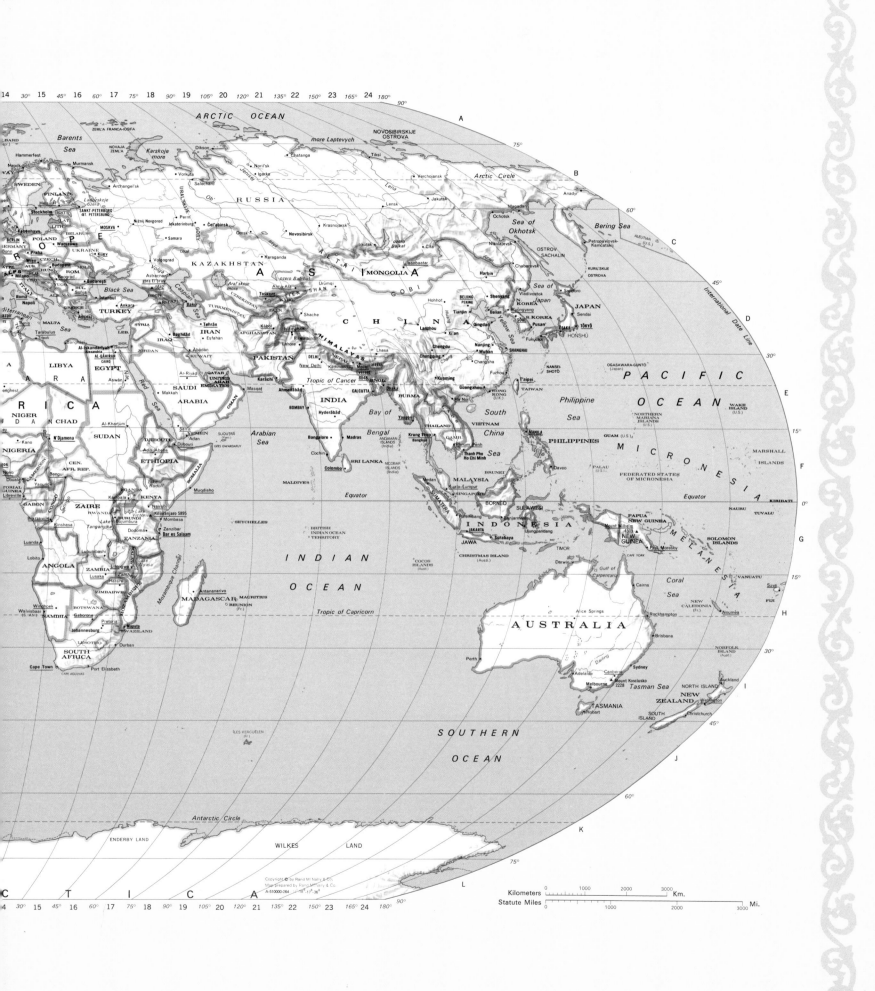

Kilometers
Statute Miles

North America

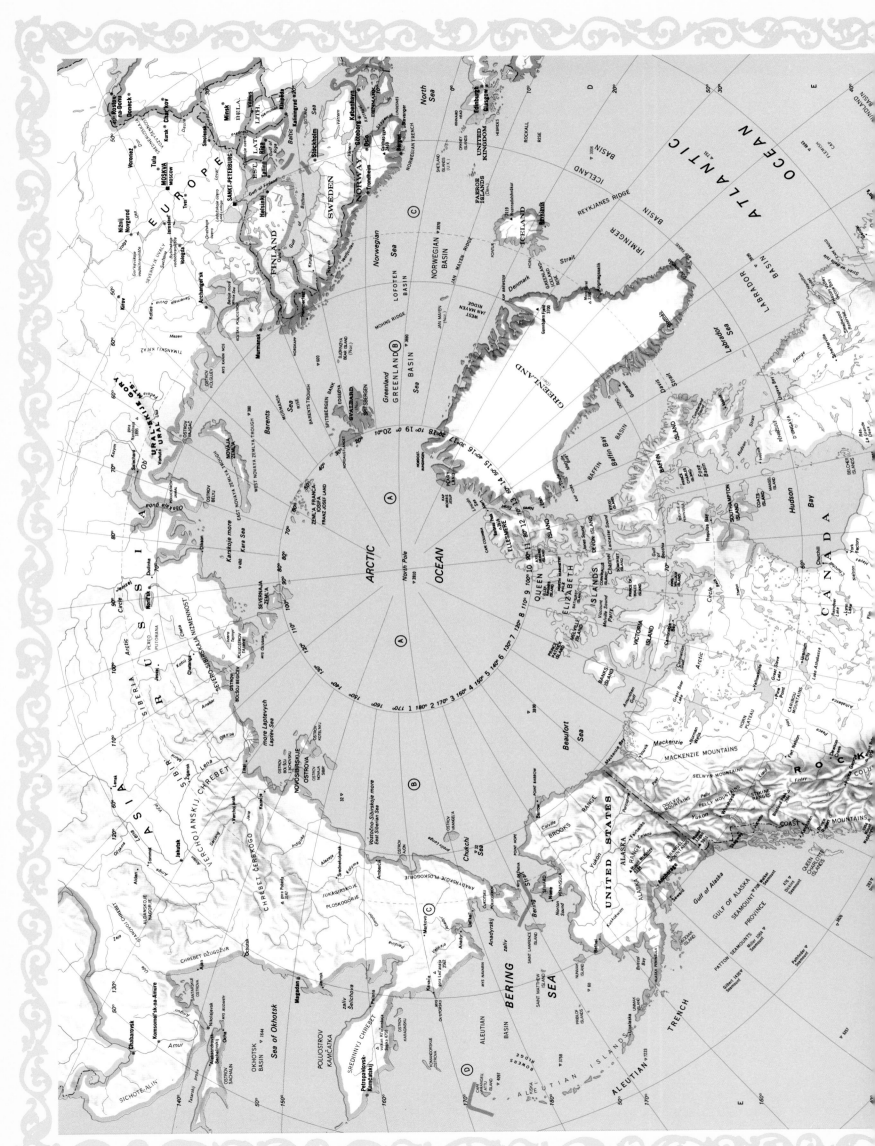

North America

United States

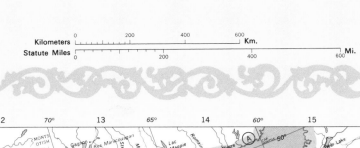

Southeastern Canada

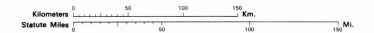

Northeastern United States

Southeastern United States

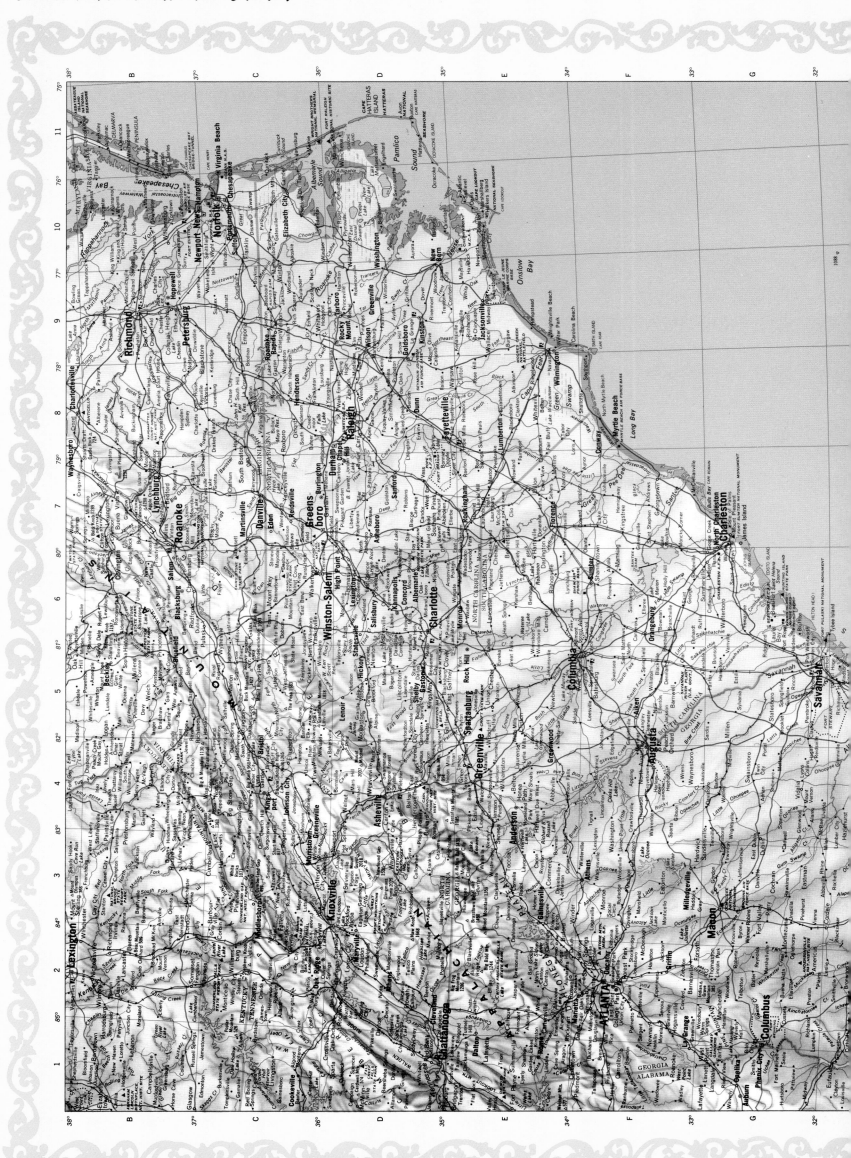

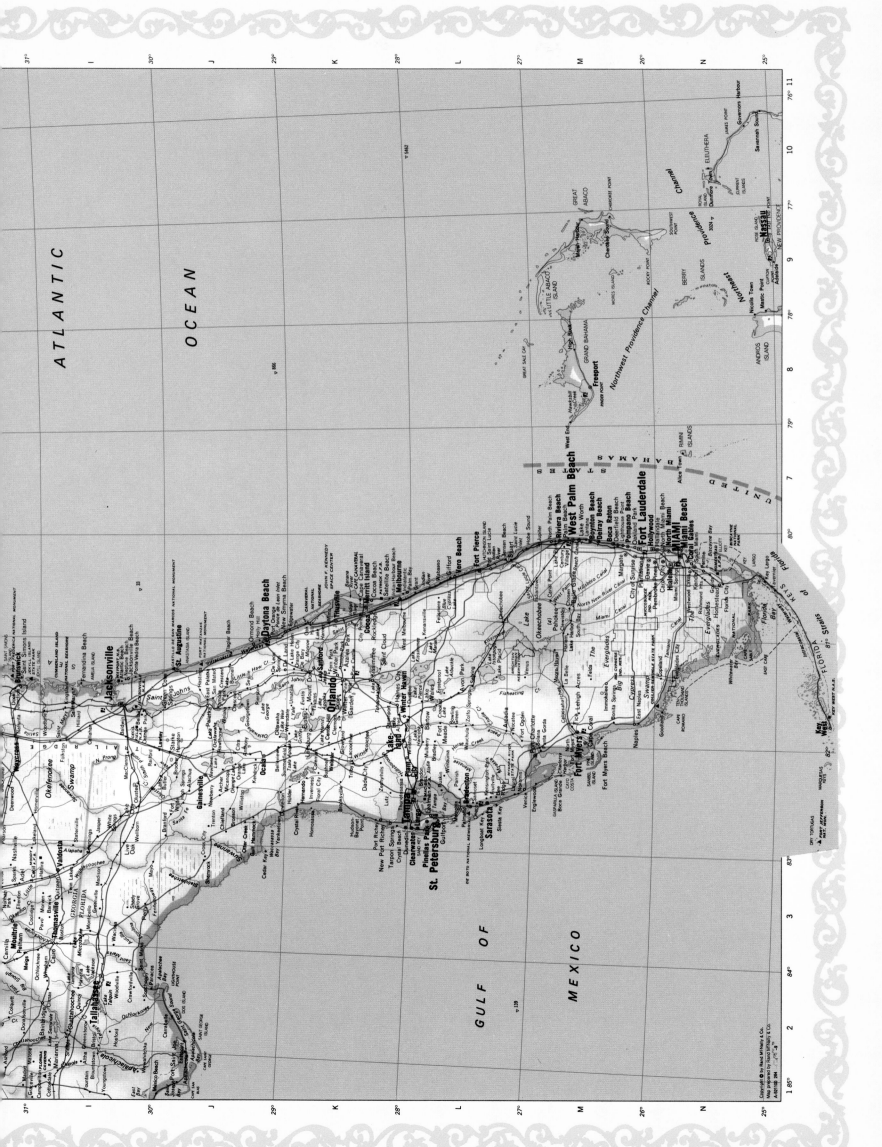

Mississippi Valley

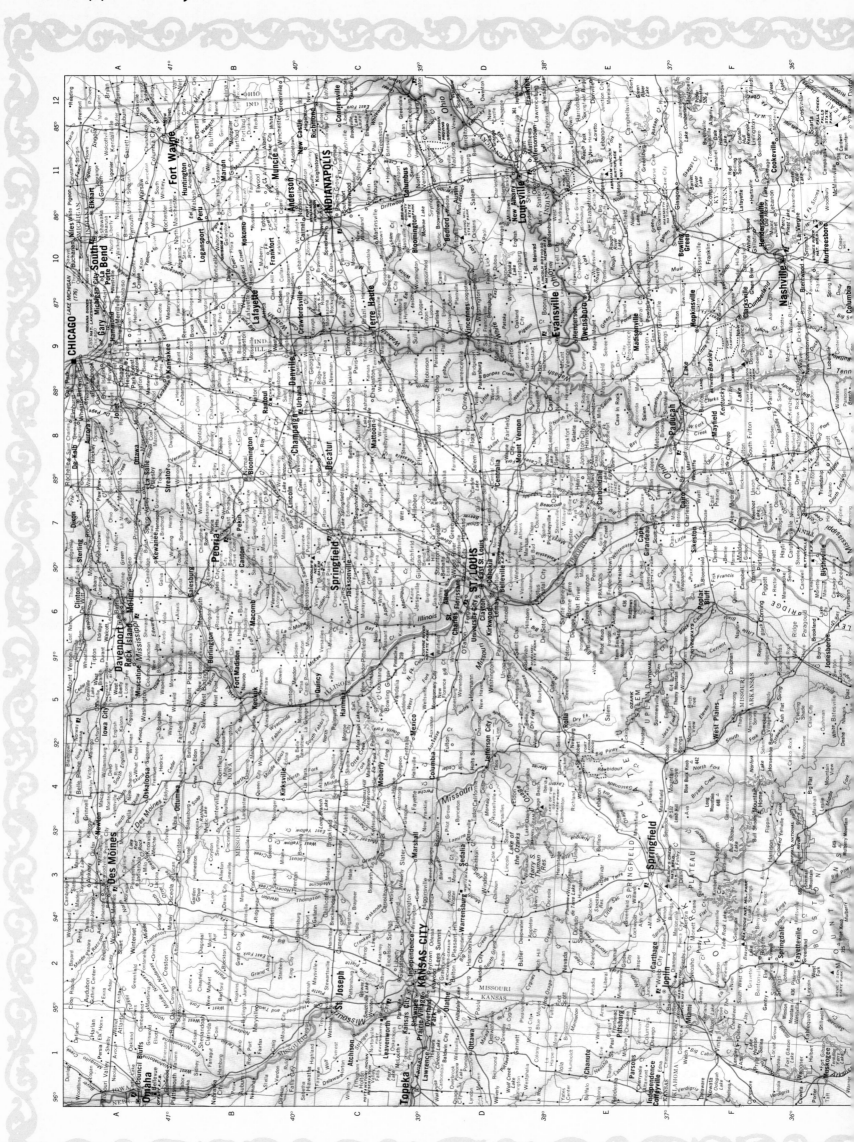

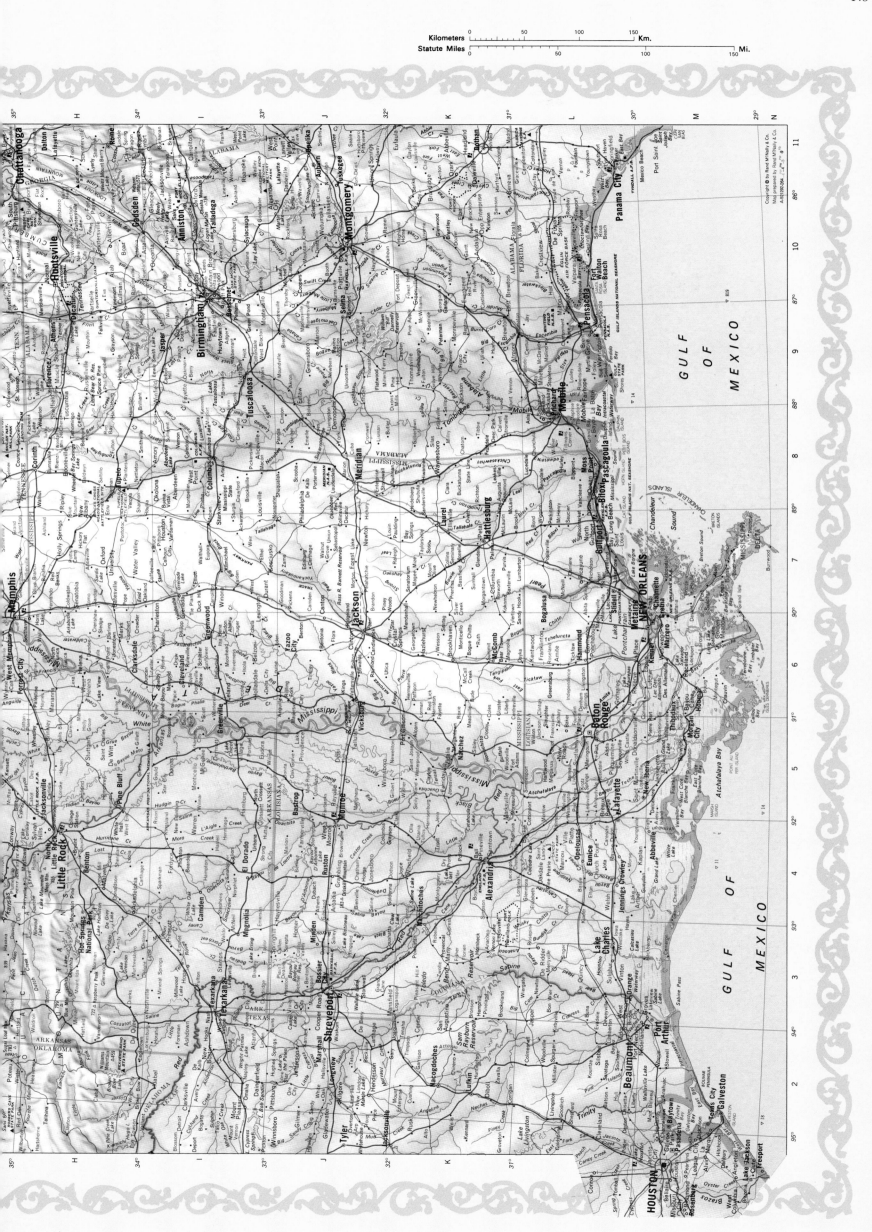

Great Lakes Region

Northern Great Plains

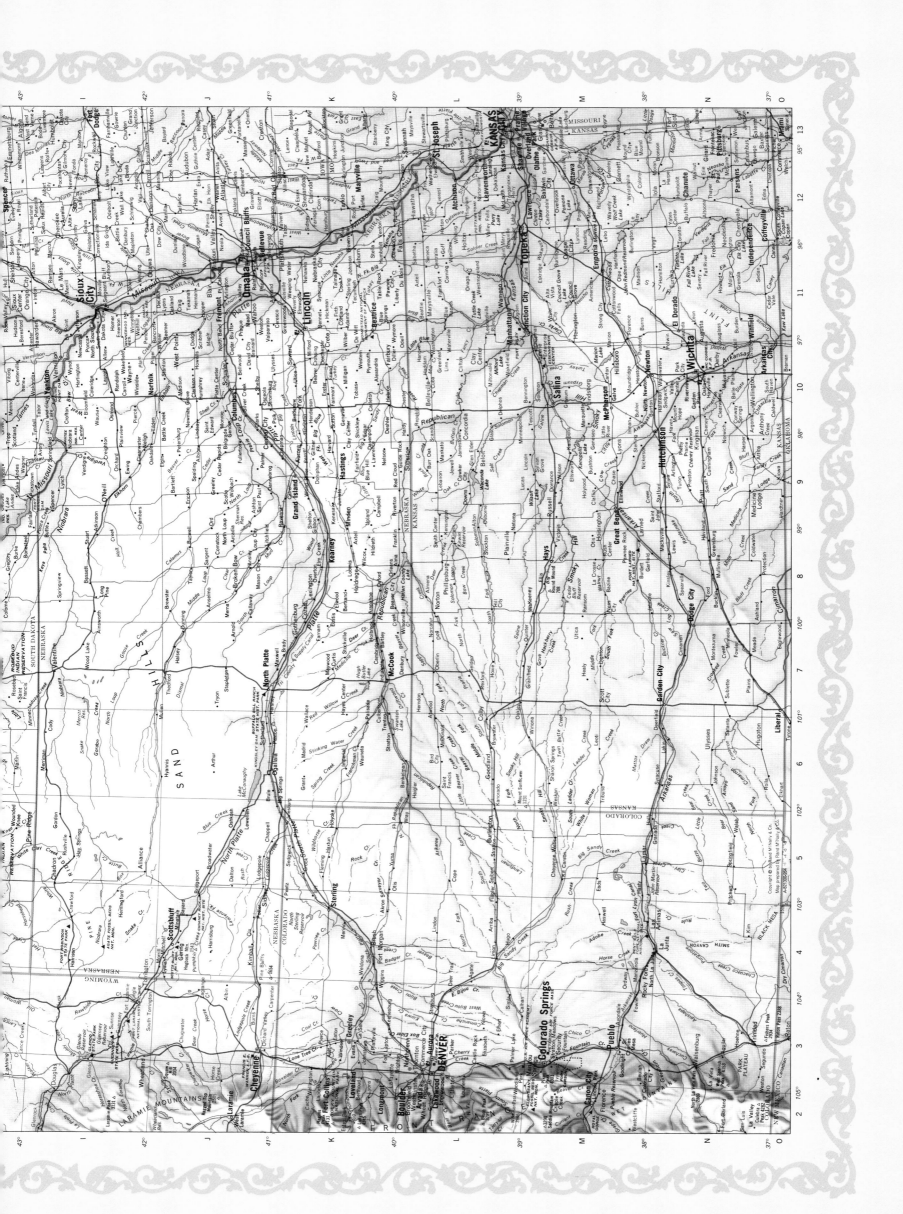

Southern Great Plains

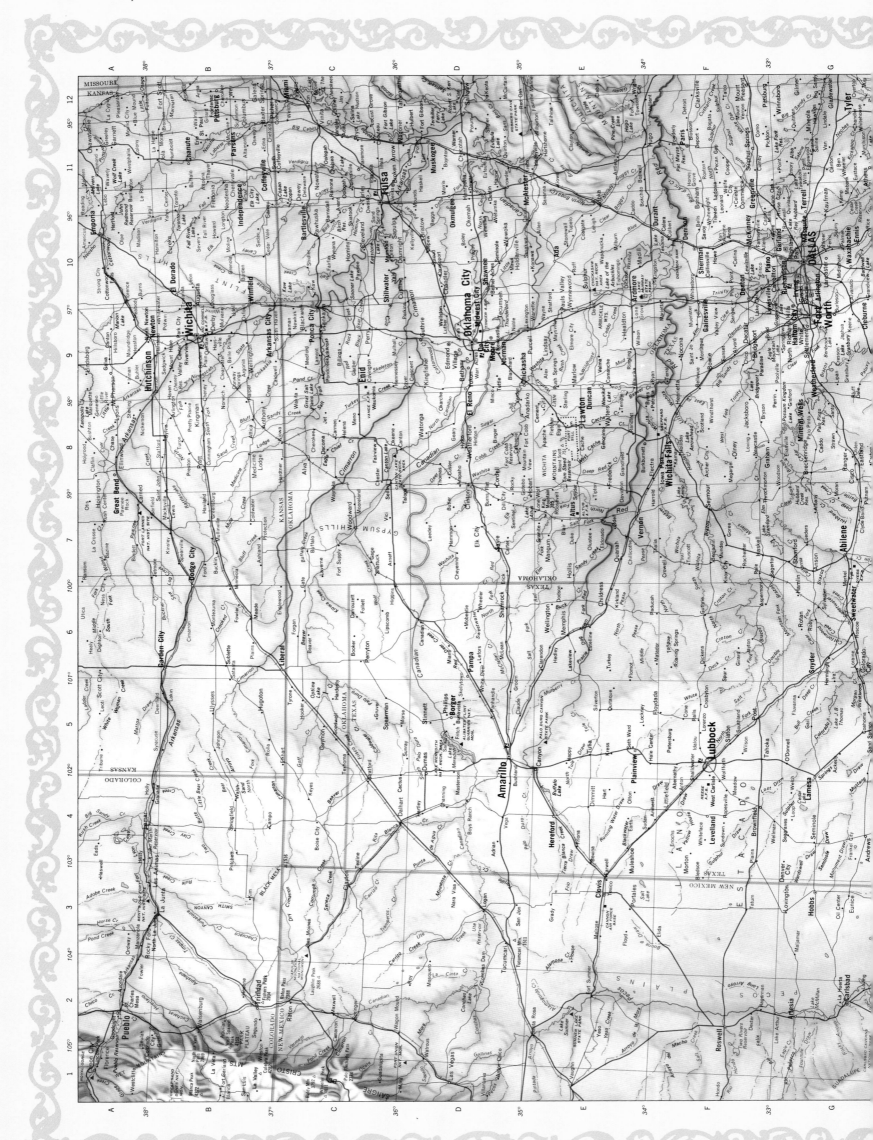

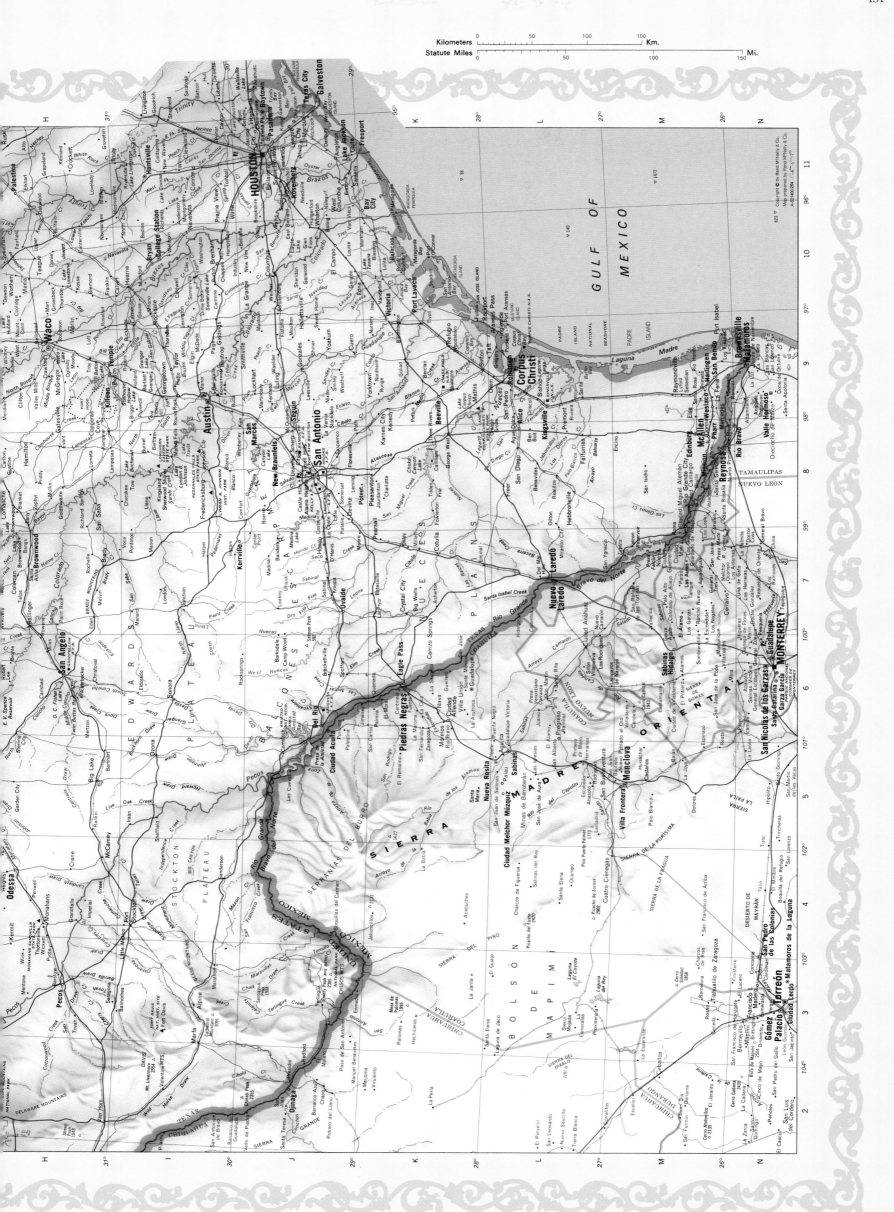

Southwestern United States

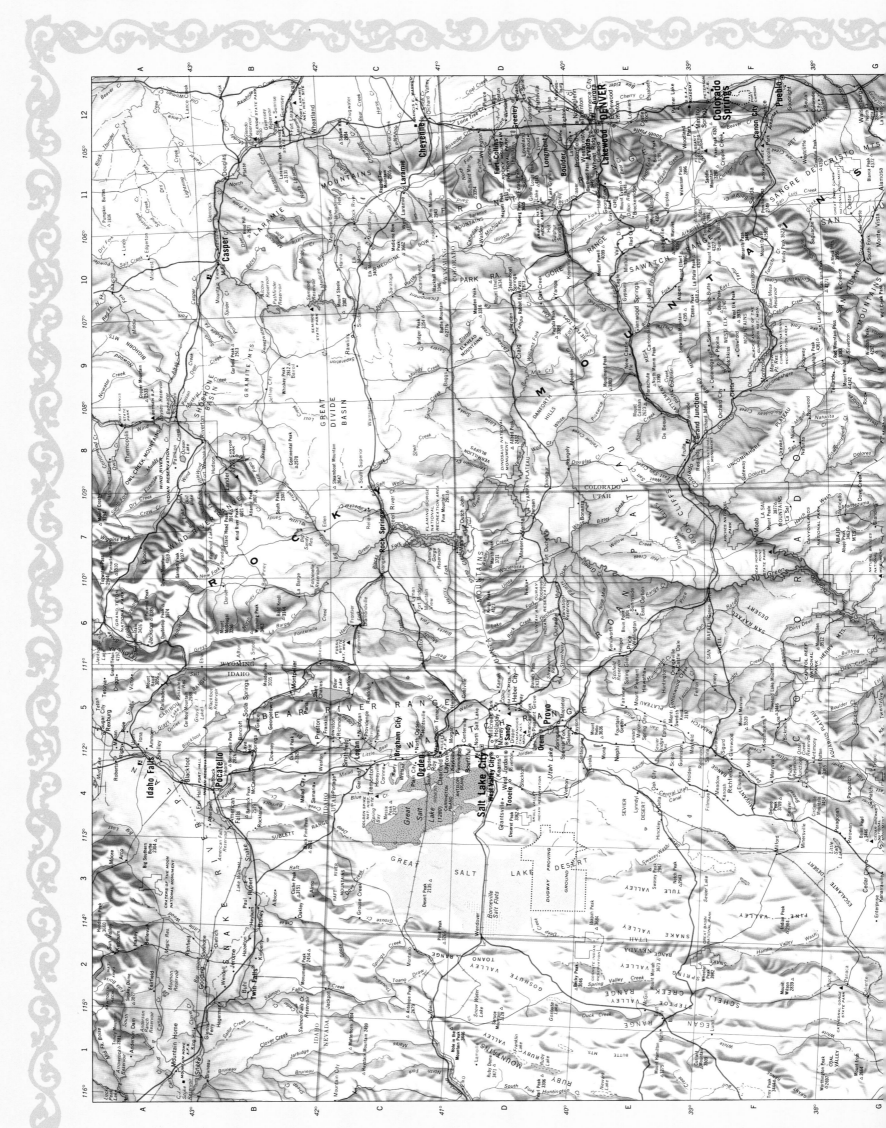

Northwestern United States

California and Nevada

Kilometers
Statute Miles

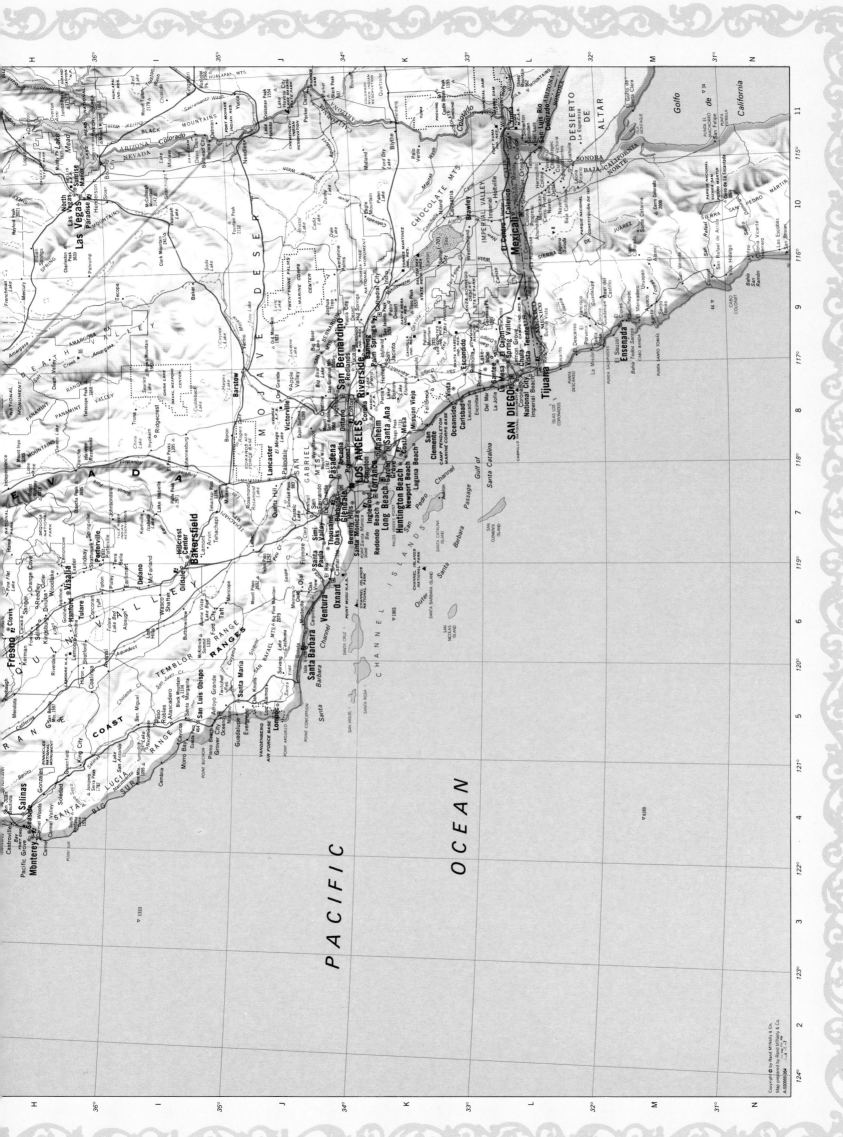

Alaska

Hawaii

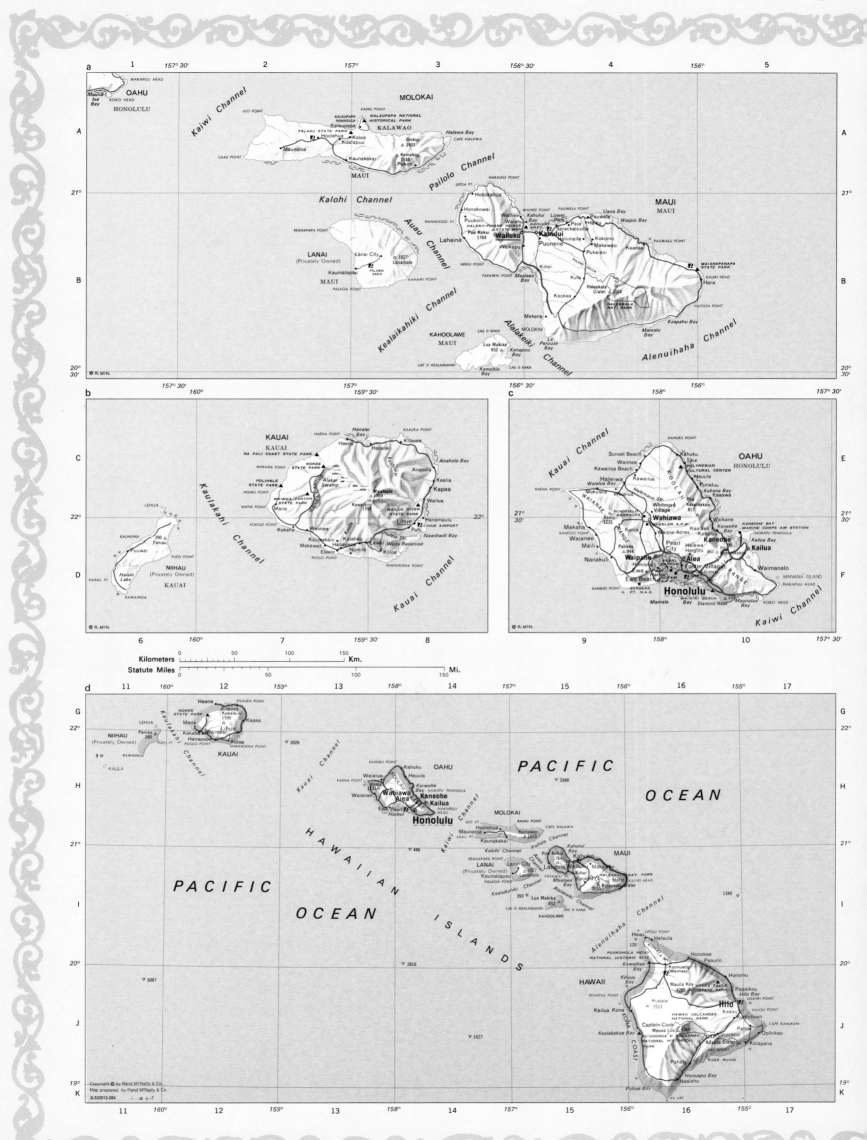

Kilometers 0 10 20 30 40 50 Km.
Statute Miles 0 10 20 30 40 50 Mi.

Kilometers 0 50 100 150 Km.
Statute Miles 0 50 100 150 Mi.

PART SEVEN

Indexes

Map Index

In a single alphabetical list, this index includes names of more than 15,000 features that appear on the reference maps. These features include populated places and physical features–such as lakes, rivers, and mountain ranges. Each name is followed by a map-reference key and a page reference.

Alphabetization and Abbreviation
The names of cities and towns appear in regular type. The names of all other features appear in *italics.* The names of physical features may be inverted, since they are always alphabetized under the proper, not the generic, part of the name. For example, Lake Erie is listed as *Erie, Lake.* Otherwise every entry, whether consisting of one word or more, is alphabetized as a single continuous entity. "Lake City", for example, appears after "Lafayette" and before "Lakehurst."

In the case of identical names, towns are listed first, followed by states, then physical features. Entries that are completely identical are sequenced alphabetically by state name. Each name is followed by a state abbreviation. Exceptions are features that cross state or international boundaries, which are, therefore, not wholly contained within one state. The state abbreviations are those used by the United States Postal Service (see list below). Other abbreviations have been adopted by Rand McNally.

On the map, abbreviations may be used in a name, but the full name will appear in the index: for example *Mt. St. Helens* on the map is *Saint Helens, Mount,* in the index.

Map-Reference Keys and Page References
The map-reference keys and page references are found in the last two columns of each entry.

Each map-reference key consists of a letter and a number. The letters appear along the side of each map and the numbers appear across the top and bottom. Inset maps are keyed separately.

Map-reference keys for point features, such as towns, cities and mountain peaks, indicate the positions of the symbols. For extensive features, such as countries or mountain ranges, positions are given for the approximate center of the feature. Those for linear features, such as canals and rivers, are given for the position of the name.

The page number generally refers to the map that shows the feature at the best scale. Countries, mountain ranges and other extensive features are usually indexed to maps that both show the features completely and also show them in their relationship to broad areas. Page references to two-page maps always refer to the left-hand page. If a page contains several maps or insets, a small letter after the page number identifies the specific map or inset.

List of Abbreviations

AK	Alaska
AL	Alabama
AR	Arkansas
AZ	Arizona
CA	California
CO	Colorado
CT	Connecticut
DC	District of Columbia
DE	Delaware
FL	Florida
GA	Georgia
HI	Hawaii
IA	Iowa
ID	Idaho
IL	Illinois
IN	Indiana
KS	Kansas
KY	Kentucky
LA	Louisiana
MA	Massachusetts
MD	Maryland
ME	Maine
MI	Michigan
MN	Minnesota
MO	Missouri
MS	Mississippi
MT	Montana
NA	North America
NC	North Carolina
ND	North Dakota
NE	Nebraska
NH	New Hampshire
NJ	New Jersey
NM	New Mexico
NV	Nevada
NY	New York
OH	Ohio
OK	Oklahoma
OR	Oregon
PA	Pennsylvania
r.	*river*
RI	Rhode Island
SC	South Carolina
SD	South Dakota
TN	Tennessee
TX	Texas
US	United States
UT	Utah
VA	Virginia
VT	Vermont
WA	Washington
WI	Wisconsin
WV	West Virginia
WY	Wyoming

Name	Map Ref.	Page
A		
Abajo Peak, UT	G7	152
Abbeville, GA	H3	142
Abbeville, LA	M4	144
Abbeville, MS	H7	144
Abbeville, SC	E4	142
Abbotsford, WI	F5	146
Aberdeen, ID	H13	154
Aberdeen, MD	H10	140
Aberdeen, MS	I8	144
Aberdeen, NC	D7	142
Aberdeen, SD	F9	148
Aberdeen, WA	D2	154
Abernathy, TX	F5	150
Abilene, KS	M10	148
Abilene, TX	G7	150
Abingdon, IL	J5	146
Abingdon, VA	C5	142
Abiquiu, NM	H10	152
Abita Springs, LA	L6	144
Absaroka Range, US	F15	154
Absarokee, MT	E16	154
Absecon, NJ	H12	140
Acadia National Park, ME	C18	140
Accomac, VA	B11	142
Accoville, WV	B5	142
Ackerly, TX	G5	150
Ackerman, MS	I7	144
Ackley, IA	H2	146
Acworth, GA	E2	142
Ada, MN	D11	148
Ada, OH	G3	140
Ada, OK	E10	150
Adair, IA	J13	148
Adair, OK	F1	144
Adairsville, GA	E2	142
Adairville, KY	F10	144
Adak, AK	K6	158
Adak Island, AK	K6	158
Adams, MA	E13	140
Adams, MN	G3	146
Adams, NE	K11	148
Adams, NY	D10	140
Adams, ND	C9	148
Adams, TN	F9	144
Adams, WI	G6	146
Adams, Mount, WA	D4	154
Adamsville, TN	G8	144
Addis, LA	L5	144
Addison, MI	I11	146
Adel, GA	H3	142
Adel, IA	I1	146
Adin, CA	C5	156
Adirondack Mountains, NY	D12	140
Admiralty Island, AK	H27	158
Adrian, GA	G4	142
Adrian, MI	I11	146
Adrian, MN	H12	148
Adrian, MO	D2	144
Adrian, OR	G8	154
Adrian, TX	D4	150
Adrian, WV	I6	140
Advance, MO	E7	144
Affton, MO	D6	144
Afognak Island, AK	G18	158
Afton, IA	A2	144
Afton, NY	E11	140
Afton, OK	F2	144
Afton, WY	B6	152
Agate, CO	L4	148
Agate Beach, OR	F1	154
Agency, IA	J3	146
Agua Dulce, TX	L9	150
Agua Fria, r., AZ	K4	152
Aguila, AZ	K3	152
Aguilar, CO	N3	148
Ahklun Mountains, AK	G14	158
Ahoskie, NC	C10	142
Aiea, HI	F10	160c
Aiken, SC	F5	142
Ainsworth, NE	I8	148
Aitkin, MN	D2	146
Ajo, AZ	L4	152
Akaka Falls State Park, HI	J16	160d
Akeley, MN	C1	146
Akiachak, AK	F14	158
Akron, CO	K4	148
Akron, IN	A10	144
Akron, IA	I11	148
Akron, NY	D8	140
Akron, OH	F5	140
Akron, PA	G10	140
Alabama, state, US	E9	136
Alabama, r., AL	K9	144
Alabaster, AL	I10	144
Alachua, FL	J4	142
Alakai Swamp, HI	C7	160b
Alalakeiki Channel, HI	B3	160a
Alameda, CA	G3	156
Alameda, NM	I10	152
Alamo, GA	G4	142
Alamo, NV	G10	156
Alamo, TN	G7	144
Alamo, r., CA	K10	156
Alamogordo, NM	L11	152
Alamo Heights, TX	J8	150
Alamo Lake, AZ	J3	152
Alamosa, CO	G11	152
Alamosa, r., CO	G10	152
Alamosa East, CO	G11	152
Alanson, MI	E11	146
Alapaha, GA	H3	142
Alapaha, r., US	I3	142
Alaska, state, US	D18	158
Alaska, Gulf of, AK	G22	158
Alaska Peninsula, AK	H15	158
Alaska Range, AK	E19	158
Alava, Cape, WA	B1	154
Alba, MI	F11	146
Alba, TX	G11	150
Albany, GA	H2	142
Albany, IL	I5	146
Albany, IN	B11	144
Albany, KY	F11	144
Albany, MN	E1	146
Albany, MO	B2	144
Albany, NY	E13	140
Albany, OH	H4	140
Albany, OR	F2	154
Albany, TX	G7	150
Albany, WI	H6	146
Albemarle, NC	D6	142
Albemarle Sound, NC	C10	142
Alberene, VA	B8	142
Alberta, AL	J9	144
Albert City, IA	I13	148
Albert Lea, MN	G2	146
Alberton, MT	C11	154
Albertville, AL	H10	144
Albia, IA	I3	146
Albin, WY	J3	148
Albion, CA	E2	156
Albion, ID	H12	154
Albion, IL	D8	144
Albion, IN	A11	144
Albion, IA	H3	146
Albion, MI	H11	146
Albion, NE	J9	148
Albion, NY	D8	140
Albion, PA	F6	140
Albion, WA	D8	154
Albuquerque, NM	I10	152
Alburg, VT	C13	140
Alcalde, NM	H10	152
Alcester, SD	H11	148
Alcoa, TN	D3	142
Alcolu, SC	F6	142
Alcorn, MS	K5	144
Alcovy, r., GA	F3	142
Alden, IA	H2	146
Alden, MN	G2	146
Alderson, WV	B6	142
Aledo, IL	I5	146
Alegres Mountain, NM	J8	152
Aleknagik, AK	G15	158
Alenuihaha Channel, HI	I15	160d
Aleutian Islands, AK	J6	158
Aleutian Range, AK	G17	158
Alex, OK	E9	150
Alexander, ND	D4	148
Alexander Archipelago, AK	H27	158
Alexander City, AL	J11	144
Alexandria, IN	B11	144
Alexandria, KY	I2	140
Alexandria, LA	K4	144
Alexandria, MN	F12	148
Alexandria, MO	B5	144
Alexandria, NE	K10	148
Alexandria, SD	H10	148
Alexandria, TN	F10	144
Alexandria, VA	I9	140
Alexandria Bay, NY	C11	140
Alexis, IL	I5	146
Alfred, ME	D16	140
Alfred, NY	E9	140
Alger, OH	G3	140
Algodones, NM	I10	152
Algoma, WI	F8	146
Algona, IA	G1	146
Algona, WA	C3	154
Algonac, MI	H13	146
Algonquin, IL	H7	146
Algood, TN	F11	144
Alice, TX	L8	150
Aliceville, AL	I8	144
Aliquippa, PA	G6	140
Allagash, r., ME	F4	138
Allardt, TN	F12	144
Allegan, MI	H10	146
Allegany, NY	E8	140
Allegheny, r., US	G7	140
Allegheny Mountains, US	I6	140
Allegheny Plateau, US	G8	140
Allegheny Reservoir, US	F8	140
Allemands, Lac Des, LA	M6	144
Allen, NE	I11	148
Allen, OK	E10	150
Allen, SD	H6	148
Allen, TX	F10	150
Allen, Mount, AK	E23	158
Allendale, IL	D9	144
Allendale, SC	F5	142
Allentown, PA	G11	140
Allerton, IA	J2	146
Alliance, NE	I5	148
Alliance, OH	G5	140
Alligator, r., NC	D10	142
Allison, IA	H3	146
Allouez, WI	F7	146
Allyn, WA	C3	154
Alma, AR	G2	144
Alma, GA	H4	142
Alma, KS	L11	148
Alma, MI	G11	146
Alma, NE	K8	148
Alma, WI	F4	146
Alma Center, WI	F5	146
Almena, KS	L8	148
Almira, WA	C7	154
Almo, ID	H12	154
Almond, WI	F6	146
Almont, MI	H12	146
Alpaugh, CA	I6	156
Alpena, AR	F3	144
Alpena, MI	E12	146
Alpena, SD	G9	148
Alpha, IL	I5	146
Alpha, MI	D7	146
Alpharetta, GA	E2	142
Alpine, AZ	K7	152
Alpine, CA	L9	156
Alpine, TX	I3	150
Alsea, OR	F2	154
Alsea, r., OR	F2	154
Alsen, ND	C9	148
Alta, IA	I12	148
Altamaha, r., GA	H5	142
Altamont, IL	C8	144
Altamont, KS	N12	148

Basi-Boga

Camd-Chic

Cour-Dove

Ettr-Fult

Name	Map Ref.	Page
Fulton, KY	**F8**	144
Fulton, MS	**H8**	144
Fulton, MO	**D5**	144
Fulton, NY	**D10**	140
Fulton, TX	**K9**	150
Fultondale, AL	**I10**	144
Fuquay-Varina, NC	**D8**	142
G		
Gabbs, NV	**F8**	156
Gackle, ND	**E8**	148
Gadsden, AL	**H10**	144
Gadsden, AZ	**L2**	152
Gaffney, SC	**D5**	142
Gage, OK	**C7**	150
Gail, TX	**G5**	150
Gainesboro, TN	**F11**	144
Gainesville, FL	**J4**	142
Gainesville, GA	**E3**	142
Gainesville, MO	**F4**	144
Gainesville, TX	**F9**	150
Gaithersburg, MD	**H9**	140
Galatia, IL	**E8**	144
Galax, VA	**C6**	142
Galena, AK	**D16**	158
Galena, IL	**H5**	146
Galena, KS	**N13**	148
Galena, MO	**F3**	144
Galena Park, TX	**J11**	150
Galesburg, IL	**J5**	146
Galesburg, MI	**H10**	146
Galesville, WI	**F4**	146
Galeton, PA	**F9**	140
Galion, OH	**G4**	140
Galiuro Mountains, AZ	**L6**	152
Gallatin, MO	**C3**	144
Gallatin, TN	**F10**	144
Gallatin, r., US	**E14**	154
Galliano, LA	**M6**	144
Gallinas, r., NM	**D2**	150
Gallinas Peak, NM	**J11**	152
Gallipolis, OH	**I4**	140
Gallup, NM	**I8**	152
Galt, CA	**F4**	156
Galva, IL	**I5**	146
Galva, IA	**I12**	148
Galva, KS	**M10**	148
Galveston, IN	**B10**	144
Galveston, TX	**J12**	150
Galveston Bay, TX	**J12**	150
Galveston Island, TX	**J12**	150
Gamaliel, KY	**F11**	144
Gambell, AK	**E9**	158
Gambier, OH	**G4**	140
Ganado, AZ	**I7**	152
Ganado, TX	**J10**	150
Gannett Peak, WY	**G16**	154
Gannvalley, SD	**G9**	148
Gantt, AL	**K10**	144
Garber, OK	**C9**	150
Garberville, CA	**D2**	156
Garden City, GA	**G5**	142
Garden City, KS	**N7**	148
Garden City, MO	**D2**	144
Garden City, TX	**H5**	150
Gardendale, AL	**I10**	144
Garden Grove, CA	**K8**	156
Garden Grove, IA	**J2**	146
Garden Lakes, GA	**E1**	142
Garden Peninsula, MI	**E9**	146
Garden Plain, KS	**N10**	148
Gardiner, ME	**C17**	140
Gardiner, MT	**E15**	154
Gardiner, OR	**G1**	154
Gardiners Bay, NY	**F14**	140
Gardner, KS	**M13**	148
Gardner, MA	**E15**	140
Gardnerville, NV	**F6**	156
Garfield, KS	**M8**	148
Garfield, NM	**L9**	152
Garfield, WA	**C8**	154
Garfield Mountain, MT	**F13**	154
Garibaldi, OR	**E2**	154
Garland, AL	**K10**	144
Garland, TX	**G10**	150
Garland, UT	**C4**	152
Garnavillo, IA	**H4**	146
Garner, IA	**G2**	146
Garner, NC	**D8**	142
Garnett, KS	**M12**	148
Garretson, SD	**H11**	148
Garrett, IN	**A11**	144
Garrett, KY	**B4**	142
Garrison, MT	**D13**	154
Garrison, ND	**D6**	148
Garrison, TX	**K2**	144
Garwin, IA	**H3**	146
Garwood, TX	**J10**	150
Gary, IN	**A9**	144
Gary, SD	**G11**	148
Gary, TX	**J2**	144
Gary, WV	**B5**	142
Gas City, IN	**B11**	144
Gasconade, r., MO	**D5**	144
Gassaway, WV	**I6**	140
Gaston, NC	**C9**	142
Gaston, Lake, US	**C8**	142
Gastonia, NC	**D5**	142
Gate, OK	**C6**	150
Gate City, VA	**C4**	142
Gatesville, NC	**C10**	142
Gatesville, TX	**H9**	150
Gateway, CO	**F8**	152
Gatlinburg, TN	**D3**	142
Gauley, r., WV	**I5**	140
Gauley Bridge, WV	**I5**	140
Gause, TX	**I10**	150
Gaylord, MI	**E11**	146
Gaylord, MN	**F1**	146
Gays Mills, WI	**G5**	146
Gearhart Mountain, OR	**H5**	154
Geary, OK	**D8**	150
Geddes, SD	**H9**	148
Geiger, AL	**J8**	144
Geistown, PA	**G8**	140
Genesee, ID	**D9**	154
Genesee, r., US	**H18**	146
Geneseo, IL	**I5**	146
Geneseo, KS	**M9**	148
Geneseo, NY	**E9**	140
Geneva, AL	**K11**	144
Geneva, IL	**I7**	146
Geneva, IN	**B12**	144
Geneva, NE	**K10**	148
Geneva, NY	**E9**	140
Geneva, OH	**F6**	140
Genoa, IL	**H7**	146
Genoa, NE	**J10**	148
Genoa, OH	**F3**	140
Genoa, WI	**G4**	146
Gentry, AR	**F2**	144
George, IA	**H11**	148
George, Lake, FL	**J5**	142
George, Lake, NY	**D13**	140
Georgetown, CO	**E11**	152
Georgetown, DE	**I11**	140
Georgetown, FL	**J5**	142
Georgetown, GA	**H1**	142
Georgetown, ID	**H14**	154
Georgetown, IL	**C9**	144
Georgetown, KY	**I2**	140
Georgetown, MS	**K6**	144
Georgetown, OH	**I3**	140
Georgetown, SC	**F7**	142
Georgetown, TX	**I9**	150
George West, TX	**K8**	150
Georgia, state, US	**E10**	136
Georgiana, AL	**K10**	144
Gerald, MO	**D5**	144
Geraldine, MT	**C15**	154
Gerber, CA	**D3**	156
Gerdine, Mount, AK	**F18**	158
Gering, NE	**J4**	148
Germantown, IL	**D7**	144
Germantown, TN	**G7**	144
Germantown, WI	**G7**	146
Germfask, MI	**D10**	146
Geronimo, OK	**E8**	150
Gettysburg, PA	**H9**	140
Gettysburg, SD	**F8**	148
Geyser, MT	**C15**	154
Geyserville, CA	**F3**	156
Gibbon, MN	**F1**	146
Gibbon, NE	**K9**	148
Gibbonsville, ID	**E12**	154
Gibsland, LA	**J3**	144
Gibson, GA	**F4**	142
Gibson City, IL	**J7**	146
Giddings, TX	**I10**	150
Gideon, MO	**F7**	144
Gifford, FL	**L6**	142
Gila, r., US	**L2**	152
Gila Bend, AZ	**L4**	152
Gila Bend Mountains, AZ	**K3**	152
Gila Mountains, AZ	**K7**	152
Gilbert, LA	**J5**	144
Gilbert, MN	**C3**	146
Gilbertown, AL	**K8**	144
Gildford, MT	**B15**	154
Gillespie, IL	**C7**	144
Gillett, AR	**H5**	144
Gillett, WI	**F7**	146
Gillette, WY	**G2**	148
Gills Rock, WI	**E8**	146
Gilman, IL	**J8**	146
Gilman, IA	**I3**	146
Gilman, WI	**E5**	146
Gilmer, TX	**G12**	150
Gilmore City, IA	**I13**	148
Gilroy, CA	**G4**	156
Giltner, NE	**K9**	148
Girard, IL	**C7**	144
Girard, KS	**N13**	148
Girard, OH	**F6**	140
Girard, PA	**E6**	140
Girard, TX	**F6**	150
Glacier Bay, AK	**G26**	158
Glacier National Park, MT	**B12**	154
Glacier Peak, WA	**B4**	154
Gladbrook, IA	**H3**	146
Glade Spring, VA	**C5**	142
Gladewater, TX	**G12**	150
Gladstone, MI	**E8**	146
Gladstone, MO	**C2**	144
Gladwin, MI	**G11**	146
Glasco, KS	**L10**	148
Glasgow, KY	**F11**	144
Glasgow, MO	**C4**	144
Glasgow, MT	**B19**	154
Glasgow, VA	**B7**	142
Glassboro, NJ	**H11**	140
Gleason, TN	**F8**	144
Glen Alpine, NC	**D5**	142
Glenburn, ND	**C6**	148
Glen Burnie, MD	**H10**	140
Glen Canyon, US	**G5**	152
Glencoe, AL	**I11**	144
Glencoe, MN	**F1**	146
Glen Cove, NY	**G13**	140
Glendale, AZ	**K4**	152
Glendale, CA	**J7**	156
Glendale, MS	**K7**	144
Glendale, OR	**H2**	154
Glendale, UT	**G4**	152
Glendale, WI	**G8**	146
Glendive, MT	**D3**	148
Glendo, WY	**B11**	152
Gleneden Beach, OR	**F1**	154
Glen Elder, KS	**L9**	148
Glen Flora, TX	**J10**	150
Glen Lyon, PA	**F10**	140
Glenmora, LA	**L4**	144
Glennallen, AK	**E22**	158
Glenns Ferry, ID	**H10**	154
Glennville, GA	**H5**	142
Glenoma, WA	**D3**	154
Glen Rock, PA	**H10**	140
Glenrock, WY	**B11**	152
Glen Rose, TX	**G9**	150
Glens Falls, NY	**D13**	140
Glen Ullin, ND	**E6**	148
Glenville, MN	**G2**	146
Glenville, WV	**I6**	140
Glen White, WV	**B5**	142
Glenwood, AL	**K10**	144
Glenwood, AR	**H3**	144
Glenwood, GA	**G4**	142
Glenwood, IA	**J12**	148
Glenwood, MN	**F12**	148
Glenwood, NM	**K8**	152
Glenwood, UT	**F5**	152
Glenwood, VA	**C7**	142
Glenwood City, WI	**E3**	146
Glenwood Springs, CO	**E9**	152
Glidden, IA	**I13**	148
Glidden, WI	**D5**	146
Glide, OR	**G2**	154
Globe, AZ	**K6**	152
Glorieta, NM	**I11**	152
Gloster, MS	**K5**	144
Gloucester, MA	**E16**	140
Gloucester, VA	**B10**	142
Glouster, OH	**H4**	140
Glover, r., OK	**E12**	150
Gloversville, NY	**D12**	140
Glyndon, MN	**E11**	148
Goat Mountain, MT	**C12**	154
Gobles, MI	**H10**	146
Godfrey, IL	**D6**	144
Goff, KS	**L12**	148
Goffstown, NH	**D15**	140
Gogebic, Lake, MI	**D6**	146
Golconda, IL	**E8**	144
Golconda, NV	**D8**	156
Gold Beach, OR	**H1**	154
Golden, CO	**E11**	152
Golden, IL	**B5**	144
Golden City, MO	**E2**	144
Goldendale, WA	**E5**	154
Golden Meadow, LA	**M6**	144
Goldfield, IA	**H2**	146
Goldfield, NV	**G8**	156
Goldonna, LA	**J4**	144
Goldsboro, NC	**D9**	142
Goldsmith, TX	**H4**	150
Goldston, NC	**D7**	142
Goldthwaite, TX	**H8**	150
Goleta, CA	**J6**	156
Goliad, TX	**K9**	150
Golovin, AK	**D13**	158
Golva, ND	**E4**	148
Gonzales, CA	**H4**	156
Gonzales, LA	**L6**	144
Gonzales, TX	**J9**	150
Goochland, VA	**B9**	142
Goodhue, MN	**F3**	146
Gooding, ID	**H11**	154
Goodland, FL	**N5**	142
Goodland, IN	**B9**	144
Goodland, KS	**L6**	148
Goodman, MS	**J7**	144
Goodman, WI	**E7**	146
Goodnews Bay, AK	**G14**	158
Goodnight, CO	**F12**	152
Goodrich, ND	**D7**	148
Goodrich, TX	**I12**	150
Good Thunder, MN	**F1**	146
Goodview, MN	**F4**	146
Goodwater, AL	**I10**	144
Goodwell, OK	**C5**	150
Goodyear, AZ	**K4**	152
Goose, r., ND	**D10**	148
Goose Creek, SC	**G6**	142
Goose Lake, US	**C5**	156
Gordo, AL	**I9**	144
Gordon, GA	**G3**	142
Gordon, NE	**I5**	148
Gordon, WI	**D4**	146
Gordonsville, VA	**I8**	140
Goree, TX	**F7**	150
Goreville, IL	**E8**	144
Gorham, ME	**D16**	140
Gorham, NH	**C15**	140
Gorman, TX	**G8**	150
Goshen, CA	**H6**	156
Goshen, IN	**A11**	144
Goshen, NY	**F12**	140
Gosport, IN	**C10**	144
Gotebo, OK	**D8**	150
Gothenburg, NE	**K7**	148
Gould, AR	**I5**	144
Gould City, MI	**D10**	146
Goulds, FL	**N6**	142
Gouverneur, NY	**C11**	140
Gove, KS	**M7**	148
Gowanda, NY	**E8**	140
Gower, MO	**C2**	144
Gowrie, IA	**I13**	148
Grace, ID	**H14**	154
Graceville, FL	**I1**	142
Graceville, MN	**F11**	148
Grady, AR	**H5**	144
Grady, NM	**E3**	150
Graettinger, IA	**H13**	148
Graford, TX	**G8**	150
Grafton, IL	**D6**	144
Grafton, ND	**C10**	148
Grafton, WV	**H6**	140
Grafton, WI	**G8**	146
Graham, NC	**C7**	142
Graham, TX	**F8**	150
Graham, Mount, AZ	**L7**	152
Grainfield, KS	**L7**	148
Grambling, LA	**J4**	144
Granada, CO	**M5**	148
Granada, MN	**G1**	146
Granbury, TX	**G9**	150
Granby, CO	**D11**	152
Granby, MO	**F2**	144
Granby, Lake, CO	**D11**	152
Grand, r., US	**C3**	144
Grand, r., MI	**G9**	146
Grand, r., OH	**F5**	140
Grand, r., SD	**F7**	148
Grand, r., WI	**G7**	146
Grand Bay, AL	**L8**	144
Grand Blanc, MI	**H12**	146
Grand Cane, LA	**J3**	144
Grand Canyon, AZ	**H4**	152
Grand Canyon, AZ	**H4**	152
Grand Canyon National Park, AZ	**H4**	152
Grand Chenier, LA	**M4**	144
Grand Coulee, WA	**C6**	154
Grand Coulee, WA	**C6**	154
Grand Coulee Dam, WA	**C7**	154
Grande, Rio (Bravo del Norte), r., NA	**F7**	136
Grande Ronde, r., US	**E8**	154
Grandfalls, TX	**H4**	150
Grandfield, OK	**E8**	150
Grand Forks, ND	**D10**	148
Grand Haven, MI	**G9**	146
Grand Island, NE	**K9**	148
Grand Island, MI	**D9**	146
Grand Isle, LA	**M7**	144
Grand Junction, CO	**E8**	152
Grand Junction, IA	**I13**	148
Grand Junction, TN	**G7**	144
Grand Lake, CO	**D11**	152
Grand Lake, NA	**G6**	138
Grand Lake, LA	**M5**	144
Grand Lake, LA	**M4**	144
Grand Lake, OH	**G2**	140
Grand Ledge, MI	**H11**	146
Grand Marais, MI	**D10**	146
Grand Marais, MN	**C5**	146
Grand Meadow, MN	**G3**	146
Grand Mesa, CO	**E8**	152
Grand Portage, MN	**C6**	146
Grand Prairie, TX	**G10**	150
Grand Rapids, MI	**H10**	146
Grand Rapids, MN	**C2**	146
Grand Saline, TX	**G11**	150
Grand Teton, WY	**A6**	152
Grand Teton National Park, WY	**G15**	154
Grand Tower, IL	**E7**	144
Grand Traverse Bay, MI	**E10**	146
Grandview, MO	**D2**	144
Grandview, TX	**G9**	150
Grandview, WA	**D6**	154
Grand View, WI	**D4**	146
Granger, TX	**I9**	150
Granger, WA	**D5**	154
Granger, WY	**C7**	152
Grangeville, ID	**E9**	154
Granite, OK	**E7**	150
Granite City, IL	**D6**	144
Granite Falls, MN	**G12**	148
Granite Falls, NC	**D5**	142
Granite Falls, WA	**B4**	154
Granite Peak, MT	**E16**	154
Graniteville, SC	**F5**	142
Graniteville, VT	**C14**	140
Grant, FL	**L6**	142
Grant, MI	**G10**	146
Grant, NE	**K6**	148
Grant, r., WI	**H5**	146
Grant, Mount, NV	**F7**	156
Grant City, MO	**B2**	144
Grant Park, IL	**I8**	146
Grants, NM	**I9**	152
Grantsburg, WI	**E3**	146
Grants Pass, OR	**H2**	154
Grantsville, UT	**D4**	152
Grantsville, WV	**I5**	140
Grantville, GA	**F2**	142
Granville, IL	**I6**	146
Granville, NY	**D13**	140
Granville, ND	**C7**	148
Granville, OH	**G4**	140
Granville, WV	**H7**	140
Grapeland, TX	**H11**	150
Grapevine Lake, TX	**G9**	150
Grasonville, MD	**I10**	140
Grass, r., NY	**C11**	140
Grass Creek, WY	**G17**	154
Grassflat, PA	**F8**	140
Grass Lake, MI	**H11**	146
Grass Range, MT	**C17**	154
Grass Valley, CA	**E4**	156
Grave Peak, ID	**D11**	154
Gravette, AR	**F2**	144
Gray, GA	**F3**	142
Gray, KY	**C2**	142
Grayback Mountain, OR	**H2**	154
Grayling, AK	**E14**	158
Grayling, MI	**F11**	146
Grays Harbor, WA	**D1**	154
Grayson, AL	**H9**	144
Grayson, KY	**I4**	140
Grayson, LA	**J4**	144
Grays Peak, CO	**E11**	152
Graysville, TN	**G11**	144
Grayville, IL	**E8**	144
Great Barrington, MA	**E13**	140
Great Basin, US	**C3**	136
Great Bend, KS	**M9**	148
Great Dismal Swamp, US	**C10**	142
Great Divide Basin, WY	**H17**	154
Great Falls, MT	**C14**	154
Great Falls, SC	**E6**	142
Great Miami, r., US	**H2**	140
Great Pee Dee, r., SC	**F7**	142
Great Sacandaga Lake, NY	**D12**	140
Great Salt Lake, UT	**C4**	152
Great Salt Lake Desert, UT	**D3**	152
Great Smoky Mountains, US	**D3**	142
Great Smoky Mountains National Park, US	**D3**	142
Greece, NY	**D9**	140
Greeley, CO	**D12**	152
Greeley, KS	**M12**	148
Greeley, NE	**J9**	148
Greeleyville, SC	**F7**	142
Green, r., US	**F7**	152
Green, r., IL	**I6**	146
Green, r., KY	**E9**	144
Green, r., ND	**D4**	148
Green, r., WA	**C3**	154
Greenacres, WA	**C8**	154
Green Bay, WI	**F7**	146
Green Bay, US	**F8**	146
Greenbrier, AR	**G4**	144
Green Brier, TN	**F10**	144
Greenbrier, r., WV	**J6**	140
Greenburg, LA	**L6**	144
Greenbush, MN	**C11**	148
Greencastle, IN	**C10**	144
Greencastle, PA	**H9**	140
Green City, MO	**B4**	144
Green Cove Springs, FL	**J5**	142
Greendale, IN	**C12**	144
Greene, IA	**H3**	146
Greene, NY	**E11**	140
Greeneville, TN	**C4**	142
Greenfield, CA	**H4**	156
Greenfield, IL	**C6**	144
Greenfield, IA	**J13**	148
Greenfield, MA	**E14**	140
Greenfield, MO	**E3**	144
Greenfield, OH	**H3**	140
Greenfield, TN	**F8**	144
Green Forest, AR	**F3**	144
Green Lake, WI	**G7**	146
Greenland, AR	**G2**	144
Greenland, MI	**D6**	146
Greenleaf, KS	**L11**	148
Green Mountains, VT	**D14**	140
Green Peter Lake, OR	**F3**	154
Green Pond, AL	**I9**	144
Greenport, NY	**F14**	140
Green River, UT	**F6**	152
Green River, WY	**C7**	152
Green River Lake, KY	**E11**	144
Greensboro, AL	**J9**	144
Greensboro, FL	**I2**	142
Greensboro, GA	**F3**	142
Greensboro, MD	**I11**	140
Greensboro, NC	**C7**	142
Greensburg, IN	**C11**	144
Greensburg, KS	**N8**	148
Greensburg, KY	**E11**	144
Greensburg, PA	**G7**	140
Greens Peak, AZ	**J7**	152
Green Springs, OH	**F3**	140
Green Swamp, NC	**E8**	142
Greentown, IN	**B11**	144
Greenup, IL	**C8**	144
Greenup, KY	**I4**	140
Green Valley, AZ	**M6**	152
Green Valley, IL	**J6**	146
Greenview, IL	**B7**	144
Greenville, AL	**K10**	144
Greenville, CA	**D5**	156
Greenville, FL	**I3**	142
Greenville, GA	**F2**	142
Greenville, IL	**D7**	144
Greenville, KY	**E9**	144
Greenville, ME	**B17**	140
Greenville, MI	**G10**	146
Greenville, MS	**I5**	144
Greenville, MO	**E6**	144
Greenville, NH	**E15**	140
Greenville, NC	**D9**	142
Greenville, OH	**G2**	140
Greenville, PA	**F6**	140
Greenville, SC	**E4**	142
Greenville, TX	**F10**	150
Greenwich, CT	**F13**	140
Greenwich, NY	**D13**	140
Greenwich, OH	**F4**	140
Greenwood, AR	**G2**	144
Greenwood, IN	**C10**	144
Greenwood, MS	**I6**	144
Greenwood, NE	**K11**	148
Greenwood, SC	**E4**	142
Greenwood, WI	**F5**	146
Greenwood, Lake, SC	**E4**	142
Greer, SC	**E4**	142
Greers Ferry Lake, AR	**G4**	144
Gregory, MI	**H11**	146
Gregory, SD	**H8**	148
Gregory, TX	**L9**	150
Grenada, MS	**I7**	144
Grenola, KS	**N11**	148
Grenora, ND	**C4**	148
Gresham, OR	**E3**	154
Gresham Park, GA	**F2**	142

Gret-Hoke

Name	Map Ref.	Page
Gretna, LA	M6	144
Gretna, VA	C7	142
Greybull, WY	F17	154
Greybull, r., WY	F17	154
Grey Eagle, MN	E1	146
Greylock, Mount, MA	E13	140
Greys, r., WY	G15	154
Gridley, CA	E4	156
Gridley, IL	J7	146
Griffin, GA	F2	142
Grifton, NC	D9	142
Griggsville, IL	C6	144
Grinnell, IA	I3	146
Griswold, IA	J12	148
Groesbeck, TX	H10	150
Groom, TX	D5	150
Grosse Pointe, MI	H13	146
Gros Ventre, r., WY	G15	154
Groton, CT	F14	140
Groton, NY	E10	140
Groton, SD	F9	148
Grottoes, VA	I8	140
Grove, OK	C12	150
Grove City, MN	F13	148
Grove City, OH	H3	140
Grove City, PA	F6	140
Grove Hill, AL	K9	144
Groveland, FL	K5	142
Grover City, CA	I5	156
Groves, TX	M3	144
Groveton, NH	C15	140
Groveton, TX	H11	150
Grovetown, GA	F4	142
Gruetli-Laager, TN	G11	144
Grulla, TX	M8	150
Grundy, VA	B4	142
Grundy Center, IA	H3	146
Gruver, TX	C5	150
Gu Achi, AZ	L4	152
Guadalupe, CA	J5	156
Guadalupe, r., TX	K9	150
Guadalupe Mountains National Park, TX	H2	150
Guadalupe Peak, TX	H2	150
Guadalupita, NM	H11	152
Gualala, CA	F2	156
Guerneville, CA	F2	156
Guernsey, WY	B12	152
Gueydan, LA	L4	144
Guide Rock, NE	K9	148
Guildhall, VT	C15	140
Guilford, ME	B17	140
Guin, AL	I9	144
Gulf Hammock, FL	J4	142
Gulfport, FL	L4	142
Gulfport, MS	L7	144
Gulf Shores, AL	L9	144
Gunnison, CO	F10	152
Gunnison, UT	E5	152
Gunnison, r., CO	F8	152
Guntersville, AL	H10	144
Guntersville Lake, AL	H10	144
Gurdon, AR	I3	144
Gustavus, AK	G27	158
Gustine, CA	G5	156
Gustine, TX	H8	150
Guthrie, KY	F9	144
Guthrie, OK	D9	150
Guthrie, TX	F6	150
Guthrie Center, IA	J13	148
Guttenberg, IA	H4	146
Guyandotte, r., WV	I4	140
Guymon, OK	C5	150
Guyot, Mount, US	D3	142
Guyton, GA	G5	142
Gwinn, MI	D8	146
Gwinner, ND	E10	148
Gym Peak, NM	L9	152
Gypsum, CO	E10	152
Gypsum, KS	M10	148

H

Name	Map Ref.	Page
Hackberry, AZ	I3	152
Hackberry, LA	M3	144
Hackensack, NJ	G12	140
Hackett, AR	G2	144
Hackettstown, NJ	G12	140
Hackleburg, AL	H9	144
Haddam, KS	L10	148
Haddock, GA	F3	142
Hadlock, WA	B3	154
Haena Point, HI	C7	160b
Hagan, GA	G5	142
Hagerman, ID	H11	154
Hagerman, NM	F2	150
Hagerstown, IN	C11	144
Hagerstown, MD	H9	140
Haggin, Mount, MT	D12	154
Hague, ND	E8	148
Hagues Peak, CO	D11	152
Hahira, GA	I3	142
Haigler, NE	K6	148
Haiku, HI	B4	160a
Hailey, ID	G11	154
Haileyville, OK	E11	150
Haines, AK	G27	158
Haines, OR	F8	154
Haines City, FL	K5	142
Halalii Lake, HI	D6	160b
Halawa, Cape, HI	A3	160a
Halawa Heights, HI	F10	160c
Hale, MO	C3	144
Haleakala Crater, HI	B4	160a
Haleakala National Park, HI	B4	160a
Hale Center, TX	E5	150
Haleiwa, HI	E9	160c
Halekii-Pihana Heiaus State Monument, HI	B4	160a
Haleyville, AL	H9	144
Halfway, MD	H9	140
Halfway, OR	F8	154
Halifax, NC	C9	142
Halifax, VA	C8	142
Haliimaile, HI	B4	160a
Hallandale, FL	N6	142
Hallettsville, TX	J10	150
Halliday, ND	D5	148
Hallock, MN	C11	148
Hallowell, ME	C17	140
Halls, TN	G7	144
Hallstead, PA	F11	140
Hallsville, MO	C4	144
Hallsville, TX	J2	144
Halsey, NE	J7	148
Halsey, OR	F2	154
Halstad, MN	D11	148
Halstead, KS	M10	148
Haltom City, TX	G9	150
Hamburg, AR	I5	144
Hamburg, IA	K12	148
Hamburg, NJ	F12	140
Hamburg, NY	E8	140
Hamburg, PA	G11	140
Hamden, CT	F14	140
Hamden, OH	H4	140
Hamilton, AL	H9	144
Hamilton, GA	G2	142
Hamilton, IL	J4	146
Hamilton, KS	N11	148
Hamilton, MI	H9	146
Hamilton, MO	C3	144
Hamilton, MT	D11	154
Hamilton, NY	E11	140
Hamilton, NC	D9	142
Hamilton, OH	H2	140
Hamilton, TX	H8	150
Hamilton, Mount, NV	E10	156
Hamilton City, CA	E3	156
Hamilton Dome, WY	A8	152
Hamlet, NC	E7	142
Hamlin, TX	G6	150
Hamlin, WV	I4	140
Hammon, OK	D7	150
Hammond, IN	A9	144
Hammond, LA	L6	144
Hammond, WI	F3	146
Hammondsport, NY	E9	140
Hammonton, NJ	H12	140
Hampden, ME	C18	140
Hampden, ND	C9	148
Hampden Sydney, VA	B8	142
Hampshire, IL	H7	146
Hampstead, NC	E9	142
Hampton, AR	I4	144
Hampton, FL	J4	142
Hampton, GA	F2	142
Hampton, IA	H2	146
Hampton, NE	K10	148
Hampton, NH	E16	140
Hampton, NJ	G12	140
Hampton, SC	G5	142
Hampton, TN	C4	142
Hampton, VA	B10	142
Hampton Bays, NY	G14	140
Hampton Butte, OR	G5	154
Hams Fork, r., WY	C6	152
Hana, HI	B5	160a
Hanahan, SC	G6	142
Hanakaoo Point, HI	B3	160a
Hanalei, HI	C7	160b
Hanamaulu, HI	D8	160b
Hanapepe, HI	D7	160b
Hanceville, AL	H10	144
Hancock, MD	H8	140
Hancock, MI	C7	146
Hancock, MN	F12	148
Hancock, NY	F11	140
Hancock, WI	F6	146
Hanford, CA	H6	156
Hankinson, ND	E11	148
Hanna, OK	D11	150
Hanna, WY	C10	152
Hanna City, IL	J6	146
Hannaford, ND	D9	148
Hannah, ND	C9	148
Hannibal, MO	C5	144
Hanover, IL	H5	146
Hanover, IN	D11	144
Hanover, KS	L11	148
Hanover, NH	D14	140
Hanover, NM	L8	152
Hanover, PA	H10	140
Hanover, VA	B9	142
Hanska, MN	G13	148
Hapeville, GA	F2	142
Happy, TX	E5	150
Happy Camp, CA	C2	156
Happy Jack, AZ	J5	152
Harbor, OR	H1	154
Harbor Beach, MI	G13	146
Harbor Springs, MI	E11	146
Harcuvar Mountains, AZ	K3	152
Hardeeville, SC	G5	142
Hardesty, OK	C5	150
Hardin, IL	C6	144
Hardin, MT	E18	154
Hardinsburg, KY	E10	144
Hardtner, KS	N9	148
Hardwick, GA	F3	142
Hardwick, VT	C14	140
Hardwood, LA	L5	144
Hardy, AR	F5	144
Hardy, NE	K10	148
Harkers Island, NC	E10	142
Harlan, IA	J12	148
Harlan, KY	C3	142
Harlan County Lake, NE	K8	148
Harlem, FL	M6	142
Harlem, GA	F4	142
Harlem, MT	B17	154
Harlingen, TX	M9	150
Harlowton, MT	D16	154
Harman, WV	I7	140
Harmony, IN	C9	144
Harmony, MN	G3	146
Harney Peak, SD	H4	148
Harper, KS	N9	148
Harper, TX	I7	150
Harrell, AR	I4	144
Harriman, TN	D2	142
Harrington, DE	I11	140
Harrington, ME	C19	140
Harrington, WA	C7	154
Harris, MN	E3	146
Harrisburg, AR	G6	144
Harrisburg, IL	E8	144
Harrisburg, NE	J4	148
Harrisburg, OR	F2	154
Harrisburg, PA	G10	140
Harrison, AR	F3	144
Harrison, ID	C9	154
Harrison, MI	F11	146
Harrison, NE	I4	148
Harrisonburg, LA	K5	144
Harrisonburg, VA	I8	140
Harrisonville, MO	D2	144
Harriston, MS	K5	144
Harrisville, MI	F12	146
Harrisville, NY	C11	140
Harrisville, WV	H5	140
Harrodsburg, KY	E12	144
Harrold, TX	E7	150
Harry S. Truman Reservoir, MO	D3	144
Hart, MI	G9	146
Hart, TX	E4	150
Hartford, AL	K11	144
Hartford, AR	G2	144
Hartford, CT	F14	140
Hartford, KS	M12	148
Hartford, KY	E10	144
Hartford, MI	H9	146
Hartford, SD	H11	148
Hartford, WI	G7	146
Hartford City, IN	B11	144
Hartington, NE	I10	148
Hartland, ME	C17	140
Hartley, IA	H12	148
Hartley, TX	D4	150
Hartselle, AL	H10	144
Hartshorne, OK	E11	150
Hartsville, SC	E6	142
Hartsville, TN	F10	144
Hartville, MO	E4	144
Hartwell, GA	E4	142
Hartwell Lake, US	E4	142
Harvard, IL	H7	146
Harvard, NE	K9	148
Harvey, IL	I8	146
Harvey, ND	D8	148
Haskell, OK	D11	150
Haskell, TX	F7	150
Hasperos Canyon, NM	K11	152
Hastings, FL	J5	142
Hastings, MI	H10	146
Hastings, MN	F3	146
Hastings, NE	K9	148
Hasty, CO	M5	148
Haswell, CO	M4	148
Hatch, NM	L9	152
Hatch, UT	G4	152
Hatchie, r., US	G7	144
Hatfield, AR	H2	144
Hatfield, MA	E14	140
Hatteras, NC	D11	142
Hatteras, Cape, NC	D11	142
Hatteras Island, NC	D11	142
Hattiesburg, MS	K7	144
Hatton, AL	H9	144
Hatton, ND	D10	148
Haubstadt, IN	D9	144
Hauula, HI	E10	160c
Havana, AR	G3	144
Havana, FL	I2	142
Havana, IL	B6	144
Havana, ND	F10	148
Havasu, Lake, US	J2	152
Havelock, NC	E10	142
Haven, KS	N10	148
Haverhill, MA	E15	140
Haviland, KS	N8	148
Havre, MT	B16	154
Havre de Grace, MD	H10	140
Havre North, MT	B16	154
Haw, r., NC	D7	142
Hawaii, HI	J16	160d
Hawaiian Islands, HI	I14	160d
Hawaii Volcanoes National Park, HI	J16	160d
Hawarden, IA	I11	148
Hawesville, KY	E10	144
Hawi, HI	I16	160d
Hawkins, TX	G11	150
Hawkins, WI	E5	146
Hawkinsville, GA	G3	142
Hawksbill, VA	I8	140
Hawley, MN	E11	148
Hawley, PA	F11	140
Hawthorne, FL	J4	142
Hawthorne, NV	F7	156
Haxtun, CO	K5	148
Hay, r., WI	E4	146
Hayden, AZ	K6	152
Hayden, CO	D9	152
Haydenville, OH	H4	140
Hayes, LA	L4	144
Hayes, Mount, AK	E21	158
Hayes Center, NE	K6	148
Hayesville, NC	D3	142
Hayesville, OR	F3	154
Hayfield, MN	G3	146
Hayfork, CA	D2	156
Haynes, AR	H6	144
Haynesville, LA	J3	144
Hayneville, AL	J10	144
Hays, KS	M8	148
Hays, MT	C17	154
Hay Springs, NE	I5	148
Haystack Mountain, NV	C10	156
Haysville, KS	N10	148
Hayti, MO	F7	144
Hayti, SD	G10	148
Hayward, CA	G3	156
Hayward, WI	D4	146
Hazard, KY	B3	142
Hazel, r., VA	I9	140
Hazel Green, WI	H5	146
Hazelton, ID	H11	154
Hazelton, ND	E7	148
Hazelwood, NC	D3	142
Hazen, AR	H5	144
Hazen, ND	D6	148
Hazlehurst, GA	H4	142
Hazlehurst, MS	K6	144
Hazleton, IA	H4	146
Hazleton, PA	G11	140
Headland, AL	K11	144
Headley, Mount, MT	C10	154
Healdsburg, CA	F3	156
Healdton, OK	E9	150
Healy, AK	E20	158
Healy, KS	M7	148
Hearne, TX	I10	150
Heart, r., ND	E6	148
Heath Springs, SC	E6	142
Heathsville, VA	B10	142
Heavener, OK	H2	144
Hebbronville, TX	L8	150
Heber, AZ	J6	152
Heber, CA	L10	156
Heber City, UT	D5	152
Heber Springs, AR	G4	144
Hebron, IL	H7	146
Hebron, IN	A9	144
Hebron, MD	I11	140
Hebron, NE	K10	148
Hebron, ND	E5	148
Hecla, SD	F9	148
Hector, MN	G13	148
He Devil, ID	E9	154
Hedley, TX	E6	150
Hedrick, IA	I3	146
Heflin, AL	I11	144
Heidelberg, MS	K8	144
Helemano Stream, r., HI	E9	160c
Helena, AR	H6	144
Helena, MT	D13	154
Helena, OK	C8	150
Helenwood, TN	C2	142
Hellertown, PA	G11	140
Hells Canyon, US	E9	154
Helper, UT	E6	152
Hemet, CA	K9	156
Hemingford, NE	I4	148
Hemingway, SC	F7	142
Hemphill, TX	K3	144
Hempstead, TX	I10	150
Henderson, KY	E9	144
Henderson, MN	F2	146
Henderson, NE	K10	148
Henderson, NV	H11	156
Henderson, NC	C8	142
Henderson, TN	G8	144
Henderson, TX	J2	144
Hendersonville, NC	D4	142
Hendersonville, TN	F10	144
Hendricks, MN	G11	148
Hendricks, WV	H7	140
Henefer, UT	C5	152
Henlopen, Cape, DE	I11	140
Hennepin, IL	I6	146
Hennessey, OK	C9	150
Henniker, NH	D15	140
Henning, MN	E12	148
Henning, TN	G7	144
Henrietta, NY	D9	140
Henrietta, NC	D5	142
Henrietta, TX	F8	150
Henry, IL	I6	146
Henry, SD	G10	148
Henry, Cape, VA	C10	142
Henry, Mount, MT	B10	154
Henryetta, OK	D11	150
Henrys Fork, r., US	C6	152
Hensley, AR	H4	144
Hephzibah, GA	F4	142
Heppner, OR	E6	154
Herculaneum, MO	D6	144
Hereford, AZ	M6	152
Hereford, TX	E4	150
Herington, KS	M11	148
Herkimer, NY	D12	140
Herlong, CA	D5	156
Herman, MN	F11	148
Herman, NE	J11	148
Hermann, MO	D5	144
Hermansville, MI	E8	146
Hermanville, MS	K6	144
Hermiston, OR	E6	154
Hermitage, AR	I4	144
Hermitage, MO	E3	144
Hermleigh, TX	G6	150
Hernando, FL	K4	142
Hernando, MS	H7	144
Herndon, KS	L7	148
Herndon, PA	G10	140
Heron Lake, MN	H12	148
Herreid, SD	F7	148
Herrin, IL	E7	144
Herring Cove, AK	I29	158
Herscher, IL	I7	146
Hershey, NE	J6	148
Hershey, PA	G10	140
Hertford, NC	C10	142
Hesperia, MI	G9	146
Hesperus Mountain, CO	G8	152
Hesston, KS	M10	148
Hetch Hetchy Aqueduct, CA	G4	156
Hettinger, ND	E5	148
Heuvelton, NY	C11	140
Heyburn, ID	H12	154
Heyworth, IL	B8	144
Hialeah, FL	N6	142
Hiawassee, GA	E3	142
Hiawatha, KS	L12	148
Hiawatha, UT	E5	152
Hibbing, MN	C3	146
Hickam Air Force Base, HI	F10	160c
Hickman, KY	F7	144
Hickman, NE	K11	148
Hickory, MS	J7	144
Hickory, NC	D5	142
Hickory Flat, MS	H7	144
Hicksville, OH	F2	140
Hico, TX	H8	150
Higbee, MO	C4	144
Higgins, TX	C6	150
Higginsville, MO	C3	144
Highland, CA	J8	156
Highland, IL	D7	144
Highland, IN	A9	144
Highland, KS	L12	148
Highland Home, AL	K10	144
Highland Park, IL	H8	146
Highland Park, TX	G10	150
Highlands, NJ	G13	140
Highlands, NC	D3	142
Highlands, TX	J11	150
Highland Springs, VA	B9	142
Highmore, SD	G8	148
High Point, NC	D6	142
High Point, NJ	F12	140
High Rock Lake, NC	D6	142
High Springs, FL	J4	142
Hightstown, NJ	G12	140
Highwood, MT	C15	154
Hilbert, WI	F7	146
Hildreth, NE	K8	148
Hill City, KS	L8	148
Hill City, MN	D2	146
Hill City, SD	H4	148
Hillcrest Center, CA	I7	156
Hilliard, FL	I5	142
Hillister, TX	L2	144
Hillman, MI	E12	146
Hills, MN	H11	148
Hillsboro, IL	C7	144
Hillsboro, KS	M10	148
Hillsboro, MO	D6	144
Hillsboro, NH	D15	140
Hillsboro, NM	L9	152
Hillsboro, ND	D10	148
Hillsboro, OH	H3	140
Hillsboro, OR	E3	154
Hillsboro, TX	G9	150
Hillsboro, WI	G5	146
Hillsboro Canal, FL	M6	142
Hillsborough, NC	C7	142
Hillsborough, r., FL	K4	142
Hillsdale, MI	I11	146
Hillsdale Lake, KS	M13	148
Hillsville, VA	C6	142
Hilo, HI	J16	160d
Hilton, NY	D9	140
Hilton Head Island, SC	G6	142
Hima, KY	B3	142
Hinchinbrook Entrance, AK	F21	158
Hinchinbrook Island, AK	F21	158
Hinckley, IL	I7	146
Hinckley, MN	D3	146
Hinckley, UT	E4	152
Hindman, KY	B4	142
Hines, OR	G6	154
Hinesville, GA	H5	142
Hingham, MA	E16	140
Hinsdale, MT	B18	154
Hinsdale, NH	E14	140
Hinton, OK	D8	150
Hinton, WV	B6	142
Hiram, ME	D16	140
Hitchcock, TX	J11	150
Hitchins, KY	I4	140
Hiwannee, MS	K8	144
Hiwassee, r., US	D2	142
Hixson, TN	G11	144
Hoback, r., WY	G15	154
Hobart, OK	D7	150
Hobbs, NM	G3	150
Hobe Sound, FL	L6	142
Hobgood, NC	C9	142
Hobson, MT	C16	154
Hocking, r., OH	H5	140
Hodge, LA	J4	144
Hodgenville, KY	E11	144
Hoehne, CO	N3	148
Hoffman, MN	F12	148
Hogansville, GA	F2	142
Hoh, r., WA	C1	154
Hohenwald, TN	G9	144
Hoisington, KS	M9	148
Hokah, MN	G4	146
Hokes Bluff, AL	I11	144

Name	Map Ref.	Page

Jewe-Lake

Loga-Mate

Mont-Newl

Oris-Pine

181

Pine-Redl

Name	Map Ref.	Page
Pine Creek Lake, OK	E11	150
Pinedale, CA	H6	156
Pinedale, WY	B7	152
Pine Grove, PA	G10	140
Pine Grove, WV	H6	140
Pine Hill, AL	K9	144
Pine Hills, FL	K5	142
Pinehurst, GA	G3	142
Pinehurst, ID	E9	154
Pinehurst, NC	D7	142
Pine Island, MN	F3	146
Pine Island, FL	M4	142
Pineland, TX	K3	144
Pinellas Park, FL	L4	142
Pine Mountain, WY	I16	154
Pine Prairie, LA	L4	144
Pine Ridge, SD	H5	148
Pine River, MN	D1	146
Pinetop, AZ	J7	152
Pinetops, NC	D9	142
Pine Valley, UT	F3	152
Pineville, KY	C3	142
Pineville, LA	K4	144
Pineville, MO	F2	144
Pineville, NC	D6	142
Pineville, WV	B5	142
Pinewood, SC	F6	142
Piney, r., TN	G9	144
Piney Woods, MS	J7	144
Pinnacle Buttes, WY	G16	154
Pinson, AL	I10	144
Pioche, NV	G11	156
Pioneer, OH	F2	140
Pipestone, MN	G11	148
Piqua, OH	G2	140
Pirtleville, AZ	M7	152
Pisgah Forest, NC	D4	142
Pisinemo, AZ	L4	152
Pismo Beach, CA	I5	156
Pit, r., CA	D3	156
Pittsboro, MS	I7	144
Pittsboro, NC	D7	142
Pittsburg, KS	N13	148
Pittsburg, TX	G12	150
Pittsburgh, PA	G7	140
Pittsfield, IL	C6	144
Pittsfield, ME	C17	140
Pittsfield, MA	E13	140
Pittsfield, NH	D15	140
Pittsford, MI	I11	146
Pittston, PA	F11	140
Pittsview, AL	J11	144
Pixley, CA	I6	156
Placerville, CA	F5	156
Plain City, OH	G3	140
Plain City, UT	C4	152
Plain Dealing, LA	J3	144
Plainfield, CT	F15	140
Plainfield, IN	C10	144
Plainfield, NJ	G12	140
Plainfield, WI	F6	146
Plains, GA	G2	142
Plains, KS	N7	148
Plains, MT	C11	154
Plains, TX	F4	150
Plainview, MN	F3	146
Plainview, NE	I10	148
Plainview, TX	E5	150
Plainville, IN	D9	144
Plainville, KS	L8	148
Plainwell, MI	H10	146
Plaistow, NH	E15	140
Planada, CA	G5	156
Plankinton, SD	H9	148
Plano, IL	I7	146
Plano, TX	F10	150
Plantation, FL	M6	142
Plant City, FL	K4	142
Plantersville, AL	J10	144
Plantersville, MS	H8	144
Plantsite, AZ	K7	152
Plaquemine, LA	L5	144
Platte, SD	H9	148
Platte, r., MN	D1	146
Platte, r., NE	J11	148
Platte, r., WI	H5	146
Platte Center, NE	J10	148
Platte City, MO	C2	144
Platteville, CO	D12	152
Platteville, WI	H5	146
Plattsburg, MO	C2	144
Plattsburgh, NY	C13	140
Plattsmouth, NE	J12	148
Playas Lake, NM	M8	152
Plaza, ND	C6	148
Pleasant, Lake, AZ	K4	152
Pleasant Gap, PA	G9	140
Pleasant Garden, NC	D7	142
Pleasant Grove, UT	D5	152
Pleasant Hill, IL	C6	144
Pleasant Hill, LA	K3	144
Pleasant Hill, MO	D2	144
Pleasanton, KS	M13	148
Pleasanton, TX	K8	150
Pleasant Plains, IL	C7	144
Pleasantville, IA	I2	146
Pleasantville, NJ	H12	140
Pleasantville, PA	F7	140
Plentywood, MT	C3	148
Plevna, MT	E3	148
Plover, r., WI	F6	146
Plumerville, AR	G4	144
Plummer, ID	C9	154
Plymouth, CA	F5	156
Plymouth, IL	B6	144
Plymouth, IN	A10	144
Plymouth, MA	F16	140
Plymouth, NE	K11	148
Plymouth, NH	D15	140
Plymouth, NC	D10	142
Plymouth, OH	F4	140
Plymouth, PA	F11	140
Plymouth, WI	G8	146
Pocahontas, AR	F6	144
Pocahontas, IL	D7	144
Pocahontas, IA	I13	148
Pocatalico, r., WV	I5	140
Pocatello, ID	H13	154
Pocola, OK	G2	144
Pocomoke, r., US	J11	140
Pocomoke City, MD	I11	140
Pocono Mountains, PA	F11	140
Pocono Summit, PA	F11	140
Point, TX	G11	150
Point Arena, CA	F2	156
Point Au Fer Island, LA	M5	144
Point Comfort, TX	K10	150
Pointe a la Hache, LA	M7	144
Point Hope, AK	B11	158
Point Imperial, AZ	H5	152
Point Marion, PA	H7	140
Point Pleasant, NJ	G12	140
Point Pleasant, WV	I4	140
Pojoaque Valley, NM	I10	152
Polacca, AZ	I6	152
Polihale State Park, HI	C7	160b
Polk, NE	J10	148
Polk, PA	F7	140
Polkton, NC	D6	142
Pollock, LA	K4	144
Pollock, SD	F7	148
Polo, IL	I6	146
Polo, MO	C2	144
Polson, MT	C11	154
Pomerene, AZ	M6	152
Pomeroy, IA	I13	148
Pomeroy, OH	H4	140
Pomeroy, WA	D8	154
Pomme de Terre, r., MN	F11	148
Pomme de Terre, r., MO	E3	144
Pomona, CA	J8	156
Pomona, KS	M12	148
Pomona Park, FL	J5	142
Pompano Beach, FL	M6	142
Pompton Lakes, NJ	F12	140
Ponca, NE	I11	148
Ponca City, OK	C9	150
Ponce de Leon, FL	L11	144
Ponchatoula, LA	L6	144
Pond, r., KY	E9	144
Pondcreek, OK	C9	150
Pondosa, CA	C4	156
Pontchartrain, Lake, LA	L6	144
Ponte Vedra Beach, FL	I5	142
Pontiac, IL	J7	146
Pontiac, MI	H12	146
Pontotoc, MS	H8	144
Pontotoc, TX	I8	150
Pony, MT	E14	154
Pooler, GA	G5	142
Poolville, TX	G9	150
Pope, MS	H7	144
Poplar, MT	C2	148
Poplar, WI	D4	146
Poplar, r., MN	D11	148
Poplar Bluff, MO	F6	144
Poplarville, MS	L7	144
Popple, r., WI	E7	146
Poquoson, VA	B10	142
Porcupine, r., NA	C23	158
Portage, MI	H10	146
Portage, UT	C4	152
Portage, WI	G6	146
Portage, r., OH	F3	140
Portageville, MO	F7	144
Portal, GA	G5	142
Portal, ND	C5	148
Portales, NM	E3	150
Port Allegany, PA	F8	140
Port Allen, LA	L5	144
Port Angeles, WA	B2	154
Port Aransas, TX	L9	150
Port Arthur, TX	M3	144
Port Austin, MI	F13	146
Port Barre, LA	L5	144
Port Byron, IL	I5	146
Port Charlotte, FL	M4	142
Port Chester, NY	F13	140
Port Clinton, OH	F4	140
Port Clyde, ME	D17	140
Porte Crayon, Mount, WV	I7	140
Port Edwards, WI	F6	146
Porter, OK	D11	150
Porter, TX	I11	150
Porterville, CA	H6	156
Porterville, MS	J8	144
Port Gamble, WA	C3	154
Port Gibson, MS	K6	144
Port Graham, AK	G19	158
Port Henry, NY	C13	140
Port Hope, MI	G13	146
Port Huron, MI	H13	146
Port Isabel, TX	M9	150
Port Jervis, NY	F12	140
Portland, AR	I5	144
Portland, IN	B12	144
Portland, ME	D16	140
Portland, MI	H11	146
Portland, ND	D10	148
Portland, OR	E3	154
Portland, TN	F10	144
Portland, TX	L9	150
Port Lavaca, TX	K10	150
Port Leyden, NY	D11	140
Port Lions, AK	H18	158
Port Neches, TX	M3	144
Portneuf, r., ID	H13	154
Port Norris, NJ	H11	140
Port O'Connor, TX	K10	150
Portola, CA	E5	156
Port Orange, FL	J6	142
Port Orchard, WA	C3	154
Port Orford, OR	H1	154
Port Richey, FL	K4	142
Port Royal, PA	G9	140
Port Royal, SC	G6	142
Port Saint Joe, FL	J1	142
Port Saint Lucie, FL	L6	142
Port Sanilac, MI	G13	146
Portsmouth, NH	D16	140
Portsmouth, OH	I4	140
Portsmouth, VA	C10	142
Port Sulphur, LA	M7	144
Port Townsend, WA	B3	154
Portville, NY	E8	140
Port Wakefield, AK	G18	158
Port Washington, WI	G8	146
Port Wentworth, GA	G5	142
Port Wing, WI	D4	146
Porum, OK	D11	150
Posen, MI	E12	146
Possum Kingdom Lake, TX	G8	150
Post, TX	F5	150
Postelle, TN	D2	142
Post Falls, ID	C9	154
Postville, IA	G4	146
Poteau, OK	G2	144
Poteau, r., US	G2	144
Poteet, TX	J8	150
Poth, TX	J8	150
Potholes Reservoir, WA	C6	154
Potlatch, ID	D9	154
Potomac, IL	B9	144
Potomac, r., US	I10	140
Potomac Heights, MD	I9	140
Potosi, MO	E6	144
Potsdam, NY	C12	140
Potter, NE	J4	148
Potterville, MI	H11	146
Potts Camp, MS	H7	144
Pottstown, PA	G11	140
Pottsville, PA	G10	140
Potwin, KS	N10	148
Poughkeepsie, NY	F13	140
Poulan, GA	H3	142
Poulsbo, WA	C3	154
Poultney, VT	D13	140
Pound, VA	B4	142
Poway, CA	L8	156
Powder, r., US	B5	136
Powder, r., OR	F8	154
Powderly, KY	E9	144
Powderly, TX	F11	150
Powell, WY	F17	154
Powell, r., US	C3	142
Powell, Lake, US	G6	152
Powell, Mount, CO	E10	152
Powellhurst, OR	E3	154
Powellton, WV	I5	140
Powers, MI	E8	146
Powers, OR	H1	154
Powers Lake, ND	C5	148
Powhatan, LA	K3	144
Powhatan, VA	B9	142
Powhatan Point, OH	H6	140
Poyen, AR	H4	144
Poygan, Lake, WI	F7	146
Poynette, WI	G6	146
Prague, NE	J11	148
Prague, OK	D10	150
Prairie, r., MN	C2	146
Prairie, r., WI	E6	146
Prairie City, IL	J5	146
Prairie City, IA	I2	146
Prairie City, OR	F7	154
Prairie du Chien, WI	G4	146
Prairie du Sac, WI	G6	146
Prairie Grove, AR	G2	144
Prairie View, TX	I11	150
Prairie Village, KS	M13	148
Pratt, KS	N9	148
Prattsburg, NY	E9	140
Prattville, AL	J10	144
Premont, TX	L8	150
Prentice, WI	E5	146
Prentiss, MS	K7	144
Prescott, AZ	J4	152
Prescott, AR	I3	144
Prescott, WI	F3	146
Presho, SD	H7	148
Presidio, TX	J2	150
Presque Isle, ME	F5	138
Presque Isle, PA	E6	140
Preston, GA	G2	142
Preston, ID	H14	154
Preston, IA	H5	146
Preston, KS	N9	148
Preston, MN	G3	146
Prestonsburg, KY	B4	142
Pretty Prairie, KS	N9	148
Pribilof Islands, AK	H9	158
Price, TX	J2	144
Price, UT	E6	152
Price, r., UT	E6	152
Prichard, AL	L8	144
Priddy, TX	H8	150
Priest, r., ID	B9	154
Priest Lake, ID	B9	154
Priest River, ID	B9	154
Primera, TX	M9	150
Primghar, IA	H12	148
Prince Frederick, MD	I10	140
Prince George, VA	B9	142
Prince of Wales, Cape, AK	D10	158
Prince of Wales Island, AK	I28	158
Princess Anne, MD	I11	140
Princeton, CA	E3	156
Princeton, IL	I6	146
Princeton, IN	D9	144
Princeton, KY	E9	144
Princeton, ME	B19	140
Princeton, MI	D8	146
Princeton, MN	E2	146
Princeton, MO	B3	144
Princeton, NJ	G12	140
Princeton, NC	D8	142
Princeton, WV	B5	142
Princeton, WI	G6	146
Princeville, IL	J6	146
Princeville, NC	D9	142
Prince William Sound, AK	F21	158
Prineville, OR	F5	154
Pritchett, CO	N5	148
Proctor, MN	D3	146
Proctor, VT	D13	140
Project City, CA	D3	156
Prophetstown, IL	I6	146
Prospect, OH	G3	140
Prosser, WA	D6	154
Protection, KS	N8	148
Provencal, LA	K3	144
Providence, KY	E9	144
Providence, RI	F15	140
Providence, UT	C5	152
Provincetown, MA	E16	140
Provo, UT	D5	152
Provo, r., UT	D5	152
Prudhoe Bay, AK	A20	158
Pryor, OK	C11	150
Pudding, r., OR	E3	154
Pueblo, CO	F12	152
Pueblo of Acoma, NM	I9	152
Pueo Point, HI	D6	160b
Puerco, r., US	I7	152
Puerco, Rio, r., NM	J10	152
Puget Sound, WA	C3	154
Puhi, HI	D8	160b
Pukalani, HI	B4	160a
Pulaski, NY	D10	140
Pulaski, TN	G9	144
Pulaski, VA	B6	142
Pulaski, WI	F7	146
Pullman, WA	D8	154
Punaluu, HI	E10	160c
Punta Gorda, FL	M4	142
Punxsutawney, PA	G8	140
Purcell, OK	D9	150
Purcellville, VA	H9	140
Purdy, MO	F3	144
Purgatoire, r., CO	N4	148
Purvis, MS	K7	144
Putnam, CT	F15	140
Putnam, TX	G7	150
Putney, GA	H2	142
Putney, VT	E14	140
Puukolii, HI	B3	160a
Puunene, HI	B4	160a
Puxico, MO	F6	144
Puyallup, WA	C3	154
Puyallup, r., WA	D3	154
Pye Islands, AK	G19	158
Pymatuning Reservoir, US	F6	140
Pyote, TX	H3	150
Pyramid Lake, NV	D6	156
Q		
Quabbin Reservoir, MA	E14	140
Quakertown, PA	G11	140
Quanah, TX	E7	150
Quantico, VA	I9	140
Quarryville, PA	H10	140
Quartz Hill, CA	J7	156
Quartz Mountain, OR	G3	154
Quartzsite, AZ	K2	152
Quebeck, TN	G11	144
Queen City, MO	B4	144
Queen City, TX	I2	144
Quemado, NM	J8	152
Quemado, TX	K6	150
Questa, NM	H11	152
Quilcene, WA	C3	154
Quimby, IA	I12	148
Quinault, r., WA	C2	154
Quincy, CA	E5	156
Quincy, FL	I2	142
Quincy, IL	C5	144
Quincy, MA	E15	140
Quincy, MI	I11	146
Quincy, WA	C6	154
Quinhagak, AK	G14	158
Quinlan, TX	G10	150
Quinn, r., NV	C7	156
Quinter, KS	L7	148
Quinton, OK	D11	150
Quitaque, TX	E5	150
Quitman, GA	I3	142
Quitman, MS	J8	144
Quitman, TX	G11	150
Qulin, MO	F6	144
R		
Rabbit Ears Pass, CO	D10	152
Raccoon, r., IA	A3	144
Raceland, LA	M6	144
Race Point, MA	E16	140
Racine, WI	H8	146
Radcliff, KY	E11	144
Radford, VA	B6	142
Raeford, NC	E7	142
Raft, r., US	H12	154
Raft River Mountains, UT	C3	152
Ragland, AL	I10	144
Rahway, NJ	G12	140
Raiford, FL	I4	142
Rainelle, WV	J6	140
Rainier, Mount, WA	D4	154
Rainy, r., NA	C14	148
Rainy, r., MI	E11	146
Rainy Lake, NA	B2	146
Raisin, r., MI	I12	146
Raleigh, MS	J7	144
Raleigh, NC	D8	142
Ralls, TX	F5	150
Ralston, NE	J11	148
Ralston, PA	F10	140
Ramah, NM	I8	152
Ramer, AL	J10	144
Ramona, CA	K9	156
Ramona, OK	C11	150
Ramona, SD	G10	148
Rampart, AK	D19	158
Ramseur, NC	D7	142
Ramsey, IL	C7	144
Ranburne, AL	I11	144
Ranches of Taos, NM	H11	152
Ranchester, WY	F18	154
Rancho Cordova, CA	F4	156
Randleman, NC	D7	142
Randlett, OK	E8	150
Randolph, AZ	L5	152
Randolph, ME	C17	140
Randolph, NE	I10	148
Randolph, NY	E8	140
Randolph, UT	C5	152
Randolph, VT	D14	140
Randolph, WI	G6	146
Random Lake, WI	G8	146
Rangeley, ME	C16	140
Rangely, CO	D8	152
Ranger, TX	G8	150
Rankin, IL	B9	144
Rankin, TX	H5	150
Ranlo, NC	D5	142
Ransom, KS	M8	148
Ranson, WV	H9	140
Rantoul, IL	B8	144
Raoul, GA	E3	142
Rapid, r., MI	D8	146
Rapid, r., MN	B1	146
Rapidan, r., VA	I9	140
Rapid City, MI	F10	146
Rapid City, SD	G4	148
Rapid River, MI	E9	146
Rappahannock, r., VA	B10	142
Rathbun Lake, IA	J2	146
Rathdrum, ID	C9	154
Rat Islands, AK	K4	159a
Raton, NM	C2	150
Raton Pass, NM	O3	148
Rattlesnake, MT	D12	154
Raven, VA	B5	142
Ravena, NY	E13	140
Ravenna, KY	B3	142
Ravenna, MI	G10	146
Ravenna, NE	J9	148
Ravenna, OH	F5	140
Ravenswood, WV	I5	140
Rawlins, WY	C9	152
Ray, ND	C4	148
Raymond, IL	C7	144
Raymond, MN	F12	148
Raymond, MS	J6	144
Raymond, WA	D2	154
Raymondville, TX	M9	150
Rayne, LA	L4	144
Raytown, MO	C2	144
Rayville, LA	J5	144
Reading, KS	M12	148
Reading, MI	I11	146
Reading, OH	H2	140
Reading, PA	G11	140
Readlyn, IA	H3	146
Readstown, WI	G5	146
Realitos, TX	L8	150
Reardan, WA	C8	154
Rector, AR	F6	144
Red, r., US	E8	136
Red, r., KY	B3	142
Red, r., NM	H11	152
Red, r., WI	E7	146
Red Bank, NJ	G12	140
Red Bank, TN	G11	144
Red Banks, MS	H7	144
Red Bay, AL	H8	144
Redbay, FL	L11	144
Red Bluff, CA	D3	156
Red Boiling Springs, TN	F11	144
Red Bud, IL	D7	144
Red Cedar, r., MI	H11	146
Red Cedar, r., WI	E4	146
Red Cliff, CO	E10	152
Red Cloud, NE	K9	148
Red Devil, AK	F16	158
Redding, CA	D3	156
Redeye, r., MN	E12	148
Redfield, IA	J13	148
Redfield, SD	G9	148
Redford, TX	J2	150
Red Hook, NY	F13	140
Redkey, IN	B11	144
Redlake, MN	D12	148
Red Lake, r., MN	D11	148
Red Lake Falls, MN	D11	148
Redlands, CA	J8	156

Redl-Sain

Name	Map Ref.	Page
Redlands, CO	E8	152
Red Level, AL	K10	144
Red Lick, MS	K6	144
Red Lion, PA	H10	140
Red Lodge, MT	E16	154
Redmond, OR	F4	154
Redmond, UT	E5	152
Redmond, WA	C3	154
Red Mountain, CA	C2	156
Red Mountain Pass, CO	G9	152
Red Oak, IA	J12	148
Red Oak, OK	E11	150
Redondo Beach, CA	K7	156
Red Rock, r., MT	F13	154
Red Rock, Lake, IA	I2	146
Red Springs, NC	E7	142
Redwater, r., MT	D2	148
Red Wing, MN	F3	146
Redwood, r., MN	G12	148
Redwood City, CA	G3	156
Redwood Falls, MN	G12	148
Redwood National Park, CA	C1	156
Redwood Valley, CA	E2	156
Reed City, MI	G10	146
Reeder, ND	E5	148
Reedley, CA	H6	156
Reedsburg, WI	G5	146
Reeds Peak, NM	K9	152
Reedsport, OR	G1	154
Reedsville, WI	F8	146
Reelfoot Lake, TN	F7	144
Reese, MI	G12	146
Reese, r., NV	D8	156
Reeseville, WI	G7	146
Reform, AL	I8	144
Refugio, TX	K9	150
Regent, ND	E5	148
Rehoboth Beach, DE	I11	140
Reidsville, GA	G4	142
Reidsville, NC	C7	142
Reinbeck, IA	H3	146
Reisterstown, MD	H10	140
Reliance, WY	C7	152
Remer, MN	C2	146
Remington, IN	B9	144
Remington, VA	I9	140
Remsen, IA	I12	148
Remus, MI	G10	146
Rend Lake, IL	D8	144
Renick, WV	J6	140
Reno, NV	E6	156
Renovo, PA	F9	140
Rensselaer, IN	B9	144
Rensselaer, NY	E13	140
Renton, WA	C3	154
Renville, MN	G12	148
Renwick, IA	H2	146
Repton, AL	K9	144
Republic, KS	L10	148
Republic, MI	D8	146
Republic, MO	E3	144
Republic, WA	B7	154
Republican, r., US	L10	148
Reserve, LA	L6	144
Reserve, NM	K8	152
Revillagigedo Island, AK	I29	158
Revillo, SD	F11	148
Rexburg, ID	G14	154
Rexford, KS	L7	148
Rexford, MT	B10	154
Reyes, Point, CA	F2	156
Reyno, AR	F6	144
Reynolds, GA	G2	142
Reynolds, ND	D10	148
Reynoldsville, PA	F8	140
Rhame, ND	E4	148
Rhine, GA	H3	142
Rhinebeck, NY	F13	140
Rhinelander, WI	E6	146
Rhode Island, state, US	C12	136
Rhode Island Sound, US	F15	140
Rib Lake, WI	E5	146
Rice, TX	G10	150
Rice Lake, WI	E4	146
Riceville, IA	G3	146
Riceville, TN	D2	142
Richards, TX	I11	150
Richardson, TX	G10	150
Richardton, ND	E5	148
Richey, MT	D2	148
Richfield, ID	G11	154
Richfield, MN	F2	146
Richfield, PA	G9	140
Richfield, UT	F4	152
Richfield Springs, NY	E12	140
Richford, VT	C14	140
Rich Hill, MO	D2	144
Richland, GA	G2	142
Richland, MI	H10	146
Richland, MO	E4	144
Richland, TX	H10	150
Richland, WA	D6	154
Richland Center, WI	G5	146
Richlands, NC	E9	142
Richlands, VA	B5	142
Richland Springs, TX	H8	150
Richmond, CA	G3	156
Richmond, IN	C12	144
Richmond, KS	M12	148
Richmond, KY	B2	142
Richmond, ME	C17	140
Richmond, MI	H13	146
Richmond, MN	F13	148
Richmond, MO	C3	144
Richmond, TX	J11	150
Richmond, UT	C5	152
Richmond, VT	C14	140
Richmond, VA	B9	142
Richmond Heights, FL	N6	142
Richmond Highlands, WA	C3	154
Richmond Hill, GA	H5	142
Richmondville, NY	E12	140
Rich Square, NC	C9	142
Richton, MS	K8	144
Richwood, OH	G3	140
Richwood, WV	I6	140
Rico, CO	G8	152
Riddle, OR	H2	154
Riddle Mountain, OR	G7	154
Ridgecrest, CA	I8	156
Ridge Farm, IL	C9	144
Ridgefield, CT	F13	140
Ridgeland, MS	J6	144
Ridgeland, SC	G6	142
Ridgely, TN	F7	144
Ridgeville, SC	F6	142
Ridgeway, MO	B3	144
Ridgeway, WI	G6	146
Ridgway, CO	F9	152
Ridgway, IL	E8	144
Ridgway, PA	F8	140
Riegelwood, NC	E8	142
Rienzi, MS	H8	144
Riffe Lake, WA	D3	154
Rifle, CO	E9	152
Rifle, r., MI	F11	146
Rigby, ID	G14	154
Riggins, ID	E9	154
Riley, KS	L11	148
Rillito, AZ	L5	152
Rimersburg, PA	F7	140
Rincon, GA	G5	142
Rincon, NM	L9	152
Ringgold, GA	E1	142
Ringgold, LA	J3	144
Ringling, OK	E9	150
Ringsted, IA	H13	148
Rio, WI	G6	146
Rio Dell, CA	D1	156
Rio Grande City, TX	M8	150
Rio Grande see Grande, Rio, r., NA	F7	136
Rio Hondo, TX	M9	150
Rio Rancho, NM	I10	152
Rio Vista, CA	F4	156
Ripley, MS	H8	144
Ripley, NY	E7	140
Ripley, OH	I3	140
Ripley, TN	G7	144
Ripley, WV	I5	140
Ripon, CA	G4	156
Ripon, WI	G7	146
Ririe, ID	G14	154
Rising Star, TX	G8	150
Rising Sun, IN	D12	144
Rising Sun, MD	H10	140
Risingsun, OH	F3	140
Rison, AR	I4	144
Ritter, Mount, CA	G6	156
Rittman, OH	G5	140
Ritzville, WA	C7	154
Rivanna, r., VA	B8	142
Riverbank, CA	G5	156
Riverdale, CA	H6	156
Riverdale, ND	D6	148
River Falls, AL	K10	144
River Falls, WI	F3	146
Riverhead, NY	G14	140
Rivermont, NC	D9	142
River Road, OR	F2	154
Riverside, CA	K8	156
Riverside, IA	I4	146
Riverside, TX	I11	150
Riverton, IL	C7	144
Riverton, NE	K9	148
Riverton, UT	D5	152
Riverton, VA	I8	140
Riverton, WY	A8	152
Riverton Heights, WA	C3	154
River View, AL	J11	144
Riverview, FL	L4	142
Riverview, KS	N10	148
Rives, TN	F7	144
Rivesville, WV	H6	140
Riviera, AZ	I2	152
Riviera, TX	L9	150
Riviera Beach, FL	M6	142
Roachdale, IN	C10	144
Roan Cliffs, US	E7	152
Roan Mountain, TN	C4	142
Roanoke, AL	I11	144
Roanoke, IL	J6	146
Roanoke, IN	B11	144
Roanoke, VA	B7	142
Roanoke (Staunton), r., US	C9	142
Roanoke Island, NC	D11	142
Roanoke Rapids, NC	C9	142
Roan Plateau, US	E6	152
Roaring Spring, PA	G8	140
Roaring Springs, TX	F6	150
Robbins, NC	D7	142
Robbins, TN	C2	142
Robbinsville, NC	D3	142
Robeline, LA	K3	144
Robersonville, NC	D9	142
Roberta, GA	G2	142
Roberta Mills, NC	D6	142
Robert Lee, TX	H6	150
Roberts, ID	G13	154
Roberts, MT	E16	154
Roberts Creek Mountain, NV	E9	156
Robertsdale, AL	L9	144
Robertsdale, PA	G8	140
Robert S. Kerr Lake, OK	D11	150
Robinson, IL	C9	144
Robinson, TX	H9	150
Robstown, TX	L9	150
Roby, TX	G6	150
Rochelle, GA	H3	142
Rochelle, IL	I6	146
Rochelle, TX	H7	150
Rochester, IN	A10	144
Rochester, MI	H12	146
Rochester, MN	F3	146
Rochester, NH	D16	140
Rochester, NY	D9	140
Rochester, TX	F7	150
Rock, MI	D8	146
Rock, r., US	I6	146
Rock, r., US	H11	148
Rockcastle, r., KY	B2	142
Rock Creek Butte, OR	F7	154
Rockdale, IL	I7	146
Rockdale, TX	I9	150
Rock Falls, IL	I6	146
Rockford, AL	J10	144
Rockford, IL	H6	146
Rockford, IA	G3	146
Rockford, MI	G10	146
Rockford, OH	G2	140
Rockford, TN	D3	142
Rock Hall, MD	H10	140
Rock Hill, SC	E5	142
Rockingham, NC	E7	142
Rock Island, IL	I5	146
Rocklake, ND	C8	148
Rockland, ID	H13	154
Rockland, ME	C17	140
Rockland, MA	E16	140
Rockland, MI	D6	146
Rockledge, FL	K6	142
Rocklin, CA	F4	156
Rockmart, GA	E1	142
Rockport, KY	E10	144
Rockport, ME	C17	140
Rockport, MA	E16	140
Rock Port, MO	B1	144
Rockport, TX	K9	150
Rock Rapids, IA	H11	148
Rock River, WY	C11	152
Rocksprings, TX	I6	150
Rock Springs, WY	C7	152
Rockton, IL	H6	146
Rock Valley, IA	H11	148
Rockville, IN	C9	144
Rockville, MD	H9	140
Rockwall, TX	G10	150
Rockwell, IA	H2	146
Rockwell, NC	D6	142
Rockwell City, IA	I13	148
Rockwood, ME	B17	140
Rockwood, PA	H7	140
Rockwood, TN	D2	142
Rocky, OK	D7	150
Rocky, r., NC	D7	142
Rocky Ford, CO	M4	148
Rocky Mount, NC	D9	142
Rocky Mount, VA	C7	142
Rocky Mountain, MT	C13	154
Rocky Mountain National Park, CO	K2	148
Rocky Mountains, NA	B4	136
Roda, VA	C4	142
Rodeo, NM	M7	152
Rodney, MS	K5	144
Roeland Park, KS	L13	148
Roff, OK	E10	150
Rogers, AR	F2	144
Rogers, TX	I9	150
Rogers, Mount, VA	C5	142
Rogers City, MI	E12	146
Rogers Lake, CA	J8	156
Rogersville, AL	H9	144
Rogersville, TN	C3	142
Rogue, r., MI	G10	146
Rogue, r., OR	H1	154
Rogue River, OR	H2	154
Roland, AR	H4	144
Roland, IA	H2	146
Rolette, ND	C8	148
Rolfe, IA	I13	148
Roll, AZ	L3	152
Rolla, KS	N6	148
Rolla, MO	E5	144
Rolla, ND	C8	148
Rolling Fork, MS	J6	144
Rolling Fork, r., KY	E11	144
Roma, TX	M7	150
Rome, GA	E1	142
Rome, IL	J6	146
Rome, MS	I6	144
Rome, NY	D11	140
Romeo, MI	H12	146
Romney, WV	H8	140
Ronan, MT	C11	154
Ronceverte, WV	B6	142
Roodhouse, IL	C6	144
Roosevelt, AZ	K5	152
Roosevelt, MN	C12	148
Roosevelt, OK	E7	150
Roosevelt, UT	D7	152
Root, r., MN	G4	146
Root, r., WI	H8	146
Roper, NC	D10	142
Ropesville, TX	F4	150
Rosalia, WA	C8	154
Rosamond, CA	J7	156
Roscoe, SD	F8	148
Roscoe, TX	G6	150
Roscommon, MI	F11	146
Rose, Mount, NV	E6	156
Roseau, MN	C12	148
Roseau, r., NA	B11	148
Roseboro, NC	E8	142
Rosebud, MT	D19	154
Rosebud, SD	H7	148
Rosebud, TX	H10	150
Roseburg, OR	G2	154
Rosebush, MI	G11	146
Rose City, MI	F11	146
Rosedale, IN	C9	144
Rosedale, LA	L5	144
Rosedale, MS	I5	144
Rose Hill, NC	E8	142
Rose Hill, VA	C3	142
Roseland, LA	L6	144
Rosenberg, TX	J11	150
Rosepine, LA	L3	144
Roseville, CA	F4	156
Roseville, IL	J5	146
Roseville, MI	H13	146
Roseville, MN	E2	146
Roseville, OH	H4	140
Rosholt, SD	F11	148
Rosholt, WI	F6	146
Rosiclare, IL	E8	144
Roslyn, WA	C5	154
Rosman, NC	D4	142
Rossford, OH	F3	140
Rossiter, PA	G8	140
Ross Lake, NA	B4	154
Ross R. Barnett Reservoir, MS	J6	144
Rossville, GA	E1	142
Rossville, IL	B9	144
Rossville, IN	B10	144
Rossville, KS	L12	148
Roswell, GA	E2	142
Roswell, NM	F2	150
Rotan, TX	G6	150
Rothsay, MN	E11	148
Rothschild, WI	F6	146
Rotterdam, NY	E13	140
Rough, r., KY	E10	144
Rough River Lake, KY	E10	144
Roulette, PA	F8	140
Round Lake, MN	H12	148
Round Mountain, NV	F8	156
Round Rock, TX	I9	150
Roundup, MT	D17	154
Rouses Point, NY	B13	140
Rowena, TX	H6	150
Rowland, NC	E7	142
Rowlesburg, WV	H7	140
Roxboro, NC	C8	142
Roxie, MS	K5	144
Roxton, TX	F11	150
Roy, NM	D2	150
Roy, UT	C4	152
Roy, WA	C3	154
Royal, IA	H12	148
Royal Center, IN	B10	144
Royal City, WA	D6	154
Royale, Isle, MI	B7	146
Royal Gorge, CO	F11	152
Royal Oak, MI	H12	146
Royalton, MN	E1	146
Royse City, TX	G10	150
Royston, GA	E3	142
Ruby, AK	D17	158
Ruby, r., MT	E13	154
Ruby Dome, NV	D10	156
Ruby Mountains, NV	D10	156
Ruby Valley, NV	D10	156
Rudyard, MI	D11	146
Rudyard, MT	B15	154
Ruffin, SC	F6	142
Rufus, OR	E5	154
Rugby, ND	C8	148
Ruidoso, NM	K11	152
Ruidoso, Rio, r., NM	K11	152
Ruidoso Downs, NM	K11	152
Rule, TX	F7	150
Ruleville, MS	I6	144
Rulo, NE	K12	148
Rum, r., MN	E2	146
Rumford, ME	C16	140
Runge, TX	K9	150
Rupert, ID	H12	154
Rupert, WV	J6	140
Rural Hall, NC	C6	142
Rural Retreat, VA	C5	142
Rush, r., ND	D10	148
Rush, r., WI	F3	146
Rush Center, KS	M8	148
Rush City, MN	E3	146
Rushford, MN	G4	146
Rushmore, MN	H12	148
Rush Springs, OK	E9	150
Rushville, IL	B6	144
Rushville, IN	C11	144
Rushville, NE	I5	148
Rusk, TX	H11	150
Ruskin, FL	L4	142
Russell, IA	J2	146
Russell, KS	M9	148
Russell, KY	I4	140
Russell, MN	G12	148
Russell, PA	F7	140
Russells Point, OH	G3	140
Russell Springs, KY	E11	144
Russellville, AL	H9	144
Russellville, AR	G3	144
Russellville, KY	F10	144
Russellville, MO	D4	144
Russian, r., CA	F2	156
Russiaville, IN	B10	144
Rustburg, VA	B7	142
Ruston, LA	J4	144
Ruth, MS	K6	144
Ruth, NV	E11	156
Rutherford, TN	F8	144
Rutherfordton, NC	D5	142
Ruthton, MN	G11	148
Ruthven, IA	H13	148
Rutland, ND	E10	148
Rutland, VT	D14	140
Rutledge, GA	F3	142
Rutledge, TN	C3	142
Ryan, OK	E9	150
Ryder, ND	D6	148
Ryderwood, WA	D2	154
Ryegate, MT	D16	154
Rye Patch Reservoir, NV	D7	156
S		
Sabetha, KS	L12	148
Sabina, OH	H3	140
Sabinal, TX	J7	150
Sabine, r., US	E8	136
Sabine Lake, US	M3	144
Sabine Pass, US	M3	144
Sable, Cape, FL	N5	142
Sabula, IA	H5	146
Sac, r., MO	E3	144
Sacajawea Peak, OR	E8	154
Sacaton, AZ	K5	152
Sac City, IA	I13	148
Sackets Harbor, NY	D10	140
Saco, ME	D16	140
Saco, MT	B18	154
Saco, r., US	D16	140
Sacramento, CA	F4	156
Sacramento, r., CA	F4	156
Sacramento, r., NM	L11	152
Sacramento Mountains, NM	L11	152
Sacramento Valley, CA	D3	156
Sacred Heart, MN	G12	148
Saddle Mountain, CO	F11	152
Saegertown, PA	F6	140
Safford, AZ	L7	152
Sagavanirktok, r., AK	B20	158
Sagerton, TX	F7	150
Saginaw, MI	G12	146
Saginaw, r., MI	G12	146
Saginaw Bay, MI	G12	146
Saguache, CO	F10	152
Sahuarita, AZ	M6	152
Saint Albans, VT	C13	140
Saint Albans, WV	I5	140
Saint Andrews, SC	G7	142
Saint Anne, IL	I8	146
Saint Ansgar, IA	G3	146
Saint Anthony, ID	G14	154
Saint Augustine, FL	J5	142
Saint Catherines Island, GA	H5	142
Saint Charles, AR	H5	144
Saint Charles, ID	H14	154
Saint Charles, IL	I7	146
Saint Charles, MI	G11	146
Saint Charles, MN	G3	146
Saint Charles, MO	D6	144
Saint Charles Mesa, CO	M3	148
Saint Clair, MI	H13	146
Saint Clair, MO	D6	144
Saint Clair, r., NA	H13	146
Saint Clair, Lake, NA	H13	146
Saint Clair Shores, MI	H13	146
Saint Clairsville, OH	G6	140
Saint Cloud, FL	K5	142
Saint Cloud, MN	E1	146
Saint Croix, r., NA	G6	138
Saint Croix, r., US	E3	146
Saint Croix Falls, WI	E3	146
Saint David, AZ	M6	152
Saint David, IL	J5	146
Saint Edward, NE	J10	148
Saint Elias, Cape, AK	G22	158
Saint Elias, Mount, NA	F24	158
Saint Elias Mountains, NA	F24	158
Saint Elmo, IL	C8	144
Saint Francis, KS	L6	148
Saint Francis, SD	H7	148
Saint Francis, WI	H8	146
Saint Francis, r., US	H6	144
Saint Francisville, LA	L5	144
Sainte Genevieve, MO	E6	144
Saint George, SC	F6	142
Saint George, UT	G3	152
Saint George Island, AK	H10	158
Saint George Island, FL	J2	142
Saint Helena, CA	F3	156
Saint Helena Sound, SC	G6	142
Saint Helens, OR	E3	154
Saint Helens, Mount, WA	D3	154
Saint Ignace, MI	E11	146
Saint Ignatius, MT	C11	154
Saint James, MI	E10	146
Saint James, MN	H13	148
Saint James, MO	E5	144
Saint James, NY	G13	140

Shas-Ster

185

Ster-Torn

Name	Map Ref.	Page
Sterling, IL	I6	146
Sterling, KS	M9	148
Sterling, MI	F11	146
Sterling, NE	K11	148
Sterling, OK	E8	150
Sterling City, TX	H6	150
Sterlington, LA	J4	144
Steubenville, OH	G6	140
Stevenson, AL	H11	144
Stevenson, WA	E4	154
Stevens Pass, WA	C4	154
Stevens Point, WI	F6	146
Stevens Village, AK	C20	158
Stevensville, MI	H9	146
Stevensville, MT	D11	154
Stewardson, IL	C8	144
Stewart, MN	F1	146
Stewartstown, PA	H10	140
Stewartsville, MO	C2	144
Stewartville, MN	G3	146
Stickney, SD	H9	148
Stigler, OK	D11	150
Stikine, r., NA	H29	158
Stillhouse Hollow Lake, TX	H9	150
Stillmore, GA	G4	142
Stillwater, MN	E3	146
Stillwater, OK	C9	150
Stillwater, r., MT	E16	154
Stillwell, OK	G2	144
Stimson, Mount, MT	B12	154
Stinking Water Creek, r., NE	K6	148
Stinnett, TX	D5	150
Stirling City, CA	E4	156
Stirrat, WV	B4	142
Stockbridge, GA	F2	142
Stockbridge, MI	H11	146
Stockdale, TX	J9	150
Stockett, MT	C14	154
Stockholm, ME	E5	138
Stockton, AL	L9	144
Stockton, CA	G4	156
Stockton, IL	H5	146
Stockton, KS	L8	148
Stockton, MO	E3	144
Stockton, UT	D4	152
Stockton Plateau, TX	I4	150
Stockton Reservoir, MO	E3	144
Stockton Springs, ME	C18	140
Stockville, NE	K7	148
Stoneboro, PA	F6	140
Stonefort, IL	E8	144
Stone Harbor, NJ	H12	140
Stone Mountain, GA	F2	142
Stoneville, NC	C7	142
Stonewall, LA	J3	144
Stonewall, MS	J8	144
Stonewall, OK	E10	150
Stonington, IL	C7	144
Stonington, ME	C18	140
Stony, r., MN	C4	146
Stony Point, MI	I12	146
Stony Point, NC	D5	142
Storm Lake, IA	I12	148
Storrs, CT	F14	140
Story, WY	F19	154
Story City, IA	H2	146
Stoughton, MA	E15	140
Stoughton, WI	H6	146
Stover, MO	D4	144
Stow, OH	F5	140
Stowe, VT	C14	140
Stowell, TX	M2	144
Strasburg, CO	L3	148
Strasburg, ND	E7	148
Strasburg, OH	G5	140
Strasburg, PA	H10	140
Strasburg, VA	I8	140
Stratford, CA	H6	156
Stratford, CT	F13	140
Stratford, IA	H2	146
Stratford, OK	E10	150
Stratford, TX	C4	150
Stratford, WI	F5	146
Strathmore, CA	H6	156
Stratton, CO	L5	148
Stratton, ME	B16	140
Stratton, NE	K6	148
Strawberry, r., AR	F5	144
Strawberry, r., UT	D6	152
Strawberry Mountain, OR	F7	154
Strawberry Point, IA	H4	146
Strawn, TX	G8	150
Streator, IL	I7	146
Streeter, ND	E8	148
Streetman, TX	H10	150
Streetsboro, OH	F5	140
Strogonof Point, AK	H15	158
Stromsburg, NE	J10	148
Strong, AR	I4	144
Strong, r., MS	J7	144
Strong City, KS	M11	148
Stronghurst, IL	J5	146
Stroud, OK	D10	150
Stroudsburg, PA	G11	140
Strum, WI	F4	146
Struthers, OH	F6	140
Stryker, OH	F2	140
Stuart, FL	L6	142
Stuart, IA	J13	148
Stuart, NE	I8	148
Stuart, VA	C6	142
Stuarts Draft, VA	A7	142
Sturgeon, MO	C4	144
Sturgeon, r., MI	E11	146
Sturgeon Bay, WI	F8	146
Sturgis, KY	E9	144
Sturgis, MI	I10	146
Sturgis, MS	I7	144
Sturgis, SD	G4	148
Sturtevant, WI	H8	146
Stuttgart, AR	H5	144
Styx, r., AL	L9	144
Sublette, KS	N7	148
Sucarnoochee, r., US	J8	144
Sudan, TX	E4	150
Suffolk, VA	C10	142
Sugar, r., US	H6	146
Sugar, r., NH	D14	140
Sugar City, ID	G14	154
Sugarcreek, PA	F7	140
Sugar Grove, VA	C5	142
Sugar Hill, GA	E2	142
Sugar Island, MI	D11	146
Sugar Land, TX	J11	150
Sugarloaf Mountain, ME	B16	140
Sulligent, AL	I8	144
Sullivan, IL	C8	144
Sullivan, IN	C9	144
Sullivan, MO	D5	144
Sulphur, LA	L3	144
Sulphur, OK	E10	150
Sulphur, r., US	I2	144
Sulphur Springs, TX	F11	150
Sulphur Springs Valley, AZ	M7	152
Sultan, WA	C4	154
Sumas, WA	A3	154
Summerfield, FL	J4	142
Summerfield, NC	C7	142
Summersville, MO	E5	144
Summersville, WV	I6	140
Summerton, SC	F6	142
Summertown, TN	G9	144
Summerville, GA	E1	142
Summerville, SC	F6	142
Summit, MS	K6	144
Summit, SD	F10	148
Summit Mountain, NV	E9	156
Summit Peak, CO	G10	152
Sumner, IA	H3	146
Sumner, MS	I6	144
Sumner, WA	C3	154
Sumrall, MS	K7	144
Sumter, SC	F6	142
Sun, r., MT	C13	154
Sunbright, TN	C2	142
Sunburst, MT	B14	154
Sunbury, NC	C10	142
Sunbury, OH	G4	140
Sunbury, PA	G10	140
Sun City, AZ	K4	152
Suncook, NH	D15	140
Suncook, r., NH	D15	140
Sundance, WY	G3	148
Sundown, TX	F4	150
Sunflower, MS	I6	144
Sunflower, Mount, KS	L5	148
Sunland Park, NM	L10	152
Sunnyside, UT	E6	152
Sunnyside, WA	D5	154
Sunnyvale, CA	G3	156
Sun Prairie, WI	G6	146
Sunray, TX	C5	150
Sunrise, WY	B12	152
Sunrise Manor, NV	H10	156
Sunset, LA	L4	144
Sunset, TX	F9	150
Sunset Beach, HI	E9	160c
Sunset Heights, TX	H4	150
Suntrana, AK	E20	158
Sun Valley, ID	G11	154
Superior, AZ	K5	152
Superior, MT	C11	154
Superior, NE	K9	148
Superior, WI	D3	146
Superior, Lake, NA	C8	146
Surf City, NJ	H12	140
Surgoinsville, TN	C4	142
Suring, WI	F7	146
Surprise, AZ	K4	152
Surprise Valley, US	C5	156
Surrency, GA	H4	142
Surrey, ND	C6	148
Surry, VA	B10	142
Susanville, CA	D5	156
Susitna, AK	F19	158
Susitna, r., AK	E19	158
Susquehanna, PA	F11	140
Susquehanna, r., US	H10	140
Sussex, NJ	F12	140
Sussex, VA	C9	142
Sutherland, IA	I12	148
Sutherland, NE	J6	148
Sutherlin, OR	G2	154
Sutter, CA	E4	156
Sutter Creek, CA	F5	156
Sutton, AK	F20	158
Sutton, NE	K10	148
Sutton, WV	I6	140
Suttons Bay, MI	F10	146
Suwannee, r., US	J3	142
Swainsboro, GA	G4	142
Swan, r., MN	C2	146
Swan, r., MT	C12	154
Swanee see Suwannee, r., US	J3	142
Swan Lake, MT	C12	154
Swannanoa, NC	D4	142
Swanquarter, NC	D10	142
Swan Range, MT	C12	154
Swansboro, NC	E9	142
Swansea, SC	F5	142
Swanton, OH	F3	140
Swanton, VT	C13	140
Swanville, MN	E1	146
Swartz Creek, MI	H12	146
Swasey Peak, UT	E3	152
Swea City, IA	H13	148
Swedish Knoll, UT	E5	152
Sweeny, TX	J11	150
Sweet Briar, VA	B7	142
Sweet Home, OR	F3	154
Sweet Home, TX	J9	150
Sweet Springs, MO	D3	144
Sweetwater, TN	D2	142
Sweetwater, TX	G6	150
Sweetwater, r., WY	H18	154
Swepsonville, NC	C7	142
Swifton, AR	G5	144
Sycamore, GA	H3	142
Sycamore, IL	I7	146
Sycamore, OH	G3	140
Sycan, r., OR	H4	154
Sykesville, MD	H10	140
Sykesville, PA	F8	140
Sylacauga, AL	I10	144
Sylva, NC	D3	142
Sylvan Grove, KS	L9	148
Sylvan Hills, AR	H4	144
Sylvania, GA	G5	142
Sylvania, OH	F3	140
Sylvester, GA	H3	142
Sylvester, TX	G6	150
Sylvia, KS	N9	148
Syracuse, IN	A11	144
Syracuse, KS	N6	148
Syracuse, NE	K11	148
Syracuse, NY	D10	140

T

Name	Map Ref.	Page
Table Rock, NE	K11	148
Table Rock Lake, US	F3	144
Tabor, IA	K12	148
Tabor, SD	I10	148
Tabor City, NC	E8	142
Tacna, AZ	L3	152
Tacoma, WA	C3	154
Taconic Range, US	E13	140
Taft, CA	I6	156
Taft, OK	D11	150
Taft, TX	L9	150
Tahlequah, OK	D12	150
Tahoe, Lake, US	E5	156
Tahoe City, CA	E5	156
Tahoe Valley, CA	F5	156
Tahoka, TX	F5	150
Tahquamenon, r., MI	D10	146
Tajique, NM	J10	152
Taku Glacier, AK	G27	158
Talbotton, GA	G2	142
Talco, TX	F11	150
Talent, OR	H3	154
Talihina, OK	E11	150
Talkeetna, AK	E19	158
Talladega, AL	I10	144
Tallahassee, FL	I2	142
Tallahatchie, r., MS	I6	144
Tallapoosa, GA	F1	142
Tallapoosa, r., US	J10	144
Tallassee, AL	J11	144
Tallmadge, OH	F5	140
Tallula, IL	C7	144
Tallulah, LA	J5	144
Talmage, CA	E2	156
Talmage, NE	K11	148
Taloga, OK	C8	150
Talpa, TX	H7	150
Tama, IA	I3	146
Tamaqua, PA	G11	140
Tamarac, r., MN	C10	148
Tamaroa, IL	D7	144
Tamiami Canal, FL	N5	142
Tamms, IL	E7	144
Tampa, FL	L4	142
Tampa Bay, FL	L4	142
Tampico, IL	I6	146
Tanacross, AK	E23	158
Tanana, AK	D18	158
Tanana, r., AK	D19	158
Taneytown, MD	H9	140
Tangier, VA	B11	142
Tangipahoa, r., US	K6	144
Tanner, AL	H10	144
Taos, MO	D4	144
Taos, NM	H11	152
Taos Pueblo, NM	H11	152
Tappahannock, VA	B10	142
Tappen, ND	E8	148
Tar, r., NC	D9	142
Tarboro, NC	D9	142
Tarentum, PA	G7	140
Targhee Pass, US	F14	154
Tarkio, MO	B1	144
Tarkio, r., US	K12	148
Tarpon Springs, FL	K4	142
Tarrant City, AL	I10	144
Tarzan, TX	G5	150
Tate, GA	E2	142
Tatitlek, AK	F21	158
Tatum, NM	F3	150
Tatum, TX	J2	144
Taum Sauk Mountain, MO	E6	144
Taunton, MA	F15	140
Tavares, FL	K5	142
Tavernier, FL	N6	142
Tawakoni, Lake, TX	G10	150
Tawas City, MI	F12	146
Taylor, AZ	J6	152
Taylor, AR	I3	144
Taylor, NE	J8	148
Taylor, TX	I9	150
Taylor, Mount, NM	I9	152
Taylors, SC	E4	142
Taylorsville, IN	C11	144
Taylorsville, KY	D11	144
Taylorsville, MS	K7	144
Taylorsville, NC	D5	142
Taylorville, IL	C7	144
Tazewell, TN	C3	142
Tazewell, VA	B5	142
Tchefuncta, r., LA	L6	144
Tchula, MS	I6	144
Teague, TX	H10	150
Teche, Bayou, r., LA	L5	144
Tecopa, CA	I9	156
Tecumseh, MI	H12	146
Tecumseh, NE	K11	148
Tecumseh, OK	D10	150
Teec Nos Pos, AZ	H7	152
Tehachapi, CA	I7	156
Tehachapi Pass, CA	I7	156
Tekamah, NE	J11	148
Tekoa, WA	C8	154
Tekonsha, MI	H11	146
Telescope Peak, CA	H8	156
Tell City, IN	E10	144
Teller, AK	D11	158
Tellico, r., US	D2	142
Tellico Plains, TN	D2	142
Telluride, CO	G9	152
Temecula, CA	K8	156
Tempe, AZ	K5	152
Temperance, MI	I12	146
Temple, OK	E8	150
Temple, TX	H9	150
Tenaha, TX	K2	144
Tenakee Springs, AK	H27	158
Tenino, WA	D3	154
Tenkiller Ferry Lake, OK	D11	150
Tennessee, state, US	D9	136
Tennessee, r., US	D9	136
Tennille, GA	G4	142
Tensas, r., LA	K5	144
Tensed, ID	C9	154
Ten Sleep, WY	F18	154
Ten Thousand Islands, FL	N5	142
Terlingua, TX	J3	150
Terra Alta, WV	H7	140
Terra Bella, CA	I6	156
Terral, OK	F9	150
Terrebonne Bay, LA	M6	144
Terre Haute, IN	C9	144
Terrell, TX	G10	150
Terrell Hills, TX	J8	150
Terry, MS	J6	144
Terry, MT	E2	148
Terry Peak, SD	G4	148
Tescott, KS	L10	148
Tesuque, NM	I11	152
Tetlin, AK	E23	158
Tetlin Lake, AK	E23	158
Teton, ID	G14	154
Teton, r., MT	C14	154
Tetonia, ID	G14	154
Teton Range, WY	G15	154
Teutopolis, IL	C8	144
Texarkana, AR	I2	144
Texarkana, TX	I2	144
Texas, state, US	E7	136
Texas City, TX	J12	150
Texhoma, OK	C5	150
Texico, NM	E3	150
Texline, TX	C3	150
Texoma, Lake, US	F10	150
Thalia, TX	F7	150
Thatcher, AZ	L7	152
Thayer, KS	N12	148
Thayer, MO	F5	144
Thealka, KY	B4	142
Thebes, IL	E7	144
The Dalles, OR	E4	154
Thedford, NE	J7	148
The Everglades, FL	M6	142
The Flat Tops, CO	D9	152
Theodore, AL	L8	144
Theodore Roosevelt Lake, AZ	K5	152
Theresa, NY	C11	140
Thermopolis, WY	A8	152
Thibodaux, LA	M6	144
Thief, r., MN	C11	148
Thief River Falls, MN	C11	148
Thielsen, Mount, OR	G3	154
Thomas, OK	D8	150
Thomas, WV	H7	140
Thomasboro, IL	B8	144
Thomaston, AL	J9	144
Thomaston, CT	F13	140
Thomaston, GA	G2	142
Thomaston, ME	C17	140
Thomasville, AL	K9	144
Thomasville, GA	I3	142
Thomasville, NC	D6	142
Thompson, IA	G2	146
Thompson, r., US	C3	144
Thompson Falls, MT	C10	154
Thompson Pass, AK	F22	158
Thompsonville, MI	F10	146
Thomson, GA	F4	142
Thomson, IL	I5	146
Thonotosassa, FL	K4	142
Thoreau, NM	I8	152
Thornapple, r., WI	E4	146
Thorndale, TX	I9	150
Thornton, AR	I4	144
Thornton, CO	E12	152
Thornton, TX	H10	150
Thorntonville, TX	H4	150
Thorp, WI	F5	146
Thorsby, AL	J10	144
Thousand Lake Mountain, UT	F5	152
Thousand Oaks, CA	J7	156
Three Fingered Jack, OR	F4	154
Three Forks, MT	E14	154
Three Lakes, WI	E6	146
Three Oaks, MI	I9	146
Three Rivers, MI	I10	146
Three Rivers, TX	K8	150
Three Sisters, OR	F4	154
Throckmorton, TX	F7	150
Thunder Bay, MI	F12	146
Thunder Bay, r., MI	E12	146
Thunderbolt, GA	G5	142
Thurmont, MD	H9	140
Tibbie, AL	K8	144
Tice, FL	M5	142
Tickfaw, LA	L6	144
Tickfaw, r., US	L6	144
Ticonderoga, NY	D13	140
Tidioute, PA	F7	140
Tie Plant, MS	I7	144
Tierra Amarilla, NM	H10	152
Tiffany Mountain, WA	B6	154
Tiffin, OH	F3	140
Tifton, GA	H3	142
Tiftona, TN	D1	142
Tignall, GA	F4	142
Tilden, IL	D7	144
Tilden, NE	I10	148
Tilden, TX	K8	150
Tillamook, OR	E2	154
Tillmans Corner, AL	L8	144
Tillson, NY	F12	140
Tilton, IL	B9	144
Tilton, NH	D15	140
Tiltonsville, OH	G6	140
Timber Lake, SD	F6	148
Timmonsville, SC	E7	142
Timms Hill, WI	E5	146
Timpson, TX	K2	144
Tims Ford Lake, TN	G10	144
Tinsley, MS	J6	144
Tioga, ND	C5	148
Tioga, PA	F9	140
Tioga, r., US	F9	140
Tionesta, PA	F7	140
Tionesta Creek, r., PA	F7	140
Tioughnioga, r., NY	E10	140
Tippecanoe, r., IN	A10	144
Tipton, CA	H6	156
Tipton, IN	B10	144
Tipton, IA	I4	146
Tipton, MO	D4	144
Tipton, OK	E7	150
Tiptonville, TN	F7	144
Tishomingo, MS	H8	144
Tishomingo, OK	E10	150
Tiskilwa, IL	I6	146
Titonka, IA	G1	146
Tittabawassee, r., MI	G11	146
Titusville, FL	K6	142
Titusville, PA	F7	140
Tivoli, TX	K10	150
Toano, VA	B10	142
Toast, NC	C6	142
Tobacco, r., MI	G11	146
Tobias, NE	K10	148
Tobyhanna, PA	F11	140
Toccoa, GA	E3	142
Toccoa (Ocoee), r., US	E2	142
Togiak, AK	G14	158
Togwotee Pass, WY	G15	154
Toiyabe Range, NV	E8	156
Toksook Bay, AK	F12	158
Toledo, IL	C8	144
Toledo, IA	I3	146
Toledo, OH	F3	140
Toledo, OR	F2	154
Toledo Bend Reservoir, US	K3	144
Tolleson, AZ	K4	152
Tolono, IL	C8	144
Toluca, IL	I6	146
Tomah, WI	G5	146
Tomahawk, WI	E6	146
Tomball, TX	I11	150
Tombigbee, r., US	K8	144
Tombstone, AZ	M6	152
Tompkinsville, KY	F11	144
Toms, r., NJ	G12	140
Toms River, NJ	H12	140
Tonasket, WA	B6	154
Tonawanda, NY	D8	140
Tonganoxie, KS	L12	148
Tongue, r., US	E19	154
Tongue, r., ND	C10	148
Tongue, r., TX	F6	150
Tonica, IL	I6	146
Tonkawa, OK	C9	150
Tonopah, NV	F8	156
Tooele, UT	D4	152
Toomsboro, GA	G3	142
Topawa, AZ	M5	152
Topeka, KS	L12	148
Toppenish, WA	D5	154
Topsham, ME	D17	140
Torch Lake, MI	E10	146
Tornillo, TX	M10	152

Subject Index

A HARD TRAIL.